NEW SAINTS AND BLESSEDS
OF THE CATHOLIC CHURCH

Volume 2

*On October 25, 1987, on the steps of St. Peter's Basilica,
Pope John Paul II enrolled the Italian physician Giuseppe Moscati
(pictured on the banner) among the saints,
with 400,000 of the faithful in attendance.*

FERDINAND HOLBÖCK

NEW SAINTS AND BLESSEDS
OF THE
CATHOLIC CHURCH

Blesseds and Saints
Canonized by Pope John Paul II
During the Years 1984 to 1987

Volume 2

Afterword by Paolo Molinari, S.J.,
General Postulator of the Society of Jesus

Translated by
Michael J. Miller, M. PHIL., M.A. THEOL.

IGNATIUS PRESS   SAN FRANCISCO

Title of the German original
Neue Heilige der Katholischen Kirche, Band 2
© 1992 Christiana-Verlag, Stein am Rhein
Switzerland

Cover photographs:
Top right: Benedetta Cambiagio Frassinello
Middle, left to right: Benedetto Menni, Edith Stein, Peter Friedhofen
Bottom, left to right: Rupert Meyer, Rafaela Ybarra de Vilallonga

Photos courtesy of
Photo-Archiv IMAGO SANCTORUM, Christiana-Verlag

Cover design by Riz Boncan Marsella

© 2003 Ignatius Press, San Francisco
ISBN 0–89870–871–0
Library of Congress control number 2003105171
Printed in the United States of America ∞

CONTENTS

SAINTS

Canonized by Pope John Paul II in the years 1984 to 1987

PREFACE

In this second volume of *New Saints and Blesseds of the Catholic Church* are depicted the lives and deaths, the struggles and battles of those men and women who were raised to the honors of the altar by Pope John Paul II during the four years from 1984 through 1987, in forty-nine beatification ceremonies and in seven canonization liturgies.

Among them are blesseds and saints from a wide variety of countries, languages, ages, and walks of life: lay people, religious, priests and bishops, confessors and martyrs. Most of them have been largely unknown until now. And yet all of them not only deserve reverence, but are without exception worthy of imitation in their striving for perfection, in their fidelity to the Catholic faith and to the Church of Jesus Christ.

The life of each one of these personages is portrayed briefly, occasionally in greater detail, followed by [excerpts from] the homily that the Successor of Peter gave at the respective beatification or canonization ceremony. This papal address presents in most cases a very contemporary commentary on the life of the new blessed or saint in question.

Anyone who reads these short biographies should be edified and touched, and spontaneously moved to give thanks, that the Church, which today is so often reviled, abandoned, and criticized, is still in our days a Mother and teacher (*mater et magistra*), the Mother of Saints, and a guide to sanctity. Finally, despite the all-too-human errors and sinfulness of her members, she is the *una, sancta, catholica et apostolic Ecclesia*, and everyone who has the good fortune and the grace to belong to her can pray and sing: "Thanks be to God, who by his grace, gave me within his Church a place. Never will I desert her."

Salzburg, Feast of Saint Thomas Aquinas, January 28, 1992

Ferdinand Holböck

Blessed Andrea Carlo Ferrari, Cardinal Archbishop of Milan

BLESSEDS

Beatified by Pope John Paul II in the years 1984 to 1987

*Pope John Paul II and the General Postulator of the Jesuits,
Father Paolo Molinari, S.J., on June 5, 1986, after the promulgation
of the decree proclaiming that a miracle was worked by God through
the intercession of Father Rupert Mayer, S.J.*

Blessed Guillaume Répin and Ninety-eight Companions in Angers

Secular Priest, Martyr

b. August 26, 1709, Thouarcé, France
d. January 2, 1794, Angers

Beatified February 19, 1984

MARTYRS D'ANGERS 1793-1794

Just as the Vendée region became a *terra martyrum* during the French Revolution, so the same can be said for the city and diocese of Angers, in western France. There the Abbé Noël Pinot, who was beatified on October 31, 1926, suffered martyrdom by decapitation on February 9, 1794—not only he, but many others who preceded or followed him in martyrdom. Ninety-eight of these heroes of faith were beatified by Pope John Paul II on February 19, 1984. At the head of the list as the eldest stands Canon Guillaume Répin.[1]

He was born on August 26, 1709, the second child of René Répin and his wife, Renée (née Gourdon), in the town of Thouarcé (département Maine-et-Loire). In 1728 he entered the seminary in Angers. After receiving Holy Orders, the newly ordained Father Répin served from 1734 to 1749 as assistant priest in the parish of Saint Julian, in Angers. He then became pastor and canon of Saint Simplician, in Matigné-Briand. He labored there for more than forty years as a zealous, fatherly, spiritual

---

[1] N. Del Re, "Répin, Guglielmo e 98 Compagni, martiri in Angers", in *Bibliotheca Sanctorum* (Rome, 1987), 1:1126–27.

guide who was a real shepherd to his parishioners and was esteemed by all who knew him well. During the pastorate of Father Répin, the parish church was renovated several times and
repeatedly redecorated.

When Canon Répin was summoned on February 10, 1791, to
take the oath of obedience to the new constitution, he left his parish so as to avoid performing an act so detrimental to the Church
and went to Angers. There, on June 17, 1792, he and many other
priests who had refused to take the oath were arrested and incarcerated. In prison Canon Répin, being the senior priest, was selected
by his fellow inmates to celebrate Mass in their name—to the extent
that that was possible—and to administer the sacraments.

When it was once again demanded of these priests that they
take a somewhat modified oath (the so-called Liberty-Equality
oath), they again resisted bravely. Now, with Canon Répin at their
head, they were locked up in the *Rossignolerie*, the former school
of the Christian Brothers. There they lived until June 17, 1793. As
a result of the courageous popular uprising in the Vendée, these
priests regained their freedom. Canon Répin went to Mauges,
then to Cholet, and from there back again to Mauges. There,
however, he was arrested once more, on December 24, 1793, and
thrown into jail in Chalonnes.

After two long hearings, Canon Répin was finally handed over
by the revolutionary committee to the military commission, *sui-
vant la loi* [according to law], to be executed by guillotine. On
January 2, 1794, Guillaume Répin, together with the pastor of
Sainte Marie, in Chalonnes, and two other victims, was executed
on the Place du Ralliement in Angers. Eventually, more than two
thousand Catholics in Angers at that time (priests, nuns, and lay
people) had to give up their lives for their fidelity to their Catholic
faith. Out of this great company of heroes, the martyrdom of
ninety-nine Catholics has been thoroughly investigated thus far
and recognized to be genuine, the consequence of hatred for
the Catholic faith. The bishop of Angers, Monseigneur Joseph
Rumeau, had already begun the process of beatification for these

ninety-nine in 1905. Not until June 9, 1983, was it brought to a successful conclusion in Rome.

Pope John Paul II undertook to beatify these ninety-nine martyrs on February 19, 1984, and on that occasion he gave the following homily:

"Who will separate us from the love of Christ?" (Rom 8:35).

Such is the question the Apostle Paul once posed in his Letter to the Romans. He had in mind at that time the sufferings and the persecutions of the first generation of disciples, witnesses of Christ. The words of distress, of anguish, of hunger, of nakedness, of danger, of persecution, of torment, of massacre "like sheep led to slaughter" described very precise realities which were—or would be—the experience of many of those who would attach themselves to Christ, or rather who would accept the love of Christ in faith. Paul himself would be able to enumerate the trials that he had already undergone (cf. 2 Cor 6:4–10) while awaiting his own martyrdom here in Rome. And the Church today, together with the martyrs of the 18th and 19th centuries, asks itself in turn "who will separate us from the love of Christ?"

Saint Paul hastens to give an unequivocal response to this question: "nothing will be able to separate us from the love of God that comes to us in Christ Jesus our Lord", nothing, neither death, nor the mysterious powers of the world, nor the future, nor any other creature (cf. Rom 8:38–39).

Because God has handed over his only Son for the sake of the world, because this Son has given his life for us, such a love does not belie itself. It is stronger than everything. It preserves in eternal life those who have loved God to the point of giving their life for him. The regimes that persecute pass away. But this glory of the martyrs remains. *"We are more than conquerors because of him who has loved us"* (Rom 8:37).

This is the victory won by the martyrs elevated today to the glory of the altars by beatification.

There are first the very numerous martyrs who, in the *Diocese of Angers*, in the time of the French Revolution, accepted death because they were determined, according to the expression of Guillaume Repin, "to preserve their faith and their religion", remaining firmly attached to the Catholic and Roman Church. Those who were priests refused to take the oath they considered schismatic; they were unwilling to abandon their pastoral charge. Those who were lay persons remained faithful to these priests, to the Mass celebrated by them, to the signs of their veneration of Mary and of the saints. Doubtless, within the context of great ideological, political and military tensions, they could be charged with suspicions of infidelity to their country. In the "notices" of their sentences they were accused of involvement with "the anti-revolutionary forces". This happens moreover in almost all persecutions, of yesterday and of today. But for the men and women whose names have been recorded—among the many others who are doubtless of equal merit—what they really lived, how they replied to their judicial interrogators, leaves not the slightest doubt about their determination to remain faithful—at the risk of their lives—to the demands of their faith, nor about the profound reason for their sentence, the hatred of that faith which their judges despised as "groundless devotion" and "fanaticism".

We remain in admiration before the decisive, calm, brief, sincere, humble replies, not seeking to provoke but firm and to the point on the essential: fidelity to the Church. Thus speak the priests, all guillotined as was their venerable dean Guillaume Repin, the religious who refuse even to allow it to appear that they have taken the oath, the four laymen. Suffice it to recall the testimony of one of them (Antoine Fournier): "You intend then to suffer death for the defense of your religion?—Yes." Thus speak these eighty women, who can hardly be accused of armed rebellion! Some had already expressed the desire to die for the name of Jesus rather than to renounce their religion (Renée Feillatreau).

True Christians, they give witness also by their refusal to hate their executioners, by their forgiveness, their desire for peace for all: "I pray the good God only for the peace and unity of the whole world" (Marie Cassin). Finally, their last moments reveal the depth of their faith. Some sing hymns and psalms all the way to the place of torment; "they request a few moments in order to make to God the sacrifice of their lives, which they would make with such fervor that their executioners themselves were astounded." Sister Marie-Anne, Daughter of Charity, comforted her Sister with these words: "We are going to have the good fortune of seeing God and of possessing him for all eternity . . . and we will be able to enjoy this without fear of being separated from it" (testimony of the Abbé Gruget).

Today these ninety-nine martyrs of Angers, in the glory of beatification, join the first of their number, the Abbé Noël Pinot, who was beatified almost sixty years ago.

Yes, the words of the Apostle Paul are splendidly verified here: "We are more than conquerors because of him who has loved us." [2]

(See Appendix for the names of the 98 companions.)

---

[2] *L'Osservatore Romano*, March 20, 1984, p. 3.

Blessed Giovanni Mazzucconi

Priest, Missionary in Oceania, Martyr

b. *March 1, 1826, Rancio di Lecco, Italy*

d. *September 7, 1855, on the shore of Woodlark Island, Oceania*

Beatified February 19, 1984

A blessed herald of the faith who left Italy and went to Oceania in keeping with Christ's missionary instruction "Go into all the world" is Giovanni Mazzucconi,[1] who was beatified on February 19, 1984, by Pope John Paul II. He was born on March 1, 1826, in Rancio di Lecco, in Italy. His destiny is often compared with that of Saint Peter Chanel because, like him, he too had to give up his life in his mission territory in Oceania.

Giovanni Mazzucconi was among the first members of the Milan Institute for the Foreign Missions. He drew up the statutes of this institute and composed its community prayers. In 1850 he was ordained a priest, and soon afterward he was sent on a mission to Oceania (Melanesia and Micronesia) to work on Rook Island (off New Guinea) as a missionary and to win the natives over to the Christian faith.

After he had labored there selflessly and zealously for three years, he became seriously ill; before he could be deployed again on the front lines in the campaign for the kingdom of God, he had to travel to Sidney, Australia, to be cured of his sickness. On

[1] G. Scurati, *Cenni del Sacerdote Giovanni Mazzucconi, missionario apostolico nella Malesia, morto per la fede il 7 settembre 1855* (Milan, 1957).

the return trip from Australia to his mission station, the missionary's boat was cast by a storm onto the shore of Woodlark Island, where Giovanni Mazzucconi, together with his guides, was massacred by the savages. It is not certain exactly when that happened—probably on September 7, 1855.

Pope John Paul II said the following about this herald of the faith and martyr at the beatification on February 19, 1984:

> A . . . testimony of adamant faith and ardent charity has been given to the Church and to the world by Father Giovanni Mazzucconi, who consummated in martyrdom his young life as priest and missionary. Among the first members of the Pontifical Institute for the Foreign Missions of Milan, he felt that the missions were "the secret desire" of his heart. On the horizon of his life he foresaw an even more profound union with Christ, a union that would unite him to the sufferings and to the cross of his Lord and Master, precisely because of his tireless commitment to evangelization: "Blessed that day when it will be granted to me to suffer a great deal for such a holy cause, but even more blessed will be the day when I might be found worthy of shedding my blood for it and of meeting death in the midst of torment."
>
> However, the Christian message that Mazzucconi was preaching to the natives of Woodlark was an open condemnation of their behavior which went as far as the horrors of infanticide. And despite the immense charity and the indefatigable dedication of the Blessed, his preaching provoked irritation and hatred. But he maintained a supernatural serenity, in the midst of hardships, fever, opposition, because he lived in intimate union with God. Paraphrasing the words of St Paul, he was able to write: "I know that God is good and that he loves me immensely. All the rest, calm and tempest, danger and safety, life and death, are nothing but changing and momentary expressions of the dear, immutable and eternal Love." [2]

[2] *L'Osservatore Romano*, March 20, 1984, p. 3.

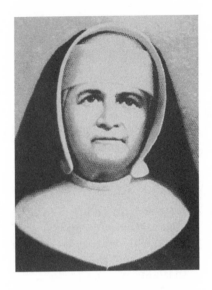

Blessed Marie-Léonie (Alodie Virginie) Paradis

Religious, Foundress

b. *May 12, 1840, L'Acadie,*
Sainte Marguérite de
Blairfindie, Quebec, Canada
d. *May 3, 1912, Sherbrooke,*
Quebec

Beatified September 11, 1984

At the beatification ceremony for Sister Marie-Léonie Paradis[1] in Jarry Park, Montreal, Canada, on September 11, 1984, Pope John Paul II said, among other things:

This new beatification of a Canadian nun reminds us how much religious communities have contributed to Canada in every sector of ecclesial and social life. They have done this through contemplative prayer, education, assistance to the poor, work in hospitals and apostolic involvement of all kinds. It is a great gift. And if, today, the concrete forms of service can be different and evolve according to need, the religious vocation as such remains a marvelous gift of God. It is a witness without parallel, a prophetic charism essential to the Church, not only because of the immeasurable services for which the sisters are responsible, but because first of all it signifies the gratuity [selflessness] of love in a spousal gift to Christ, in a total consecration to his redemptive work. I would ask this of all the Christians gathered

---

[1] E. Nadeau, *Mère Léonie* (Montreal, 1952); and *Montre-moi tes chemins* (Sherbrooke, 1974).

20

here: Are the Canadian people still able to appreciate this gift? Do they help religious women to find and to strengthen their vocation? And you, dear sisters, do you appreciate the greatness of the call of God and the fundamentally evangelical life-style which corresponds to that gift?[2]

Alodie Virginie Paradis, who was born on May 12, 1840, into the humble home of simple, pious parents in L'Acadie, Quebec, Canada, thought very highly of religious life from early childhood on, and at the age of only fourteen—prompted by her countryman Camillo Lefèbvre, then a newly ordained priest of the Holy Cross Congregation—she entered the Congregation of the Marist Sisters of the Holy Cross, founded by Father Basil Moreau. She made her religious profession with this community of nuns as Sister Marie-Léonie on August 22, 1857, in the presence of Father Moreau, who was staying then in Canada. From then on she took her holy religious vows very seriously and was meticulous at all times about her fidelity to them.

After teaching girls in various houses of her congregation from 1857 to 1862, Sister Marie-Léonie was sent to the United States of America in 1862 to work as a governess at Saint Vincent's Orphanage in New York. She remained at this assignment until 1870.

In 1869, the Marist Sisters of the Holy Cross who lived in North America separated from the motherhouse of their congregation in France and founded an independent, autonomous congregation, the Sisters of the Holy Cross.

These sisters, at the request of the Holy See, had begun quite some time previously to devote themselves exclusively to teaching, a complete change from the task to which their founder, Father Basil Moreau, had assigned them at first, namely, to serve as housekeepers in the houses of the Holy Cross Fathers. Nevertheless, since the Marists of the Holy Cross in Notre Dame Province in Indiana wanted at least some members of the community to

[2] *L'Osservatore Romano*, October 1, 1984, p. 8.

continue this housekeeping work, Sister Marie-Léonie gladly accepted the offer made to her in 1870 to transfer to Notre Dame. When Father Camillo Lefèbvre, the founder of Saint Joseph's College in Memramcook, New Brunswick, Canada, asked Sister Marie-Léonie to take responsibility for the religious instruction of the girls whom he had recruited to perform various services in the college that he had founded, she went there with another sister on September 22, 1874. Under her direction, these girls at Saint Joseph's College in Memramcook coalesced into a community of nuns from which a new religious congregation developed, the Congregation of the Little Sisters of the Holy Family.

Until 1904 Sister Marie-Léonie still belonged, strictly and canonically speaking, to the Congregation of the Marists of the Holy Cross. On October 2, 1904, however, she finally assumed the religious habit of the Little Sisters of the Holy Family and with it the responsibility of leading them as general superior; she remained in this office until the end of her life. On May 3, 1912, in the motherhouse in Sherbrooke, Canada, she was called to her eternal reward. The principal duty of the Little Sisters of the Holy Family remains, even today, housekeeping in monasteries, seminaries, and colleges.

At the beatification of Mother Marie-Léonie, Pope John Paul II said the following about her personality:

Today, to this living record of the saints and the blessed which has been in this land for centuries, a new name is being added, that of Sister Marie-Léonie Paradis.

This woman is one of you, humble among the humble, and today she takes her place among those whom God has lifted up to glory. I am happy that for the first time, this beatification is taking place in Canada, her homeland.

Born of simple, poor and virtuous parents, she soon grasped the beauty of religious life and committed herself to it through her vows with the Marist Order of the Holy Cross. She never once questioned that gift to God, not even during the difficult periods of community life in New York and in Indiana. When she was appointed to serve in a college in Memramcook in Acadia, the richness of her religious life drew young women to her who also wanted to dedicate their life to God. With them and thanks to the understanding of Bishop Larocque of Sherbrooke, she founded the Congregation of the Little Sisters of the Holy Family, which is still thriving and is still very much appreciated.

Never doubting her call, she often asked: "Lord, show me your ways", so that she would know the concrete form of her service in the Church. She found and proposed to her spiritual daughters a special kind of commitment: the service of educational institutions, seminaries and priests' homes. She never shied away from the various forms of manual work, which is the lot of so many people today and which held a special place in the Holy Family and in the life of Jesus of Nazareth himself. It is there that she saw the will of God for her life. It was in carrying out these tasks that she found God. In the sacrifices which were required and which she offered in love, she experienced a profound joy and peace. She knew that she was one with Christ's fundamental attitude: he had "come not to be served, but to serve". She was filled with the greatness of the Eucharist and with the greatness of the priesthood at the service of the Eucharist. That is one of the secrets of her spiritual motivation. Yes, God looked upon the holiness of his humble servant Marie-Léonie, who had been inspired by Mary's openness and receptivity. And henceforth, from age to age, her Congregation and the Church will call her blessed (cf. Lk 1:48).[3]

[3] Ibid.

Blessed
Clemente Marchisio

Secular Priest, Rural Pastor,
Founder

b. March 1, 1833, Racconigi, Italy
d. December 16, 1903, Rivalba,
Italy

Beatified September 30, 1984

On September 30, 1984, Pope John Paul beatified at Saint
Peter's in Rome a simple priest from a rural Italian parish, thus
raising to the honors of the altar the secular priest Clemente
Marchisio.[1]

He was born on March 1, 1833, in Racconigi (archdiocese of
Turin), the first of nine children of a craftsman and his wife, and
very early on he sensed his calling to the priesthood. He entered
the seminary at Bra and, after completing his theological studies,
was ordained a priest on September 20, 1856, in Turin. At the
Ecclesiastical Institute in Turin, he deepened his theological
knowledge through a further two-year course in moral and pastoral theology, under the direction of the saintly priest Joseph
Cafasso. To him Blessed Clemente Marchisio in later years would
gratefully attribute his entire priestly formation.

The young diocesan priest Clemente Marchisio first served as
an assistant (*viceparroco*) in Cambiaso, then in Viganò; finally, he

---

[1] D. Franchetti, *Il santo prevosto di Rivalba Torinese, Don Clemente Marchisio* (Turin,
1933); J. Cottino, *Un parroco di campagna* (Turin, 1952); N. Sarale, *Teologia della semplicità*
(Rome, 1975).

became a pastor in Rivalba, where he worked tirelessly in a zealous and fruitful ministry for forty-three years, until his death.

A wise spiritual guide, he took special care of young women. He had observed that many of the girls who came to the city of Turin seeking work went astray and were ruined. Therefore, he founded in his parish a shelter for girls and set up a workshop for them, a weaving mill. To look after the girls he first brought nuns from the Institute of Vincentian Sisters of the Immaculate Virgin Mary (founded by Blessed Federico Albert) into his parish. These nuns, however, were withdrawn; after making a pilgrimage to Lourdes and seeking the advice of Archbishop Gastaldi of Turin, he set about founding his own congregation of women religious, the Institute of the Daughters of Saint Joseph (*Istituto delle Figlie di San Giuseppe*).

While helping out as a preacher and a confessor in the great archdiocese of Turin, Father Clemente Marchisio was in a position to observe that quite often there was a lack of cleanliness in the linens and vestments used in the celebration of the Eucharistic Sacrifice, that bread and wine of poor quality were consecrated, and even that invalid matter was used occasionally. So he made it the special duty of his nuns, the Daughters of Saint Joseph, to foster a great reverence and love for the Holy Eucharist and to look after the hosts and the altar wine, the linens and vestments, as well as the candles and cloths used on altars in the rural churches. While employed in these beautiful tasks, the sisters not only met with the approval of the clergy in the archdiocese, but also received the income necessary to support themselves. In this way, furthermore, they gained many novices and eventually were able to found communities throughout Italy. Their founder, Father Clemente Marchisio, taught the sisters his own distinctive spirituality: leading a life of poverty and simplicity in the service of our Lord in the Most Holy Sacrament, one must serve him with a strong faith and the greatest reverence.

Four years after the death of Father Clemente Marchisio, which took place on December 16, 1903, in Rivalba, the religious institute of the Daughters of Saint Joseph of Rivalba obtained definitive approval from Pope Pius X, the saintly pope of the Eucharist. While he was still bishop of Mantua, he had come to know and respect the rural pastor Don Clemente Marchisio, and, as patriarch of Venice, he had continued his benevolence toward him.

Pope John Paul II characterized this simple, zealous, and quite eucharistically-minded diocesan priest as follows at the beatification on September 30, 1984:

The image of Christ the Good Shepherd . . . shines in Blessed Clemente Marchisio: always concerned to be "an example to believers in speech and conduct, in love, in faith" (1 Tim 4:12), he was careful to progress in the grace with which every priest is endowed in Christ, thus becoming every day a more valid and living instrument of Jesus, the Eternal Priest.

A man of prayer, as every priest must be, he was aware of the duty to invoke God, the Lord of the universe and of his life, but he was also aware that true adoration, worthy of the infinite sanctity of God, is attained above all through the Sacrament of the Body and Blood of Christ. Therefore he always had great zeal in devoutly celebrating the Eucharistic mystery, in assiduously making adoration, and in taking care of the beauty of the various liturgical celebrations. He was in fact persuaded that the Church is built up above all by the Eucharist; by their participation in it, the members of the Christian community identify themselves mystically with Christ and become a single body among themselves.[2]

[2] L'Osservatore Romano, October 29, 1984, p. 6.

Blessed
Federico Albert

Rural Pastor, Founder

b. *October 16, 1820, Turin*
d. *September 30, 1876,*
    Lanzo Torinese

Beatified September 30, 1984

An exemplary Italian pastor and a friend of Saint Don Bosco, who even assisted him at his death, Federico Albert[1] was beatified on September 30, 1984, by Pope John Paul II.

He was born on October 16, 1820, in Turin, the first son of a high-ranking officer in the general staff of the Sardinian army. It was understood that, when he came of age, the young man would enter the military academy, as his father had provided. One day, however, as Federico Albert was praying before the reliquary of Blessed Sebastiano Valfré, the Apostle of Turin, he suddenly and unexpectedly sensed a vocation to the priesthood. He became a cleric and was included by King Carlo Alberto among the clergy at the court. At the University of Turin he completed a doctorate in theology. On June 10, 1843, he was ordained a priest by the heroic Bishop Franzoni and was appointed chaplain at the royal court. He held this office until the year 1852. During that time, the young court chaplain preached a Lenten sermon in the castle of Moncalieri, in the presence of King Victor Emmaneul II, the

[1] J. Cottino, *Il venerabile Federico Albert* (Turin, 1954).

royal family, and the entire court. He took as his text the Gospel account of the woman caught in adultery and spoke with such audacious clarity that everyone could tell that the preacher was alluding to the adulterous escapades of the king. The royal courtiers were horrified; the king himself, however, appreciated the apostolic courage of the court chaplain and said to him as he departed, "Thank you! You have always told me the truth."

After a short interlude devoted to the pastoral care of souls in the Church of San Carlo in Turin—from which the Servite Fathers had been driven—on April 18, 1852, Father Federico Albert became vicar of Lanzo Torinese, an extensive, populous, and troublesome mountain parish, which demanded of its priests a strong spirit of sacrifice. Here he applied himself very quickly to the urgently needed renovation of the dilapidated church, and with his own hands he gathered the requisite building materials. Then he sought to improve the religious and moral life there and in the surrounding parishes, and with tremendous zeal for souls he scheduled devotions and preached popular missions. In order to provide suitable shelter for orphans and other needy individuals, he founded Maria Immaculata Hospice. Somewhat later, to care for the children housed there, Father Federico Albert founded the Congregation of the Vincentian Sisters of Mary Immaculate, who were later called the Albertines, after their founder. He then founded a boarding school for boys also, which he entrusted to Don Bosco, with whom he had extremely cordial relations. As a pastor, Father Federico Albert proved more and more to be a thoroughly apostolic man, of unwavering equanimity, who had a great love for the poor, a profound capacity for empathy, and a delicate, kindly way with everyone.

In 1873 Father Federico Albert was named bishop of Pinerolo by the pope. He tearfully begged the pope, however, not to burden him with this responsibility.

In the midst of the many and various activities involved in establishing an agricultural colony for youngsters, which was intended to help the pastors in the region to tend the cultivated lands within their parish benefices, he suffered an accidental injury that would bring his life to an end. As he was painting the ceiling of the chapel, he attempted to avert a situation that endangered a youngster who was helping him, but he lost his footing and came crashing to the ground. For two days he lay in agony, assisted by Don Bosco and Blessed Don Michele Rua, the priest who would one day succeed Don Bosco. Father Albert died on September 30, 1876.

Pope John Paul spoke as follows about this exemplary Italian pastor at his beatification on September 30, 1984:

> Blessed Federico Albert . . . [was] totally dedicated to the good of the souls entrusted to him and to the needs of the poor. He, having received the vocation to the priesthood in adult life, did not have the opportunity to attend a seminary; but he prepared himself to become a priest in such a way as to be proposed today as a valid model for priests, who can admire his deep spiritual life, nourished by a constant communion with Christ, and his generous commitment to acquire a solid cultural formation which would allow him to be proposed as a sure guide in the midst of the People of God.
>
> His spirit of faith, his unconditional obedience to the Pope and his bishop, and his priestly charity made him an element of balance among the members of the priesthood and a zealous pastor, particularly attentive to youth and the poor. Looking at the new [Blessed], we are made quite clearly aware how it is possible to respond to the concrete demands of mankind, provided we are faithful servants of Christ and the Church.[2]

---

[2] *L'Osservatore Romano*, October 29, 1984, p. 6.

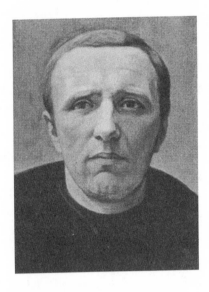

Blessed
Isidore of Saint Joseph
De Loor

Passionist Lay Brother

b. *April 18, 1881, Vrasene,*
   Belgium
d. *October 6, 1916, Kortrijk,*
   Belgium

Beatified September 30, 1984

A Flemish lay brother in the Passionist order of Saint Paul of the Cross, to whom the many cancer patients of our time could look as an intercessor with God and as an encouraging example in enduring this painful illness, is Brother Isidore of Saint Joseph De Loor.[1] He was born on April 18, 1881, in Vrasene, in the diocese of Ghent, Belgium, the son of Alois De Loor and his wife, Camilla, née Hutsebaut. His parents were simple but deeply pious Catholic farmers. Growing up in a good Catholic atmosphere, Isidore became a pious and industrious lad, but he was sickly. He was not really suited for the hard work on the farm. Instead, after receiving the sacrament of confirmation, on May 25, 1894, he helped the pastor teach catechism.

In 1907, a preacher from the Redemptorist order of Saint Alphonsus Liguori, Father Bouckaert, gave a mission in Isidore's native village. Afterward the famous missionary advised the young man to enter the Passionist community in Ere (diocese of Tournai) as a lay brother. Isidore did this with a joyful heart, and on Sep-

---

[1] P. Angelus, *Een heilig kloosterbroeder Passionist, Broeder Isidoor van den H. Jozef* (Wezembeek/Oppem, 1916).

tember 13, 1908, he consecrated himself to his suffering, crucified Lord Jesus Christ by taking perpetual vows as a religious.

In 1910 Brother Isidore was assigned by his superiors to the Passionist monastery at Wezembeek-Oppem, near Brussels, to work as cook, gardener, and porter. Here, too, he fulfilled his duties obediently and in a spirit of self-denial, in reparation to and out of love for the Crucified Savior.

In early 1911, Brother Isidore had to have his right eye surgically removed. The cancer had started to work in him, and it would not go into remission again. Brother Isidore may well have suspected this; the doctors and the superiors knew it. Nevertheless, after his operation Brother Isidore gladly returned to his work.

On August 11, 1912, Brother Isidore was transferred to Kortrijk (archdiocese of Brussels), to the Passionist monastery there. Here again, he bravely and devoutly performed his assigned tasks as cook, porter, and alms-gatherer. In doing so he was always extremely conscientious and faithful to the rule, and he also enjoyed an admirably intimate union with God. Thus he became—despite the illness that crept through him like poison—more and more an example of religious perfection for the Passionist lay brothers. In September 1916, the cancer spread to the inner organs, especially to his intestines. The growth of the metastases caused him horrible pains. He was a stranger to moaning and complaining, though; he endured everything with resignation to the will of God, often with the ejaculation on his lips, "Yes, Father, for the sake of paradise!" After all, paradise, heaven, "once earned, is earned for ever", the cancer patient used to say. Those were also his last words before his death on October 6, 1916.

After the death of Brother Isidore, many Catholics in Belgium began to pray with confidence to this faithful departed religious. Many remarkable answers to prayer were reported to the superiors of the Passionist order, so that they were prompted to begin the process of beatification. This was successfully concluded in 1984.

At the beatification on September 30, 1984, Pope John Paul II said:

The new Blessed, Isidore De Loor, is surely a fascinating and providential example for our era (taken up with freedom which is sometimes quite equivocal), of a growing conformity to the will of the heavenly Father in following Christ Jesus. Because of his life, the witnesses of the life of Brother Isidore of St Joseph called him "the Brother of God's Will".

In Blessed Isidore De Loor it is given to us to contemplate above all the face of the suffering Christ, in whom the infinite love of God is revealed. This new [Blessed] knew how to accept the supreme and absolute value of the will of God, and he undertook to fulfil it in his own life with love and trust, according to the example of Jesus Christ, who always set out to do what was pleasing to the Father, even when it was to take up the cross. Such was the willingness and promptness with which Blessed [Isidore] De Loor abandoned himself in everything to the will of the Lord, to follow Jesus crucified and risen, that he was called "Brother of God's Will". Stricken with one of the most widespread illnesses of our century, cancer, Brother Isidore prepared for death with the same docility with which he had lived, accepting this dramatic trial as an opportunity to conform himself fully to the Redeemer, the object of his continuous and prolonged meditations.

The new [Blessed] invites each one of us to the feet of Christ, who died for love, exhorting us to unite our toils and sufferings to those of Christ, in order to find in this way the salvific and constructive meaning of work, suffering and toil, and to receive valid answers to the questions of life (cf. *Salvifici Doloris*, 31).[2]

[2] *L'Osservatore Romano*, October 29, 1984, p. 6.

Blessed
Rafaela Ybarra
de Vilallonga

Wife, Foundress

b. January 16, 1843, Bilbao, Spain
d. February 23, 1900, Bilbao

Beatified September 30, 1984

A daughter was born to a wealthy but devout Basque couple, Gabriel Maria Ybarra y Gutiérrez de Cabiedas and Rosaria de Arambarri y Mancebo, on January 16, 1843 in Bilbao, Spain. The following day she received in baptism the name Rafaela Maria Stefania[1] and from then on grew to be a shining example among the saints of the Basque people, as Pope John Paul II declared at the beatification on September 30, 1984.

Even as a very small child, Rafaela showed extraordinary signs of piety. At the age of eleven, she received her First Holy Communion, which made a truly profound impression upon her. On that occasion—as she noted in her diary—she wept for joy over the profound experience of encountering Christ. If you think that little Rafaela grew up to be a nun, you're wrong. She wanted to demonstrate, in a genuinely Christian marriage, that you can also love God fervently when you deliberately include Christ as the third party to the marriage covenant. At the age of eighteen,

---

[1] A. Chavarria y Arrondo, *Nació para ser Madre: La Vida y la Obra de Rafaela y Ibarra de Vilallonga, Fundadora de la Congregación de los Santos Angeles Custodios* (Buenos Aires, 1953).

Rafaela married the son of a wealthy Christian family, José Vila-llonga, and together with him led a Christian married life in the best sense. She loved her husband in God and for God's sake, and likewise her children and adopted nieces and nephews. She lovingly took in her aged parents and other relatives as well, not forgetting meanwhile to carry out apostolic work in a wider circle. In the true spirit of the apostolate, she used her great wealth to establish Holy Family Hospice in Bilbao for women in difficult straits and girls who were at risk. To care for such girls she also founded a religious congregation, the Sisters of the Holy Guardian Angels (*Congregación de los Santos Angeles Custodios*), and this was her chief accomplishment.

Under the prudent spiritual direction of the Jesuit priest Francisco de Sales Muruzábel, and with her husband's approval, Señora Rafaela Ybarra de Vilallonga took vows of poverty, chastity, and obedience, to which in 1890 she added the vow of always preferring what is most pleasing to God, which would include—as soon as her family situation permitted—consecrating herself completely to God as a religious.

Señora Rafaela Ybarra Vilallonga died on February 23, 1900, in her house in Bilbao. She was renowned for her sanctity, which the Pope confirmed at her beatification on September 30, 1984. On that occasion John Paul II said the following:

Another reflection of the infinite perfection of Christ is seen in Blessed Rafaela Ybarra, who tried always to grow in Christ, in order to build herself up in charity (Eph 4:15f.). Her unconditional dedication to God and others in the different circumstances of her life is admirable: as a young person, as a wife, and as foundress of a religious institute.

From the cross and prayer she was able to draw the strength to offer herself on the altars of Christian love. How many persons benefitted from her capacity of self-giving for Christ! How many, because of her gentleness with the needy, never called her anything but "Mother"!

She, from her privileged position, knew how to look with human and Christian sensitivity at the society of her time. From this attitude various social and apostolic initiatives were begun, which directed her action to hospitals, maternity homes, women's prisons, and young people without work or in moral danger. Precisely for the defence and the human and Christian promotion of young women, she created the Institute of the Holy Guardian Angels. She is an excellent example for our society of today and for all who want to live for God, helping at the same time to build the Kingdom of Christ in this way! To the Christians of the Basque people I want to say to them in their own language: "Follow the example of the new Blessed." [2]

[2] *L'Osservatore Romano*, October 29, 1984, pp. 6–7.

Blessed
Elizabeth of the Trinity
(Catez)

Carmelite Nun, Mystic

b. *July 18, 1880, Camp d'Avor,*
Bourges, France
d. *November 9, 1906, Dijon,*
France

Beatified November 25, 1984

Long before her beatification in 1984, the life of this modern
Trinitarian mystic had been described in detail and publicized by
the Swiss theologian Hans Urs von Balthasar, by the important
Dominican theologian Marie-Michel Philippon, and also by the
author of this work in his anthology on Trinitarian saints. We
should take note here also of the very beautiful illustrated volume
compiled by Conrad de Meester. In these works[1] it is rightly
emphasized that this blessed learned to make the mystery of the
indwelling of the Holy Trinity in her soul more and more central
to her spiritual life. She discovered that her calling in life was to
unfold the Trinitarian riches of her baptismal call and thus to
become a living "praise of the glory of the Triune God".

Elizabeth Catez was born on July 18, 1880, in Camp d'Avor,
Bourges, France, the daughter of an officer who died very soon

[1] Hans Urs von Balthasar, *Two Sisters in the Spirit: Thérèse of Lisieux and Elizabeth of
the Trinity* (San Francisco: Ignatius Press, 1992); Marie-Michel Philippon, O.P., *The
Spiritual Doctrine of Sister Elizabeth of the Trinity* (Newman Press, 1948); Ferdinand
Holböck, *Ergriffen vom dreieinigen Gott: Trinitarische Heilige aus allen Jahrhunderten der
Kirchengeschichte* (Stein am Rhein, 1981), pp. 337–43; Conrad de Meester, *Elisabeth
von Dijon: Ein Lied für Gott: Eine Biographie in Bildern* (St. Ottilien).

after, leaving his wife with two daughters, Elizabeth and Marguerite. Elizabeth was a gifted youngster, especially talented in music. Despite her receptivity for all that is beautiful, and despite her involvement in apostolic and charitable works, she was strongly drawn to the Carmel of Dijon; at a very early age she was already in contact with the prioress there. She visited the exemplary prioress on a regular basis and from her obtained counsel about her progress in the spiritual life.

August 2, 1901, was the day of Elizabeth's entrance into the Carmel of Dijon. She took the religious name Elizabeth of the Most Holy Trinity. She now saw that the entire program of her inner spiritual growth and maturation was to be the realization of her name in religion: "House-of-God, in which the Holy Trinity dwells". In a letter from the end of September 1903, she wrote, "All of my efforts consist in entering my inner self and losing myself in those Three who are there!" She continued to deepen her comprehension of the mystery of the indwelling of the Triune God in her soul, which was filled with more and more mystical graces. A special proof of this is her moving "Prayer to the Holy Trinity", which she wrote down at one sitting on November 21, 1904, without the slightest correction, impelled by God's grace. In this prayer we can find all the essential and characteristic spiritual traits of this gifted Carmelite who, in five short years of religious life, attained sanctity. There is her fascination with the mystery of the Holy Trinity; her prayer life, which consisted almost exclusively in the worship of the Triune God; her passionate and delicate love for Christ, who is, by the Holy Spirit, the incarnate and eternal Word of the Father; then, too, her irresistible advance toward the Three Divine Persons who had taken up residence in her soul; her joy in the presence of these Three within her and in their desire for her worship.

At the start of Lent in 1906, as Sister Elizabeth reached for the letters of Saint Paul after midday recreation, as was her custom, she opened—seemingly quite by chance—to the passage in the Letter to the Philippians: "that I may know him and the power of his resurrection, and may share his sufferings, becoming like him in his death" (Phil 3:10).

That would now be fulfilled in her in a striking manner. She showed symptoms of a serious stomach illness and was confined to bed. On Palm Sunday in 1906, Sister Elizabeth's condition suddenly took a turn for the worse when she suffered a violent hemorrhage. In a letter from May 1906 she wrote, "On the evening of Palm Sunday I had a very serious crisis, and believed that at last the hour had come, in which I would soar away into the infinite regions, so as to behold unveiled the Blessed Trinity which has already taken up residence in me here on earth. In the stillness and silence of the night I received the anointing of the sick and a visit from my Lord."

The final months of this thoroughly Trinitarian soul, up to the day of her journey home, November 9, 1906, were then filled, day by day, with the thought of the Crucified Lord; she wanted to be a little host, united in suffering with him, to the "praise of the glory of the Holy Trinity".

In this name, "Praise of the Glory of the Holy Trinity", which Sister Elizabeth of Dijon assumed during the final weeks of her earthly life, and in the manner in which she comprehended and actualized this name as her life's work, are reflected "the fundamental ideas of her interior life and all the chief traits of her spirituality: silence, absolute self-renunciation, love for the Triune God, radical abandonment to the divine will, as well as an ever more ardent striving for union with the soul of the crucified Savior", whom she had grown to resemble in her suffering and death.

Pope John Paul II characterized the Carmelite nun Elizabeth of the Most Holy Trinity as follows at her beatification on November 25, 1984:

Almost a contemporary of Theresa of the Child Jesus, Elizabeth of the Trinity had a profound experience of the presence of God which she brought to perfection in an impressive manner in a few years of life among the Carmelites. In her, we salute one who was filled with natural gifts: she was intelligent and sensitive, accomplished as a pianist, appreciated by her friends and delicate in her affection for those who were close to her. Behold how she *blossomed in the silence of contemplation*; she shone with the happiness of a total forgetting of self. Without reserve, she received the gift of God, the grace of Baptism and of Reconciliation. In an admirable way she received the Eucharistic presence of Christ. To an exceptional degree, she was conscious of the communion offered to every creature by the Lord.

Today, we dare present to the world this cloistered religious woman who led a "life hidden in God with Jesus Christ" (Col 3:3) because she is a brilliant witness of the joy of being rooted and founded in love (cf. Eph 3:17). She celebrated God's splendour because she knew that in the most intimate part of her being there *dwelt the presence of the Father, the Son and the Holy Spirit* in whom she recognized the reality of a love infinitely alive.

Elizabeth also knew physical and moral *suffering*. United to Christ crucified, she made a total *offering* of herself and completed in her flesh the passion of the Lord (cf. Col 1:24), as she was always certain of being loved and of being able to love. In peace, she offered the gift of a wounded life.

To our disoriented humanity which no longer knows how to find God or which disfigures him, which searches for a word on which to found its hope, Elizabeth [of the Trinity] gives witness to a *perfect openness to the Word of God*. She assimilated this Word to the point of truly nourishing with it her prayer and reflection, to the point of finding therein all her reasons for living and of consecrating herself to the praise of the glory of this Word.

And this contemplative, far from isolating herself, knew how to *communicate* to her sisters and to those close to her the riches of her mystical experience. Her message flows abroad today with prophetic force. We invoke her, the disciple of Theresa of [the Child] Jesus and of John of the Cross, that she may inspire and sustain the entire Carmelite family; that she may assist many men and women, lay and religious, to receive and to share the "streams of infinite charity" which she received "at the Fountain of Life." [2]

[2] *L'Osservatore Romano,* December 10, 1984, pp. 2, 12.

Blessed
José Manyanet y Vivès

Diocesan Priest, Founder,
Author

b. January 7, 1833, Tremp, Spain
d. December 17, 1901, Barcelona

Beatified November 25, 1984

The Spanish priest José Manyanet y Vivès,[1] the founder of two
religious congregations, who in all his foundations had the ideal of
the Holy Family of Nazareth constantly in mind, was beatified by
Pope John Paul II on November 25, 1984.

He was born on January 7, 1833, in Tremp (diocese of Lérida,
in Spain), the oldest of nine children of Antonio Manyanet, a
farmer of modest means, and his wife, Bonaventura, née Vivès.

At the age of twelve, the intelligent youngster was sent to the
boarding school in Barbastro, which was run by the Piarist Fathers. At the end of his secondary schooling, he became, first, an
extern student at the seminary of Lérida and, then, a theology
student at the seminary of Seo de Urgel (diocese of Lérida). He
paid for his studies by tutoring, doing chores for the Piarists, and
by working as the bishop's valet.

On April 9, 1859, José Manyanet was ordained a priest. Bishop
José Caixal y Estrade had followed with great interest the progress of José Manyanet y Vivès while he was a candidate for the

---

[1] C. Baraut, *José Manyanet, apostol de la familia i de la joventut* (Barcelona, 1969); R.
Oromi, *Vida compendiada del P. José Manyanet y Vivés* (Barcelona, 1929).

priesthood and had come to have an exceptionally high opinion of him on account of his valuable aptitudes and abilities. Therefore, he bestowed upon the newly ordained priest two benefices in Tremp, his hometown, and simultaneously appointed him manager of his estate and seminary librarian.

For five years José Manyanet remained a resident in the episcopal palace and earned for himself during this time the reputation of being a good advisor and spiritual director. In his pastoral work in his hometown, Tremp, during the same time, he emphasized two goals: the eucharistic education of the youth and the sanctification of families. In this connection, José Manyanet founded in his native place a boarding school, which became the starting point for the Sons of the Holy Family, the congregation he established in 1864.

For the purpose of educating girls, the zealous priest also recruited young women. Now the bishop gave him the additional responsibility of caring for the spiritual formation of Mother Ana Maria Janer y Anglarill (d. 1885) and her sisters in religion, so that he might foster ties between his own congregation, the Sons of the Holy Family, and the community of nuns headed by Ana Maria Janer y Anglarill and someday unite them. He obeyed, but the project assigned to him by the bishop did not succeed. Eventually the two congregations developed quite well, but separately, as religious communities placed under the patronage of the Holy Family.

Compelled by the political situation in Spain, José Manyanet moved in 1872 to Barcelona. In this city and in the surrounding areas he established parochial schools, boarding schools, and workshops for apprentices. During his years of pastoral activity in Barcelona, he also became a successful author of catechetical works. His most important publications, in which he gave expression to his thoughts on pastoral theology, are as follows: *La Escuela de Nazareth* (The school of Nazareth), *Máximas de perfección cristiana* (Maxims of Christian perfection), *Preciosa joya de familia* (The precious jewel of the family), *El espíritu de la Sagrada Familia* (The

José Manyanet, the great devotee of the "earthly trinity":
Jesus—Mary—Joseph.

spirit of the Holy Family), *Visitas a San José* (Visits with Saint Joseph). Furthermore, the Blessed founded in 1899 the periodical *La Sagrada Familia* (The Holy Family), which found a wide readership and which in 1929 was declared by the Holy See to be the mouthpiece of the *Pia Associatio familiarum christianarum* [Pious association of Christian families]. José Manyanet y Vivès also left a voluminous correspondence of more than one thousand letters, which reveal that this priest was an exceptionally enterprising and successful apostle of devotion to the Holy Family in Spain. This devotion spread then from Spain throughout all of Europe, especially after Pope Leo XIII placed himself squarely behind this movement with his apostolic letter *Neminem fugit* of June 14, 1892.

To this zeal for spreading devotion to the Holy Family we can also attribute the magnificent and still not entirely completed construction of the Church of the Holy Family in Barcelona; the architect for this project, Antonio Gaudi, was seeking to realize the idea that José Manyanet had presented to Bishop Caixal in a letter of June 24, 1869. The Sagrada Familia, Spain's largest and most distinctive church,[2] is still incomplete after one hundred years of construction work because Blessed José Manyanet, who initiated the plans, and the architect Gaudi wanted to ensure that only donations would be used for its construction.

Blessed José Manyanet had to overcome many great difficulties, too, in carrying out all of his plans. Finally, he came down with several illnesses. On December 17, 1901, in Barcelona (San Andrès de Palomar), he died a holy death.

Pope John Paul II paid him the following tribute at his beatification, calling him a heroic witness

> whom the Church places before us . . . to offer him as an example of the model worker for the kingdom of God in Christ . . . Blessed José Manyanet y Vives, a distinguished son of Catalonia in Spain.

[2] See E. Mendoxa, *Die Stadt der Wunder* [The city of miracles] (Frankfurt: Suhrkamp Verlag, 1989).

The reason for the exaltation of this priest and founder of two religious congregations is none other than his heroic commitment to the love of God and to the cause of Christ in the service of his neighbour. He succeeded in exerting all his efforts—despite the limitations of his infirmity—to promote above all "the honour of the Holy Family and the good of families and children". This is the precise charism which permeates his whole life, steeped in the mystery of an evangelical vocation learned from the examples of Jesus, Mary and Joseph in the silence of Nazareth.

At a difficult historical moment, when certain ideologies aimed at penetrating society through the breakdown of the family, the new Blessed looked with farsightedness at the examples of Nazarene sanctity which the Holy Family teaches. From here was born his apostolic commitment to try to bring that message to the world and to make every home a Nazareth. How hard he worked for it by inviting every family—the most precious jewel, as he called it—to look to Nazareth and to build a model of life following God's plan, based at the same time on genuine human values!

Along the same line, he enthusiastically dedicated himself to offering to children and young people the teaching of the Gospel of Nazareth, with great love and respect for each one's vocation, with a view to their harmonious education. How much the new Blessed can teach our present society!

And now a word in the Catalonian language for the fellow countrymen of the new Blessed. Beloved pilgrims, try to be faithful to the example of life and the message of your fellow countryman. Take the model of the Holy Family to your homes. Make each home a Nazareth, following the apostolic aspiration of Blessed Joseph Manyanet.[3]

---

[3] *L'Osservatore Romano*, December 10, 1984, p. 2.

Blessed
Daniel Alex Brottier

Priest, Religious,
Missionary to Africa,
Father of Orphans

b. *September 7, 1872,*
  La Ferté-Saint-Cyr, France
d. *February 28, 1936, Paris*

Beatified November 25, 1984

A French missionary to Africa who first labored to evangelize
Senegal but then provided for orphans and became a father to
them, Blessed Daniel Alex Brottier[1] was raised to the honors of
the altar on November 25, 1984.

Son of a family of modest means but strong faith, he was born
on September 7, 1872, in La Ferté-Saint-Cyr, in the diocese of
Blois, France. From early childhood he showed a deep piety and a
tender devotion to the Mother of God. In 1890 Daniel entered
the seminary after one year of military service, which had not
dampened his enthusiasm for the priestly vocation at all but, rather,
had increased it. On September 22, 1899, he was ordained a priest
in Blois.

The newly ordained priest received an appointment as professor
at the ecclesiastical college in Pontlevoy. He sensed, however, that
this was not his specific calling. For a long time he had been
certain that he ought to proclaim the good news to unbelievers as

---

[1] P. Delgado, *Un grand ami des enfants, le P. Brottiers* (Paris, n.d.).

a missionary. Therefore, on September 24, 1902, he began his novitiate in the Congregation of the Holy Ghost Fathers (Spiritans) at Orly, near Paris. One year later he took religious vows. Soon afterward, he was sent to the mission in Senegal, Africa.

His missionary activity, unfortunately, did not continue for long. Because of constant, very painful migraines, he had to leave Africa. After returning to France, he did get better again, but he was constantly tormented by homesickness for Africa. In January 1907, he was permitted therefore to return to Senegal. He entered into his mission field again, but the debilitating effects of his recurring illness made it impossible for him to fulfill his duties as a missionary satisfactorily. Now he returned to France again for good. His missionary love for Senegal continued, however. That is why he founded the work entitled *Souvenir Africain* for the construction of the cathedral in Dakar.

When World War I broke out in 1914, Daniel Brottier immediately offered his services as a military chaplain. For four long years he performed his duties heroically on the killing fields in Lorraine, along the Somme River, at Verdun, and in Flanders; there he demonstrated to his comrades an admirable degree of self-denial and willingness to sacrifice, with no fear whatsoever of the dangers to his own life. After the First World War he founded the national association of French combat veterans.

In 1923 Father Brottier became director of the project for orphaned apprentices in Auteuil. This work grew considerably under his leadership. All told, he selflessly and paternally looked after more than two thousand orphans.

On February 28, 1936, Daniel Brottier died, exhausted by his many labors and cares on behalf of his orphans. He had finally earned for himself the honorable title of an "apostle of charity", who devoted himself with humble dedication and great zeal to his work.

Pope John Paul II spoke about this noble, selfless priest at the beatification ceremony in Rome on November 25, 1984, in the following words:

Daniel Brottier . . . joined the Congregation of the Holy Ghost Fathers in order to respond in the most intense way to *the missionary call*. When he departed for Africa he devoted himself without compromise to the service of the Christian community of Saint Louis in Senegal, most especially to the service of youth. His *apostolic zeal* led him incessantly to undertake new initiatives so that the Church might be a living reality and the Good News might be heard. Even when he was far distant from this field of his activity he did not cease to aid the building up of the Church in Senegal.

He was a disciple of Christ also through *the ordeal of suffering*. He was never free from physical pain. As a volunteer on the front he cared for and comforted the wounded by his courageous presence, and he brought God's aid to dying soldiers. When the war ended, he strove to prolong the *fraternity* which had grown up among these men in their privation and their heroic gift of self.

When he received [assumed] the care of the *orphans of Auteuil*, he resolutely plunged into a most overwhelming activity on their behalf which made him known far beyond Paris. *Nothing impeded his charity* when it was a question of receiving, nourishing and clothing children who were bruised and abandoned by life. He gathered innumerable associates in this profoundly evangelical labour. Since it was necessary to house these youths and place them in a warm environment, to aid them in learning a trade and building their future, Père Brottier multiplied his appeals and established a *chain of active solidarity* which is alive even today.

As a priest and religious, his great activity "flowed from his love of God", as one witness testified. Both humble and genuine, active to the limits of endurance, an unselfish servant, Daniel Brottier proceeded with boldness and simplicity because he worked "as if everything depended on him, but he also knew that everything depends on God". He entrusted the children of Auteuil to *Saint Theresa of the Child Jesus* whom he called on familiarly for help, certain of her efficacious help to all those for whom she had offered her own life.

Blessed Daniel Brottier perfected his work on earth with a courageous *fiat*. We know today that he is ready to aid the poor who call upon him, because he is in communion with the love of the Saviour, which animated all of his priestly ministry.[2]

---

[2] *L'Osservatore Romano*, December 10, 1984, p. 2.

Blessed María Mercedes de Jesus Molina y Ayala

Foundress

b. 1828, Baba, Ecuador
d. June 12, 1883, Riobamba, Ecuador

Beatified February 1, 1985

The Latin American country of Ecuador gained a second patroness on February 1, 1985—in addition to the "Lily of Quito", Saint Mariana de Jesus (d. May 26, 1645)—when Pope John Paul II beatified María Mercedes de Jesus Molina[1] in Guayaquil, Ecuador.

She was born in the year 1828 in Baba, Los Rios, Ecuador, and grew up in Guayaquil. After the death of her parents, Mercedes led a rather worldly life. A bad fall from a horse, however, brought about her conversion to genuine piety and strict penance. From then on she devoted her life to the care of abandoned children. Then she volunteered her services to the Jesuits in the evangelization of the savage Indians of the Jivaras tribe. When the missionaries from the Society of Jesus had to give up this mission territory, however, Mercedes Molina settled in Riobamba. There, after taking vows of poverty, chastity, and obedience in the presence of the bishop, she founded the Sisters of Saint Mariana de Jesus, on April 14, 1873. This institute provided care for orphaned children and also shelter for converts [from paganism] and for women and girls

[1] Isidor da Villapadierna, "Molina, Maria Mercedes di Gesù", in *Bibliotheca Sanctorum* 9:536–37.

who were at risk or who had been released from prison. Purified by many sufferings and proven in the practice of the Christian virtues, especially love of neighbor, the foundress and former missionary assistant died a holy death in the Lord on June 12, 1883, in Riobamba.

John Paul II said the following about this Ecuadoran woman at the beatification ceremony on February 1, 1985, in Guayaquil:

[I]t is a joy for all the Christian people of Ecuador that from now on they can venerate, together with the "Lily of Quito", Saint Mariana de Jesus, the "Rose of Baba and Guayaquil", Blessed Mercedes de Jesus. They are the fragrance of sanctity and powerful heavenly intercession, model and incentive for an authentic Christian life for all the children of this land.

Jesus Christ, in today's Gospel, addresses his heavenly Father with unique words: "Everything has been given over to me by my Father. No one knows the Son but the Father, and no one knows the Father but the Son—and anyone to whom the Son wishes to reveal him" (Mt 11:27). And at the same time, the Son "offers praise" to the Father, "for you have revealed these things to the merest children" (Mt 11:25). Mother Mercedes de Jesus received this revelation completely. . . .

She could well repeat with the author of the Book of Sirach: "When I was young and innocent, I sought wisdom. She came to me in her beauty, and until the end I will cultivate her . . ." (Sir 51:13–14).

"From earliest youth I was familiar with her. . . . Since in this way I have profited, I will give my teacher grateful praise" (Sir 51:15–17).

Mercedes Molina sought wisdom from her youth. The first sufferings which changed her adolescence into a profound encounter with God were a first ray of divine wisdom. She put on a scale the pleasures that the world offered and the self-giving that the Gospel demanded. And with decisiveness she chose Christ Crucified, the Wisdom of God, as the Spouse of her soul.

At first she lived consecrated to God in the midst of the world, under the guidance of outstanding priests and following in the footsteps of the then Blessed Mariana de Jesus. In this way she sought to identify herself, by prayer and penance, with Christ Crucified, whom she had chosen above any other human love.

This was the slow preparation by which she was predisposed *to give glory to the One who had given her Wisdom.* . . .

Following the way of love, Mercedes Molina, who took the title "de Jesus" to show her total surrender to Christ, very quickly began working to the glory of her Spouse.

She did this first as mother and teacher of orphans in Guayaquil; later, following in the footsteps of her confessor, as a courageous and loving missionary among the "Jibaros" Indians of Gualaquiza; and again as educator and protectress of abandoned children in Cuenca. All of this was a providential preparation in which her charism as foundress was forming and which finally received the approval of the Bishop of Riobamba on Easter Monday of 1873, when the Congregation of the Sisters of Mariana de Jesus, the Marianites, was officially born.

The Spirit of Wisdom had purified in love and in sorrow the charism of a spiritual fruitfulness transmitted to her daughters by the example of her life, along with her direct care for the first religious sisters, personally tending the "rosebush" of Christ Crucified and of the Virgin Mary, Seat of Wisdom. . . . [L]ike an immense rose bush, [her congregation], following the dream and the inspiration of the mother[-foundress], has already spread to various nations, enriching the Church in Latin America with its apostolate. . . .

[S]*anctity consists in love.*

This was in reality the sanctity of this woman of the coast of Ecuador: living the love of Jesus in the love of her neighbour. The contemplative gaze of Mother Mercedes was captivated by the poverty of the Child of Bethlehem, by the suffering on the pained face of the Crucified. She wanted to be simply and clearly *love for suffering*, according to the motto recounted in early biographical notes: "As much love for as many sufferings as there are in the world"; to practice charity toward all those who, in poverty, suffering, and abandonment, reflected the mystery of the poor child of Bethlehem or of Christ suffering on Calvary.

She was mother and educator of orphans, a poor missionary and peacemaker among the Indians, foundress of a religious family. To her daughters she transmitted her same spirit, which identifies sanctity with apostolic love for the most poor, the most disdained, the most abandoned. It was her mission "to announce salvation to the poor without shelter and support", to dry the tears of contrite hearts, to call for the liberation of those suffering imprisonment or condemnation, to comfort all the afflicted. This was love without limits, able to bring aid and comfort, as Mother summarized in her constitutions, *"to as many afflicted hearts as there are in the world"*.

In this manner Jesus Christ, by means of his humble servant Mercedes Molina, has become especially near to the people here in Ecuador; he has been made present in a special way. . . .

The Holy Spirit has sketched on the face of Mother Mercedes the traces of Christ gentle and humble, merciful and kind. In her the true preferential option for the poor shines forth clearly. It is the option of Christ and of the Church throughout all ages. It is the special preference for the most lowly that the Holy Spirit stirs up in the hearts of saints. . . .

Blessed Mercedes teaches us that in the poor there is Christ the poor man, that in all who suffer there is mirrored the loving and suffering face of Jesus. . . .

For the Church in Ecuador, for those responsible for the society of this nation, Blessed Mercedes is not only an honour, she is a model for living. Her example speaks to us of a charity that sprang from the contemplation of the Gospel, from communion with the Eucharist, which was translated into works of mercy. For this reason, like the presence of Christ in this land, it offers us a challenge to practice the Gospel of charity in the same areas where she was able to carry out her commitment of love for Christ from the very start.[2]

[2] *L'Osservatore Romano*, March 11, 1985, pp. 9–10.

Blessed
Ana de los Angeles
Monteagudo

Dominican Nun

b. around 1600, Arequipa, Peru
d. January 10, 1686, Arequipa

Beatified February 2, 1985

In addition to the Third Order Dominican Saint Rose of Lima (d. August 24, 1617), the Latin American country of Peru received a blessed of the Second Order of Saint Dominic as well, when Pope John Paul II beatified Sister Ana de los Angeles[1] in Arequipa.

She was born around 1600 in Arequipa and educated at the Dominican convent in the same locality. She then entered the convent, and, as a nun and finally as superior, she actually spent the rest of her life in that cloister, leading an intense prayer life and also performing works of charity for her neighbors and glorifying God after the example of the saint to whom her convent was dedicated, namely, Saint Catherine of Siena (d. April 29, 1380). She died on January 10, 1686, at the advanced age of eighty-six, rich in merits, as Pope John Paul II emphasized in the beatification homily:

> In Sister Ana we admire above all the exemplary Christian, the contemplative Dominican nun of the famous monastery of St Catherine, a monument of art and devotion of which the

[1] M. C. de Ganay, *Le Beate Dominicane*, vol. 2 (Rome, 1933), 158.

people of Arequipa rightfully feel proud. She carried out in her life the Dominican programme of light, of truth, of love, and of life, summed up in the well-known phrase [*contemplata aliis tradere*]: "contemplate and transmit what is contemplated."

Sister Ana de los Angeles carried out this programme with an intense, austere, radical surrender to the monastic life, according to the manner of the Order of Saint Dominic, in the contemplation of the mystery of Christ, the Truth and Wisdom of God.

But at the same time her life held a singular apostolic irradiation. She was a spiritual leader and faithful implementer of the norms of the Church that urgently sought the reform of the monasteries. She knew how to accept everyone who turned to her, teaching them the paths of pardon and the life of grace. Her hidden presence became noticed, beyond the walls of her convent, by the fame of her sanctity. With her prayer and her advice she helped bishops and priests; with her prayer she accompanied travellers and pilgrims who came to her.

Her long life was spent almost entirely within the walls of the monastery of St Catherine; first as a student and later as a religious and superior. In her last years she spent herself in a painful identification with the mystery of Christ Crucified.

Sister Ana de los Angeles confirmed with her life the apostolic fruitfulness of the contemplative life in the Mystical Body of Christ which is the Church, a contemplative life which took root very quickly here as well, from the very beginning of evangelization, and continues to be a mysterious wealth of the Church in Peru and of all of Christ's Church.

By her name in religion, Blessed Ana de los Angeles reminds us of those first fruits of creation, our "fellow servants", the holy Angels. She knew how eager they are to help and how ardently they desire to lead us to God and to guard us from the Evil One.

Certainly Sister Ana spent her life following this maxim of St John the Evangelist: "If God has loved us so, we must have the same love for one another" (1 Jn 4:11).

In the school of the Divine Master her heart was being patterned to learn the meekness and humility of Christ. . . .

Imitating the charity and ecclesial sense of her patroness, Catherine of Siena, she had a gentle and humble heart open to the needs of all, especially of the poorest.

Everyone found in her a genuine love. The poor and the lowly found a gracious welcome; the rich, an understanding that did not neglect the need for conversion; pastors found prayer and counsel; the sick, relief; the sorrowful, comfort; travellers, hospitality; the persecuted, pardon; the dying, fervent prayer.

Present in a special way in the prayerful and effective charity of Sister Ana were the dead, the souls in Purgatory whom she called "her friends". In this way, enlightening the ancestral devotion for the dead with the teaching of the Church, following the example of St Nicholas of Tolentino [d. September 10, 1305], to whom she was devoted, she extended her charity to the dead with prayer and petition.

Therefore, recalling these intimate details of the life of the new Blessed, her penance and almsgiving, her constant and fervent prayer for everyone, we have called to mind the words of the Book of Tobit: "Prayer and fasting are good, but better than either is almsgiving accompanied by righteousness. It is better to give alms than to store up gold. . . . Those who regularly give alms shall enjoy a full life" (Tobit 12:8–9), as she did, who died at an advanced age, full of virtues and merits.[2]

[2] *L'Osservatore Romano*, March 18, 1985, p. 8.

Blessed
Maria Caterina Troiani

Religious, Foundress

b. *January 19, 1813,*
   Giuliano di Roma, Italy
d. *May 6, 1887, Cairo*

Beatified April 14, 1985

Just as in our time the Ursuline nun Sister Emmaneula takes into her care the street children and the destitute of Cairo in Egypt, so too, one hundred years ago in that same great city, did Blessed Maria Caterina Troiani, who was raised to the honors of the altar by Pope John Paul II on April 14, 1985.

Costanza Domenica Troiani[1]—that was the baptismal name of this new blessed—was born on January 19, 1813, in Giuliano di Roma (diocese of Ferentino, Italy), the third child of her parents, Tommaso Troiani and Teresa Panici Cantoni. When tragedy struck her family and the three-year-old girl lost her mother, she was taken to Ferentino on July 18, 1816, and her upbringing and education were entrusted to the Sisters of Charity, who lived there according to the Rule of Saint Clare. At age sixteen Costanza Domenica entered this community of nuns and on December 8, 1829, took the religious name of Maria Caterina di Santa Rosa di Viterbo.

Sister Maria Caterina bore within her an ardent desire to go to the missions. Eventually, a request from the apostolic vicar of

---

[1] A. Pierotti, *Clausura e missione: Madre Maria Caterina Troiani de S. Rosa da Viterbo* (Rome, 1952); Sr. Antonia Falchi, *Mamma Bianca in terra d'Africa* (Rome, 1960).

Cairo reached the nuns of Ferentino, asking that some of them come to his mission in Cairo and look after abandoned girls there. In 1854 Sister Maria Caterina was able to travel to Cairo with a small group of her sisters in religion. After overcoming enormous difficulties, Sister Maria Caterina succeeded in opening a home and a school there for girls of every skin color and religious affiliation. Gradually, as the number of girls in their care (and of those still to be cared for) continued to increase, the sisters from Ferentino had a growing need for reinforcements from their motherhouse. No such help was granted them, however, to the great sorrow of Sister Maria Caterina, who had been elected abbess at the chapter in 1863, and so it happened that the nuns working in Cairo separated from their motherhouse in Ferentino. They became autonomous, and their community now called itself the Congregation of the Third Order Franciscan Missionaries of Egypt; in 1950 they received the name of Franciscan Missionary Sisters of the Immaculate Heart of Mary.

Sister Maria Caterina devoted herself unstintingly to the care of poor, abandoned, and endangered children. She managed to expand the house and the school in Clot-Bey, the suburb of Cairo where the community's work had begun, and also to establish additional houses in Egypt. At last, something that the blessed had dreamed of for years was realized: she was even able to open a house in Jerusalem (1885). She was not ashamed, either, to go begging when there was a financial need. By doing so she won over several very distinguished patrons, such as the viceroy of Egypt, Ismail Pascha; then, the sultan of Constantinople; Emperor Franz Joseph [of Austria-Hungary]; and the engineer who built the Suez Canal, Ferdinand de Lesseps.

The spirituality of Sister Maria Caterina and her community was markedly Franciscan and included a special veneration of the Sacred Heart of Jesus and an extraordinary love for the Virgin Mother of Jesus Christ and for her spouse, Saint Joseph, as well as a confident devotion to the Holy Guardian Angels. At the death of Sister Maria Caterina on May 6, 1887, it became apparent that she was esteemed and loved as "the white Mama", not only by Christians, but also by Muslims.

Pope John Paul II spoke as follows about this nun as he raised her to the honor of the altars:

Faith and charity shine forth also in the life of Sister Caterina Troiani, the foundress of the Franciscan Sisters of the Immaculate Heart of Mary. She was completely open to God's plan, and was called by Providence to leave the monastery of the Poor Clares of Ferentino and settle with some sisters in Egypt, there to attend to the human and Christian education of the children of that land abroad. Mindful of the vow taken in the first years of her religious profession to "live always in obedience and in disregard of self", she dedicated herself with missionary zeal to her new service in the city of Cairo.

She was confronted by a mountain of misery and suffering which seemed to reflect a synthesis of human pain: slavery, hunger, poverty, abandonment of infants and of the ill, exploitation and neglect. Sister Caterina did not limit herself to pointing out to others how much had to be done for those unfortunate people. Like the Good Samaritan of the Gospel parable, she halted beside every brother and sister suffering in body or spirit, lovingly offering her helping hand and paying personally. Her love towards every victim of suffering, of sickness and of distress never knew bounds: Catholics, Orthodox and Muslims found in her welcome and aid, because in every person marked by suffering Sister Caterina saw the suffering face of Christ. It was not for nothing that the little sister, rather than by her own name, was known as the "Mother of the poor", and was called the "white mother" by the women of the place who had been freed from slavery.

Nor did the risk of sickness and even of death itself by contagion check the ardour of Sister Caterina's charity. Twice there were cholera epidemics, and in such dramatic situations the Blessed and her sisters were concerned only with assisting those struck by the disease. Some of them paid with their lives for such a service of dedication and love.

Just when the works she had instituted seemed to be prospering in peace, the war of 1882 suddenly broke out, which seemed to sweep everything away. Even in these circumstances the Blessed's shining faith, indomitable courage and ardent charity stood out. With unshakeable hope in Providence she continued to behave in every circumstance according to the principle dear to her: "Diffidence towards oneself, trust in God".

Blessed Caterina Troiani entered into the service of the Church with a style of her own. As an attentive and faithful disciple of Saint Clare and Saint Francis of Assisi, she succeeded in uniting in herself the contemplative life of the one with the itinerant apostolate of the other. In full and total dedication to the Lord and to her brothers and sisters, she was a missionary in the cloister and a contemplative in the missions.[2]

---

[2] *L'Osservatore Romano*, May 13, 1985, p. 7.

Blessed
Pauline von
Mallinckrodt

Foundress

b. *June 3, 1817, Minden,*
    Westphalia, Germany
d. *April 30, 1881, Paderborn*

Beatified April 14, 1985

This German blessed[1] was the oldest of four children of an Evangelical Lutheran finance officer, Detmar von Mallinckrodt, a descendant of an ancient noble line in Westphalia, and a devout Catholic woman, Bernhardine von Hartmann; the child was born on June 3, 1817, in Minden, in Westphalia, and was baptized Pauline.

The foundation for Pauline's later charitable activity was laid by the example of her mother, whom she accompanied even as a child on visits to the poor and the sick.

In 1824 the family moved to Aachen. There, from 1827 to 1831, Pauline attended Saint Leonhard's Girls' School, where at that time the teacher and poet Luise Hensel (d. 1876) was doing great good. The latter understood how to awaken in her pupils—contrary to the prevailing trends of the time—a profound sense of religion; as a result, many of her pupils embraced religious life, for example, Pauline's classmate Clara Fey, the foundress of the Sisters of the Poor Child Jesus, and Franziska Schervier, the foundress of

[1] Sr. M. Renate Rautenbach, S.C.C., *Idee und Gestalt des Erziehungs- und Bildungswesens der Congregatio Sororum Christianae Caritatis Filiarum Immaculatae Conceptionis* (Bonn, 1987).

the Poor Sisters of Saint Francis. Pauline had a deep respect for her teacher and stayed in contact with her for the rest of her life, since she owed to Luise Hensel—a close friend of [now Blessed] Anna Katharina Emmerick—the development of her religious and charitable inclinations.

A fundamental attitude of kindness and beneficence characterized Pauline's entire life from then on. When her mother died of typhoid fever, in 1834, Pauline considered entering a religious order. That did come about, but by a peculiar path, leading to an order that she herself founded.

After her father was pensioned, the Mallinckrodt family moved in 1839 to Böddeken Estate, in the vicinity of Paderborn. In the winter months the family lived in the city of Paderborn, in the former presidential house, beside the Busdorf church. Here Pauline began her life's work. She soon saw poverty and need all around her, and she joined the Ladies' League for the Care of Poor Invalids in their Houses and also the League of Nurses to Keep Voluntary Vigils. As a result of Pauline's efforts, a child-care center was formed in 1840, in which untended children below school age were taken in and protected from becoming wayward. Pauline assumed the direction of this institution and the greater part of the expenses involved; she raised money, among other ways, through benefit performances.

On April 4, 1842, Pauline's father died. Now she moved to Paderborn for good. In that same year, 1842, she took in her first blind children, who had been living in miserable conditions, and with the support of the regional physician, Dr. H.-J. Schmidt, she founded the private Institute for the Education of Blind Children. Pauline learned about various possibilities for instructing the blind while on a trip through Germany, Austria, and northern Italy together with her sisters in 1843. From then on the care and education of the blind was the chief duty among her charitable works.

In order to expand further the institute for the blind, Pauline von Mallinckrodt looked for a suitable religious community that she herself would enter, so as to place her life entirely at the service of her fellow men. Auxiliary Bishop Anton Gottfried Claessen (1788–1847) of Cologne, a friend of the Mallinckrodt family, advised Pauline to found her own religious community instead. She did in fact resolve to do so in 1849, and, together with four like-minded women, she founded the Congregation of the Sisters of Christian Charity of the Daughters of the Immaculate Conception (*Congregatio Sororum Christianae Caritatis Filiarum Immaculatae Conceptionis*, SCC).

Pauline von Mallinckrodt remained the superior of this religious congregation until the end of her life. Eventually, the sisters not only worked at the institute for the blind in Paderborn, but also in later years were in charge of general schools, as well as orphanages and child-care centers, in many German cities. At the time of her religious profession on November 4, 1850, Mother Pauline, as she was now called, declared that she wanted "to consecrate her time, her energies, her health, and her life to the service of the blind, of children, and of the needy".

Mother Pauline set great store by the solid formation and training of the sisters who entered her congregation. Above all, however, she demanded that the sisters lead a genuine spiritual life of true piety and that they go about educating the children entrusted to them with great love. The following statement of hers is characteristic: "Love for the children is the best teacher of pedagogy; one can entrust children only to someone who loves them. Love in your heart, love in your tone of voice, love in your conduct toward the children—that attracts them with an irresistible force, and it also draws down God's blessing upon them and us."

Placing education upon a religious foundation is one of the preeminent hallmarks of the pedagogy of Pauline von Mallinckrodt. A deep respect for the human person characterized her relations with all people, especially with the children entrusted to her care. One must accept the youngster as she is, she would say, must have understanding for her, believe in the good that is within her and in her fundamental capacity to develop.

In 1871 the *Kulturkampf* began in Germany; in the course of this "cultural war", Pauline von Mallinckrodt lost the German houses of her religious congregation. She now moved these communities abroad, to neighboring countries. In Mont Saint Guibert, near Brussels, she established a new motherhouse for the congregation. She also took on new fields of endeavor in North and South America: in 1873 the first sisters traveled to the United States of America; in 1874 others went to Chile to take charge of schools and kindergartens there. During 1879 and 1880, Pauline von Mallinckrodt visited all her daughters across the Atlantic. The trip took her almost an entire year. After returning, she also visited the sisters who remained in Germany, and on December 28, 1880, she called at the former motherhouse in Paderborn; since the disbanding of the convent there, her brother Georg had rented the building from the state as a residence for elderly, sick nuns. Meanwhile, there was a relaxation in the *Kulturkampf* laws; later, the sisters were able to return to their former places of work in Germany.

When Pauline von Mallinckrodt died at the age of sixty-three, on April 30, 1881, in Paderborn, she left behind an extensive educational apostolate that had finally flourished again, even in Germany. At the death of the foundress, the congregation comprised 45 houses—of which 26 were in North America and 8 in Chile—in which a total of 402 sisters (284 of them in the United States) were performing good deeds in various fields of duty, all in the spirit of the "pedagogy of love" that Pauline von Mallinckrodt had practiced.

At the beatification of this great German woman on April 14, 1985, Pope John Paul II paid the following tribute to the new blessed:

> The spiritual message of the new Blessed, Pauline von Mallinckrodt, can be summed up in a very relevant and concrete philosophy of life: to follow Christ unreservedly in unshakeable faith; to love God and lovingly to dedicate oneself to the most lowly and poor, for the sake of Christ.

Mother Pauline von Mallinckrodt had many natural gifts: a simple, friendly character; confidence and trust in others; perseverance in pursuing her goals; enduring fidelity to the fundamental choices of her life—even in trials and great difficulties—and a sense of sacrifice, by which she magnanimously sought to give of herself unreservedly to everyone.

These rich gifts with which God so liberally endowed her were completed by a deep and developed spirit of faith. This gift of grace, which she received at Baptism, developed wonderfully under the guidance of her mother and her teachers. She grew up in the peaceful environment of a family in which love and mutual respect ruled, in a climate which nevertheless was not without silent suffering, because her parents belonged to different confessions: her mother was a believing Catholic and her father a convinced Protestant. With the help of grace, Pauline's fidelity to the Lord was strengthened as she came to terms with this situation.

However, there was also a period of crisis in her youth, a time of great anguish, full of scruples, anxieties and uncertainties. She could overcome these only by entrusting herself fully and completely to God in deep and constant prayer. And God was near to her and illumined her soul with such a clear light of faith that it can rightly be called a special "grace of faith". This new vision, given her by God, allowed her to exclaim: "I was so penetrated by this clear and solid faith that I would have believed it rather than my own eyes" (cf. *Autobiography*).

As a contemporary of hers testifies, this faith made Pauline's character a whole—clear and transparent as light, and just as simple (cf. Schlüter). Thus already at the age of eighteen she was able to recognize with unequivocal certainty that her purpose in life was determined by a special call from God.

Hers was a conscious and courageous faith. It allowed her to endure pain, bitterness and many trials, and it showed itself in her complete and unreserved love for Jesus Christ and his Mother Mary. Full of confidence and trust she left herself in their hands. Striving for God and his greater glory she grew in grace, for she constantly drew strength from prayer in the context of a profound eucharistic life.

Her love of neighbor grew naturally and spontaneously from her love of God. With great tenderness she devoted herself to unfortunate blind children, to whom she wished to give an inner light, a ray of the divine light. She founded her Congregation of the Sisters of Christian Charity for this service of love for the sake of Christ. Together with these children she took charge of other people who were in need of help: in her and her foundation everyone found help, consolation, and above all love. This same love made her also include education of youth among the tasks of her Congregation. She believed that this was a true missionary work, especially required by the needs of the time.

Her plans were daring; but she knew how to wait in quiet and humble restraint for the time which God would choose. Her work grew successful, though only amid continual struggles and difficulties. The time of its greatest growth also saw the coming of a destructive storm, persecution under the laws of the *Kulturkampf*. But here too Mother Pauline showed her interior openness to the will of God and was ready and able to encounter trials, and make her Way of the Cross.

The life of Mother Pauline is an example to us. In answer to the anxious unrest of modern man she shows us a way to inner peace: by courageously and trustingly seeing God in one's suffering brother and sister. Thus her message has relevance today too, for the search for God is always relevant.[2]

---

[2] *L'Osservatore Romano*, May 13, 1985, pp. 6–7.

Blessed [Saint] Benedetto (Angelo Ercole) Menni

Priest, Religious, Restorer of His Order

b. *March 11, 1841, Milan*
d. *April 24, 1914, Dinan*

Beatified June 23, 1985
[Canonized November 21, 1999]

For a long time the Order of the Hospitaller Brothers, which Saint John of God had called into existence, was forbidden and disbanded and had died out in the many countries of Europe—including Portugal and Spain, where it had originated; yet in the last third of the nineteenth century it was revived by Benedetto Menni,[1] who was raised to the honors of the altar on June 23, 1985 [and later canonized, in 1999].

This new blessed was born on March 11, 1841, in Milan, the son of devout Catholic parents, Luigi and Luisa Menni, née Figini, and on the same day he was baptized with the name of Angelo Ercole.

In 1859, at the age of eighteen, the young man attended to wounded soldiers on the battlefield of Magenta as a volunteer medic. He helped transport the wounded from the train station in Milan to the hospital in that city run by the Hospitaller Brothers, and then he assisted and cared for the bedridden soldiers. The

---

[1] F. Bilbao, *Biografia del Reverendissimo Padre Fr. Benito Menni, Priore e Restauratore dell'Ordine di S. Giovanni di Dio: Fondatore delle Suore Ospedaliere del S. Cuore di Gesù* (Rome, 1939).

example of the Hospitaller Brothers, which he was able to observe, made a great impression on him and awakened in him the desire to emulate their life and work in the service of the sick. On May 1, 1860, he entered the Order of the Hospitaller Brothers, and on May 13, 1860, he received the habit and the religious name of Benedetto [Benedict]. On May 15, 1861, he took temporary vows and on May 17, 1864, his solemn perpetual vows in religion. He then studied theology at the seminary in Lodi. As a member of the Order of Hospitallers he needed medical and surgical training; in order to deepen his knowledge of these disciplines, he practiced medicine at the same time in the order's hospital in Lodi.

Called to Rome, he took another course there to complete his training, and then, on October 14, 1866, he was ordained a priest.

Father Giovanni Alfieri, then the general prior of the Order of Saint John of God, recognized the abilities of the young religious priest and entrusted to him a very special task: he was assigned to reestablish and reactivate the suppressed, disbanded, and extinct hospitals and communities of the order in Spain, Portugal, Latin America, and the Philippines. One day, the general prior, Father Alfieri, introduced the young Father Benedetto Menni to the Pope of the Immaculata, Pius IX. The latter, as though by an inspiration from on high, with extraordinary kindness, took the hands of the young religious priest in his own and said to him, "Go, my son, with heaven's blessing, to reestablish and to renew your order in the place where its cradle once stood." Then, in a few key phrases, the Pope gave him the guidelines along which this restoration of the order was to proceed: "A life in community lived to perfection: very poor, very chaste, and very obedient!" (*Vita perfettamente commune, molto povera, molto casta, e molto obbediente!*)

On the day of his religious profession, Benedetto Menni had prayed that he might glorify God: "O Lord, I want to labor for my order until my final breath!" Animated by this resolution and strengthened by the papal blessing, Father Benedetto Menni set out on January 16, 1867, from Rome. He stayed for a few months in the houses of his order in Lyons and Marseilles, so as to learn something of the spirit in which the restoration of the order had been carried out there after the French Revolution. In April 1867, Father Benedetto Menni arrived in Barcelona, without money and without any knowledge of the language.

At first, in Barcelona, even Archbishop Montserrat y Navarro was opposed to the plan of reestablishing the Order of the Hospitaller Brothers in Spain. Soon, however, he took the young religious priest under his wing and helped him very effectively in carrying out this plan. With two brothers of the order who had accompanied Father Benedetto, a children's hospital for abandoned children with rickets was founded in Barcelona in December 14, 1867.

Sickness and the tumult of war subsequently forced Father Benedetto Menni several times to leave Spain. He finally succeeded, nevertheless, not only with the children's hospital in Barcelona, but also in establishing a similar hospital in Madrid. Then came—after the necessary personnel had enlisted in the order— the foundation of hospitals in Granada, Seville, Málaga, Valencia, Gibraltar, and Carabanchel Alto; still other houses followed in Guadalajara in Mexico, as well as in Lisbon and Aldeja da Ponte in Portugal.

In 1884 Father Benedetto Menni, with a wonderful band of religious brothers whom he had recruited for the apostolate and then formed by his word and example, received permission from the Holy See to erect the Latin American province of his order. He himself became the first provincial, and he was reelected to this post five times by the general chapter of the order. In March 1903, at the end of his career as provincial, this province numbered fourteen houses and hospitals, which he had founded and placed on a firm footing; the many projects that he had planned and attempted to put into action are not included in this figure.

The hospitals and communities that Father Benedetto Menni had founded were designed for men only. Requests came in again and again from the various local authorities, however, that the institutions of the Hospitaller brothers should be made available for women, too, especially the psychiatric wards. Thus the idea matured in the mind of this dynamic religious of founding a separate and independent branch of the Order of the Hospitallers for women. Two young women, natives of Granada, Josefa Recio and Maria de las Angustias Jiménez, placed themselves at his disposal for this purpose. Together with them he founded the Congregation of the Hospitaller Sisters of the Sacred Heart of Jesus, which in 1901 was approved by the Holy See. The number of foundations of these sisters increased very rapidly; they soon spread to Europe, America, and Africa.

After Father Benedetto Menni concluded his service as provincial, in 1903, he was almost exclusively concerned with the growth and consolidation of the congregation of sisters that he had called into existence.

In 1909 Father Benedetto Menni was called to Rome and was appointed by the Holy See apostolic visitator for the entire Hospitaller order. After fulfilling this duty successfully, he became the general prior of the order on April 21, 1911. He remained in this post only until June 11, 1912, however, when he received the title of general prior emeritus.

Soon after that he was sent to Paris. There he had an unexpected attack of paralysis, and then a second one in Dinan, where he eventually died on April 24, 1914.

As for the personality of this great restorer of the Hospitaller Order of Saint John of God, we should note that all of the admirable apostolic and charitable activities of Blessed Benedetto Menni proceeded from his ardent love of God, which in turn was rooted in a diligently cultivated interior life and an intense prayer life. The principles that gave purpose and guidance both to his ascetical practices and also to his indefatigable activity were as follows, as he himself formulated them: "Love God and serve him, while mistrusting yourself; place all your trust instead in Jesus and throw yourself entirely into his arms. Pray, work, suffer, be patient, love God, and be silent!"

Pope John Paul II, at the beatification of Father Benedetto Menni, said about this new blessed:

Father Menni fully understood [the] need to dedicate one's own life to Christ. He had read and made his own the words of the divine Master . . . : "Whenever you did these things to one of the least of these my brothers, you did them to me" (Mt 25:40). Among "these things" which the Lord considers as done to himself, Father Menni chose in a particular way the loving care of the sick, especially of children and the mentally ill.

Nourishing himself deeply on the spirituality of the Order of the Hospitallers of St John of God, which he had entered while still youthful, he was the restorer of this Order after the sad period of the Napoleonic suppressions and of the political regimes opposed to the Church, which had continued up to his own days. He is therefore a glory of the Order of the Hospitaller Brothers, who have in him a luminous example of the service of the sick, identified with Christ.

Father Menni, apart from this, knew how to bring to marvellous fruit some possibilities latent in the spirituality of the Order, becoming the founder of a new Congregation of Sisters dedicated to the care of mentally ill women: the Hospitaller Sisters of the Sacred Heart of Jesus, who rejoice today [at this beatification ceremony] as they see the virtues of the one whom they venerate as father and master, solemnly recognised by the Church in the month dedicated to the Divine Heart to whom they are consecrated.

The beatification of their Founder, which they have ardently longed for, should serve to stimulate their undertaking to serve Christ in the person of the sick women, according to the charism proper to the Institute.

The work accomplished by Father Menni to alleviate the suffering of so many people, had a great effect in the various countries in which he exercised his charitable activities; and, particularly, in Spain where he spent a significant part of his life.

But even in our days, his work continues to be well-deserving and providential in a society which, unfortunately, tends frequently to isolate the weak and the suffering.

[Blessed Benedetto Menni]—like all the followers of Christ—did not escape misunderstandings and suffering, even from people very close to him. However, Father Menni, convinced of his good reasons and comforted by his profound communion with Christ and the Church, was able to resist the attacks and carry on his fruitful work in the service of society and of the Kingdom of God.

His extraordinary activity was constantly sustained and animated by an intimate and profound devotion to the Sacred Heart of Jesus, and by a particular veneration for the Mother of God, especially under the title of Our Lady of the Sacred Heart of Jesus.

His exemplary humility placed him in a constant attitude of conversion and limitless trust in the power of Divine Providence.

He was untiring in his efforts to follow [in] Christ's footsteps, a good Samaritan, imitating in a unique way a merciful behaviour towards those who suffer, without giving importance to class or social condition; for in the sufferer he would always see one of those "least" brethren in whom the divine Saviour remains hidden.

"Let us ask Jesus"—he wrote in one of his letters—"to inflame us with his Love. Let us ask the Queen of Love, the Immaculate Virgin, to enkindle within us this divine fire."

Without this "divine fire", that is to say, the fire of the Holy Spirit, the Blessed could not have done all those things that he so splendidly accomplished.[2]

---

[2] *L'Osservatore Romano*, July 22, 1985, p. 6.

Blessed
Peter Friedhofen

Chimney Sweep, Founder

b. *February 25, 1819,*
   Weitersburg, Rheinland
d. *December 21, 1860, Koblenz*

Beatified June 23, 1985

In the diocese of Trier at the beginning of the nineteenth century, because of the prevailing French laws, Church organizations for the care of the poor and the sick had been laid to rest almost without exception. In August of 1802, the Alexian Brothers of Trier, too, who had looked after the sick and the poor especially, were driven from their friary. In the entire diocese not one single religious community remained that was devoted to the care of the sick. Only in the 1830s was it possible again to found ecclesiastical communities for the purpose of charitable and social work. Among the most noteworthy communities of this sort is the foundation by the layman Peter Friedhofen,[1] whom Pope John Paul II raised to the honors of the altar on June 23, 1985.

Peter Friedhofen was born on February 25, 1819, in Weitersburg, near Vallendar, in the Rheinland, the son of a prolific farming family. His father, who had the same name, died young in 1820, soon after Peter's birth; his mother, Anna Maria, née Klug,

---

[1] Hans von Meurers, *Peter Friedhofen, Schornsteinfeger und Ordensstifter* (Mönchen-Gladbach, 1935); F. Amoroso, *Dalle fuliggini dei camini alla gloria degli altari* (Rome, 1985).

followed her husband eight years later to her death. Thus Peter's life as an orphan was marked by material need and deprivation from an early age. He grew up in poverty, in extremely wretched conditions, yet he received a solid religious education; most important, his piety was characterized by a strong Marian devotion.

At the age of fourteen, Peter went to be an apprentice to his brother Jakob, who worked in Ahrweiler as a chimney sweep. During this time, Peter, inspired by the customary prayers of the parish, developed a special devotion to the patron saint of youth, Aloysius of Gonzaga. Later, he recruited other like-minded youngsters to form a brotherhood whose members made it their duty to promote the practice of the faith and to lead a moral, chaste life. During his three years as a journeyman after his apprenticeship, Peter traveled through the regions of Eifel, Moselland, and Westerwald.

After working with his brother Jakob again for a while, Peter, who had earned the title of master chimney sweep, settled in Vallendar in 1842 to ply that trade. He was sick rather often during that time, however, and so he was unable to carry out his career plans. Nevertheless, he tried all the more to recruit members for his Brotherhood of Saint Aloysius.

While searching for a more suitable way of life that would have a definite religious character, Peter Friedhofen gave up his occupation in Vallendar and in October of 1845 spent a short time in the Redemptorist community in Wittem/Limburg; the experience made a deep impression on him, but he was not meant to stay there.

After the death of his brother Jakob in November 1845, Peter Friedhofen took over his position as master chimney sweep in Ahrweiler, chiefly in order to support his widowed sister-in-law and her eleven children. During this stay in Ahrweiler, he devoted himself even more intensively than before to the Brotherhood of Saint Aloysius that he had founded, for which he had drawn up a rule while in Vallendar.[2]

[2] *"Neues Feuer": Schriften und Korrespondenz des P. Friedhofen* (Trier, 1953), pp. 16, 18–31.

In 1847, by the good offices of members of the brotherhood, Peter Friedhofen contacted Ignatius Liess, who was secretary to the bishop of Trier, Wilhelm Arnoldi, and presented to him his ideas about the further development of his Brotherhood of Saint Aloysius. One year later he received, together with several of his brethren, an audience with Bishop Arnoldi, who approved the brotherhood and confirmed its rule.

Unfortunately, that same year the brotherhood went through a crisis—perhaps because of the excessively strict demands of its founder—with the result that several members withdrew. Friedhofen himself wanted to resign. During this crucial year of 1848–1849, the call to religious life matured within him. At first he thought of gathering together the Saint Aloysius brethren to live in community, and for this purpose he built a house in his home parish of Weitersburg that he called the "little cloister" (*Klösterchen*). On November 3, 1849, he informed the bishop's secretary, Liess, of his intentions. Afterward the house was to be dedicated to the Mother of God: "In that very spot we should begin the strict life of the saintly monks of old. I want to make a start and go on ahead of the others with courage and trust. With the grace of God, people will see me next year wearing penitential garb. I feel an enormous drive within me to do this, and I cannot resist it. Neither mockery nor persecution, nor poverty, nor contradictions can prevent me, because, as I hope, the Lord is with me." Friedhofen then went on to say that he wanted to go to a cloister first for a few months, "so as to learn how to do everything right, and then move into the house wearing a religious habit".

Promptly on November 7, 1849, the bishop's secretary replied on behalf of the bishop. The latter welcomed the plan of founding the Institute of the Brothers of Charity to care for the sick in the diocese of Trier. He recommended that Peter Friedhofen have his orientation and training with the Alexian Brothers in Aachen, Cologne, or Neuss. In the winter of 1849 and 1850, Friedhofen went to Dernbach to visit Blessed Katharina Kasper, who, shortly before that, under the most difficult conditions, had founded the

Society of the Poor Handmaids of Christ to do social work. From this venture Friedhofen drew fresh courage for his own plans. He wanted to do without the visit to the Alexian Brothers' community, which the bishop had advised him to make, and begin on his own.

Immediately after his return from Dernbach, he presented his new reflections to Liess, the bishop's secretary. He said that he felt called to begin something independent, to unite himself closely to Jesus, to work for the conversion of sinners, and to promote Marian devotion, and for the sake of these goals "to care for the sick out of Christian charity". He emphasized his willingness, however, to comply in all things with the bishop's orders. Only a few days later, the answer arrived from Trier. Bishop Arnoldi agreed to the plan for a foundation in Friedhofen's home in Weitersburg and recommended finishing the construction of the house that had been begun. He required, however, that Peter Friedhofen receive training in a hospital to become a nurse. On July 13, 1850, Peter Friedhofen traveled to Aachen, with his friend

Karl Marchand, to the Alexian Brothers, where he was introduced to the care of the mentally ill, as well as to the care of the sick in hospital wards and in their homes.

The experience that he gained until December 1, 1850, strengthened Peter Friedhofen in his decision to undertake a new and independent foundation: "I am not taking on an old rule, but rather am writing with new fire and new impetus a rule that will serve as our guide and according to which we will live", he wrote to Liess, the bishop's secretary. He wanted to place the intended foundation under the patronage of the Mother of God and thus promote devotion to her. At the end of 1850, he moved into the unassuming house in Weitersburg with Karl Marchand and one other collaborator. Weitersburg, however, soon proved to be unsuitable for the new foundation; soon it was transferred to Koblenz. There the young pastor Philipp de Lorenzi, at the church of Our Lady (*Liebfrauenkirche*), took an active interest in the new foundation and served as its commissioner. Soon plenty of work was found, too, for the Brothers of Charity of Mary, Help of Christians, as the members of Peter Friedhofen's foundation were finally called.

Gradually their number grew, so that in 1858 the brotherhood could begin to venture abroad. The new affiliates (the first of which was in Luxembourg) overwhelmed Peter Friedhofen with duties. To him, however, the religious character of his brethren seemed more important than the mere external growth of his work. Since tuberculosis of the lungs prevented him, from 1857, from undertaking long journeys, he communicated with the brothers in the affiliated houses through the letters he sent to them. In his correspondence he urgently recommended that the brothers cultivate the spiritual life and persevere in the spirit of poverty.

Besides the numerous letters, the blessed left to his companions in religion a Spiritual Testament as well, composed in the year 1860.

After an illness that lasted six weeks, Peter Friedhofen died on December 21, 1860, at the early age of forty-one, deeply mourned by his brothers and by the inhabitants of the city of Koblenz. His simple origins and his weak health had not prevented this young man, who felt called to his work, from building great things in the service of the sick and the poor. At his death, the congregation founded by Peter Friedhofen numbered thirty-nine members and eight postulants in five houses.

"The love of Christ constrains us"—this is what St Paul avows of himself. It was this same love that constrained the newly-beatified Peter Friedhofen at the age of thirty to consecrate his life totally to God and to the service of the sick. Although himself poor and in bad health, he gave up his lay calling as a chimney-sweep, in order to make a new start out of his religious conviction and his burning love of neighbour.

Thus Pope John Paul II began his *laudatio* to Blessed Peter Friedhofen at the beatification ceremony in Saint Peter's Basilica in Rome on June 23, 1985:

[This Blessed] saw the wretched situation of uprooted, sick and needy people, and recognized his own apostolic mission. Thus, he founded in 1850 the community of the "Brothers of Charity of Mary, Help of Christians" with the task of serving God in poor, sick and old people.

God's providence had prepared Peter Friedhofen through the school of a hard life to recognize the signs of the times in the great social upheaval of the nineteenth century, and to reply to this out of the spirit of the Gospel. As an orphan, he had as a child to experience in his own life suffering and material need.

The house of his parents and his native Rhineland gave him a deep religious life, above all an intimate veneration of the Immaculate Virgin Mary. Already in the period of his professional education, he was inspired by a great apostolic zeal. He gathered like-minded young people about himself in a Brotherhood of St Aloysius, in order to encourage them to live in the fear of God, according to the Gospel. In this apostolate among youth, in the striving for personal sanctification, and in the special care and readiness to help needy people, his religious vocation gradually matured until it found its full development in the founding of the community of brothers: a vocation to follow Christ as closely as possible, to lead people to Christ, to plant the love of Mary in people's hearts, and to serve the sick out of Christian love.

The work of founding his Order was accompanied by great difficulties and trials, in which Blessed Peter Friedhofen showed himself to be a man of unshakeable faith and trust in God's providence and Mary's help. This was the supernatural source that gave force and foundation to his astonishing decisiveness and firmness in the development of his plans, despite his increasing bodily sickness, and it was thus that he gave form and spiritual instruction to his religious community in the service of Christian love of neighbour.[3]

[3] *L'Osservatore Romano*, July 29, 1985, p. 6–7.

Blessed
Marie Clementine
Anwarite Nengapeta

Religious, Martyr

b. December 29, 1939 Wamba, Zaire

d. November 29, 1964 Isiro, Zaire

Beatified August 15, 1985

On August 15, 1985, in Kinshasa, Pope John Paul II beatified the first black nun: Sister Marie Clementine Anwarite Nengapeta.[1] She was born in 1939 in Wamba, in the African country of Zaire, the former Belgian Congo. She received baptism together with her mother and two older sisters in 1943. In February 1953 she went to school with the Sisters of the Holy Family (Jamàa Takatifu) in Bafwabaka, who provided her with a solid education. In 1956 she earned a teacher's diploma. In the same year she began her novitiate with the sisters who had taught her. On August 5, 1959, she was admitted to her profession of vows. Already since 1956 Sister Clementine Anwarite had been teaching in the lower elementary grades at the mission school in Bafwabaka. In 1960 she earned an additional diploma from the École d'Apprentissage Pédagogique and took a few courses also at the École Ménagère. She was quite well trained, then, as a teacher and educator. With her straightforward, firm character and her willingness to help others, however, she was also firmly committed to her religious community.

[1] R. F. Esposito, *Clementina Anuarite Nengapeta* (Bari, 1978); "Nengapeta, Clementina Anuarite", in *Bibliotheca Sanctorum* 1:963–64.

Besides her teaching duties, she was also active as a catechist in her own school and in the neighboring villages. Furthermore, she managed to infuse spirit and life into the Saint Francis Xavier Society and the Legion of Mary. With great love and fidelity she was committed to her black African heritage, but even more so to her religious congregation. Her mother was abandoned by her husband and had serious difficulties in raising her other children. When she remarked to Sister Clementine Anwarite, who had consecrated herself to God, that she should give up religious life and come home to help her mother and her brothers and sisters by applying her fine education as a teacher, the nun, already firmly anchored in her religious vocation, replied: "Whoever puts his hand to the plow and looks back is unworthy of the kingdom of heaven and sorely offends God!"

And so the twenty-three-year-old nun proved her mettle when she fell into the hands of a diabolical tempter. During the midday hour of November 29, 1964, she, together with her fellow sisters, was abducted by members of the Simba tribe to Ibamhi and from there to Isiro. There the black chieftain Pierre Olombe attempted to rob her of her consecrated virginity. When he did not succeed, because the nun resisted bravely, the lecher murdered her in cold blood. Thus the young nun became a martyr of consecrated purity and virginity.

In January 1978, the canonical process was begun in the diocese of Isiro-Niangara, as well as in Wamba and in Bafwabaka, and then in Brussels also; in the course of the investigations, the nun's murderer confessed his wicked intentions, so that no doubt remained as to the authenticity of the martyrdom.

Pope John Paul II, at the solemn beatification on August 15, 1985, in Kinshasa, which was attended by an immense crowd of people and by representatives of the ecclesiastical and civil authorities in the Republic of Zaire, gave the following remarkable homily:

I am particularly united with the Archbishop of Kinshasa, Cardinal Malula, and with all my brothers in the episcopacy. I thank them also for the zeal with which they have prepared the beatification.

See here that God "has regarded the low estate of his handmaiden" (cf. Lk 1:48) and the undivided love of a daughter of this land. . . .

One day Anwarite wrote these words in her notebook: "to love the Lord, because he has done great things for me, so great is his kindness". There she expresses the meaning of her life, taking the very prayer of Mary. . . .

We can admire her and take her as our model . . . ; she is truly representative of your Christian community which she illustrates by her merits and her holy fidelity to the Lord.

Anwarite spent her whole life in Haut-Zaïre, between Wamba and Bafwabaka. She did not seem to be endowed with any extraordinary talents. A modest child, accepting her limits but working perseveringly to overcome them, she sometimes had a rather lively, joyous temperament. At others times she knew worry and suffering. Quite spontaneously she showed herself available to others, simply loving to help them and receiving them courteously.

As a child, she received baptism at the same time as her mother. Faith grew in her and became a powerful motive in the direction of her life. *While still young, she wanted to consecrate her life to the Lord as a religious.* To the community of Jamaa Takatifu, the Congregation of the Holy Family, particularly dedicated to the task of teaching, she brought her constancy in work, her sense of service, love for her young students, her concern for the poor and sick, the joy which she knew how to impart, and a desire to grow spiritually. Present here today, the members of her family and her congregation are happy to be able to attest to these qualities.

Anwarite set about to follow the Lord unreservedly; *she had given her fidelity and consecrated her virginity.* Day after day with affection and profundity, she prayed to the Mother of Christ. She could be seen deep in prayer near the image of Our Lady, where she was attentive to say the rosary with her sisters or the children who were assigned to her care. . . . One touching sign was her attachment to a statuette which she kept on herself, even at her death.

When the hour of trial comes, this young religious faces it; her faith, her sense of commitment, the primary value she places on virginity, an intense prayer life and the support of her community enable her to remain steadfast. In face of the terrible anxiety of seeing her purity attacked, in the threats against her very life, Anwarite says, "My soul is troubled now." These words recall those of Jesus (cf. Jn 12:27) and show us how much the Gospel has penetrated the life of this consecrated young girl. She overcomes the shock of the agony: her courage is without weakness, sustained by the loving presence of her superiors and sisters.

The Pope calls Blessed Clementine Anwarite "the perfect fruit of the grace of holy baptism" in her land. All of the baptized have a spiritual forefather, John the Baptist, who even received from God the grace to baptize his Son in the Jordan.

Anwarite *shows a bravery worthy of the martyrs* who, since Stephen in Jerusalem, mark the history of the Church by their heroic imitation of Christ. She dares to say, in order to defend her superior who was threatened because of her refusal, "You will kill only me." When the mortal blows fall on her, her sisters clearly hear her say to the one who was attacking her, "I forgive you, because you do not know what you are doing"; and "That is how I wanted it to be." In the most direct manner Anwarite follows Christ to whom she gave herself; like him she pardons; like him she completes her sacrifice. I myself, in the name of the whole Church, I forgive with all my heart.

In the Gospel, when Mary arrived at the threshold of Zachary's house, Elizabeth "exclaimed in a loud cry . . . *blessed* is she *who believed* that there would be a fulfillment of what was spoken to her from the Lord" (Lk 1:42, 45).

She as well, this daughter of your land, Anwarite Nengapeta, believed in the fulfilment of God's promise on her behalf; she was one of those who chose not to marry for the Reign of God. She had meditated on the example of the ancient virgin-martyrs, she had been impressed by the sacrifice of Maria Goretti and the martyrs of Uganda. Anwarite knew the price her fidelity would cost her. She heard the world of Christ, "greater love has no man than this, that a man lay down his life" (cf. Jn 15:13).

In the time of danger she does not hesitate to put her *consecration to Christ in perfect chastity* above everything else. On the eve of her death in the Blue House in Isoro she had said, "I renewed my vows, I am ready to die." Anwarite is a firm witness of the irreplaceable value of a commitment made to God and sustained by his grace.

Blessed is she who, near to our day, showed the beauty of the total gift of self for the kingdom. The *grandeur of virginity* is the offering of one's total capacity to love, so that, free from all other bonds, the whole being is able to love the Lord as a spouse and those whom the Lord loves. It is not a disdain for conjugal love; we know how Anwarite always tried to help the couples close to her to remain faithful to their own commitment, the beauty of which she often praised.

It is the primary value of fidelity which led to her martyrdom. That is precisely what martyrdom means, "to be a witness". Anwarite is a part of those witnesses who inspire and sustain the faith of their brothers and sisters. When on the night of 30 November 1964 all of the religious of the community are threatened, beaten and wounded, the sacrifice of Anwarite, rather than frightening them, encourages them in their steadfastness and helps them to endure their trial in peace. The death of one of their own had been an eloquent sign of the witness of hope. . .

Dear Brothers and Sisters, you can all sing this canticle of thanks and praise with Anwarite; here is, in effect, the first fruit of the Baptism of your country, the centenary of which we celebrated together a short time ago: the *perfect fruit of the grace of holy baptism*, the first Zairese that the Church solemnly proclaims blessed, martyr for the faith among you![2]

[2] *L'Osservatore Romano*, September 9, 1985, pp. 7–8.

Blessed [Saint] Virginia Centurione Bracelli

Wife, Mother, Foundress

b. April 2, 1587, Genoa
d. December 15, 1651, Genoa

Beatified September 22, 1985
[Canonized May 18, 2003]

An aristocratic daughter of a doge of Genoa, who lived and worked in that famous Italian port during the latter part of the sixteenth and the first half of the seventeenth centuries, became an evangelist of charity worthy of the honors of the altar, as Pope John Paul II solemnly declared at the beatification of Virginia Centurione Bracelli.[1]

This blessed from the city of Genoa was born on April 2, 1587, the daughter of the Doge Giorgio Centurione and Leila, née Spinola, who likewise belonged to the Genovese nobility.

Obeying her father's will, Virginia was married at the age of fifteen to the young son of a renowned family, Gaspare Bracelli by name. He indulged altogether too much in gambling and pleasure and shortened his earthly existence by a life of vice. The unfaithful husband gave Virginia two daughters but abandoned his family. Virginia Centurione Bracelli lovingly pursued him with patience and humility until she succeeded at last in bringing him back to the fold before he died and reconciling him with God.

---

[1] F. Stano, *Virginia Centurione Bracelli, a lei Genova rispose* (Genoa, 1985); N. Ferrante, "Centurione, Virginia, vedova Bracelli", in *Bibliotheca Sanctorum* 1:304–5.

After a few short, unhappy years of married life, Virginia became a widow in 1607. Her father wanted to give her away in marriage a second time. The daughter vehemently refused, however, and devoted herself at first to solitary prayer and penance. Then she began to serve as a dedicated lay apostle. First, she looked after abandoned and ruined country churches and had them renovated. Then, gradually, she started to care for abandoned youngsters, founding four schools for them. After providing for her own two children, with the help of her mother-in-law, Maddalena Lomellini, and the Capuchin priest Padre Mattia Bovoni, she began to spend the entire day serving the poor and the sick. Her work could be called a full-time apostolate, especially around the year 1630, when plague, famine, and war left Genoa and all of northern Italy in dire need. In 1626 Virginia gave up her remaining wealth for the sake of the poor.

She opened wide her motherly heart in leading the association of the Hundred Ladies of Mercy (*Cento Signore della Misericordia*), who had consecrated themselves to the Patronage for the Poor of Jesus Christ. Together with these women, Virginia helped wherever she could and brought comfort by her ardent words, which burned with a magnanimous love of God.

The apostolate that she had begun eventually developed into the Work of Refuge (*Opera del Rifugio*), which was designed as a place to shelter and assist abandoned and endangered youngsters. Virginia took such young people into her own house, and when this became too small, she rented a vacant convent in that quarter of the city of Genoa known as Monte Calvario. Here she sheltered forty youngsters, whom she placed under the protection of Our Lady of Refuge. It was the thirteenth day of April, 1631. From then on this date was considered the anniversary of the founding of two religious orders that originated in the work of Virginia Centurione Bracelli: the Sisters of Our Lady of Refuge on Mount Calvary (*Suore di Nostra Signora del Rifugio in Monte Calvario*) and the Daughters of Our Lady of Mount Calvary (*Figlie di Nostra Signora al Monte Calvario*).

Virginia knew how to interest Church officials and the civil authorities in her work. Furthermore, at her insistence, the Virgin Mother of God was proclaimed the Queen of Genoa. She petitioned the cardinal-archbishop of Genoa for the introduction of the Forty Hours devotion in the city of Genoa; she also requested the preaching of missions, and for this purpose the congregation of the Missionaries of Saint Charles was founded. Besides this, she performed a great service as a peacemaker between the feuding factions in the city and saw to it that a serious dispute between the doge and the cardinal-archbishop of Genoa was settled.

On December 15, 1651, this highly meritorious woman died and was deeply mourned by the inhabitants of the republic of Genoa. Unfortunately, with the passage of time, she was entirely forgotten, so that not even her spiritual daughters knew that Virginia Centurione Bracelli was the foundress of their religious community. Instead of calling themselves the Bracelli Sisters, after her, they used the name of one of their early patrons, Emmaneule Brignole, and were known as the Brignolines. On September 20, 1801, however, on the occasion of the 150th anniversary of her death, her grave was opened, and her body was found to be completely incorrupt; then people remembered again this great woman and apostle of charity of the seventeenth century, at a time of great distress in Genoa.

In 1931 the cause for beatification was begun, and on July 6, 1985, it was successfully concluded by a decree promulgating a miracle attributed to the intercession of Virginia. On September 22, 1985, Pope John Paul II beatified her in Genoa, and on that occasion he gave the following impressive homily, which is quoted here in abridged form:

"If any one would be first, he must be last of all and servant of all" (Mk 9:35).

These demanding and powerful words of the Gospel . . . allow us to outline a synthesis of the singular model of life of Virginia Centurione Bracelli, whom I have today proclaimed

Blessed in this her city, where she was born and where she laboured, and where her body lies.

The Son of God embraced the mission of being servant of all, becoming the suffering "servant" of the Father for the redemption of the world.

With an admirable gesture, Jesus illustrates the meaning he wishes to give to the word "servant": and he teaches the disciples, who were preoccupied with knowing "who was the greatest among them", that it is instead necessary to put oneself in the last place, at the service of the least. *"And he took a child, and put him in the midst of them; and taking him in his arms, he said to them, 'Whoever receives one such child in my name receives me' "* (Mk 9:37).

To welcome a child could signify, especially in that day, to dedicate oneself to the persons of least consideration; with profound esteem, a fraternal heart and love, to concern oneself with those whom the world neglects and society casts out.

In this way, Jesus reveals himself to be the model of those who serve the littlest and the poorest. He identifies himself with those who are at the lowest level of society, he conceals himself in the hearts of the humble, the suffering, the outcasts, and for this reason affirms: "Whoever receives one such child in my name receives me."

The whole of Virginia Centurione's life seems to unfold in the light of this message: to renounce one's own possessions in order to serve and welcome the humble, the beggars; to dedicate oneself to the least, to the persons most neglected by mankind.

Widowed at a very young age, she welcomed the Lord's invitation to serve him in his poor. "I want to serve you alone, who cannot die"; this was Virginia's prayer before the crucifix. "I want you to serve me in my poor", was the Lord's response.

Virginia first dedicated herself to the abandoned girls of her city, in order that they might not fall victim, because of the social misery, to still more humiliating moral miseries. In order to assure them of what they needed for a decent life, she first gave them shelter in her home, and from the noblewoman that she was, she herself became a beggar. Her passion for charity led her, even in the midst of a noble, rich society jealous of its privileges, to imitate Christ, who "though he was rich, for our sake became poor" (cf. 2 Cor 8:9). Meditation on the mystery of Calvary allowed her to comprehend in a concrete and active way the wise message of the book of Tobit: "Prayer is good when accompanied by fasting, almsgiving and righteousness. . . . It is better to give alms than to treasure up gold" (Tob 12:8).

Having thus made herself poor for love of Christ living in his poor, Virginia gave life to a type of charity that was not limited merely to relief, but that programmed an effort towards true human promotion. She wanted to do everything possible to assure the beggars of acceptable social conditions and promise for the future. In this way, she ingeniously anticipated the modern notion of assistance, teaching how to bring to fruition the gifts of charity and helping the destitute, with delicate pedagogy, to find a way out of the sad mentality induced by poverty and to become responsible for themselves.

The seeking out of the poor to this end, even in their homes, in the heart of the most humble and miserable neighborhoods of the city, was a special undertaking that she reserved for herself when she led the "Ladies" and the "Auxiliaries of Mercy" to lend their service to the needy, because she had understood that the charity of Christ does not await the downtrodden, but seeks them out, pursues them in their indigence, out of pure love.

If we ask ourselves where the strength and the courage for such great devotion and so much work came from, we find that at the centre of her life the contemplation of Christ Crucified was at work; the Jesus of Calvary, always present, loved and invoked especially in the most critical moments of her personal life and of that of her foundations. She was able to say with the Apostle Paul: *"I live by faith in the Son of God, who loved me and gave himself for me"* (Gal 2:20).

The Lord knows how to bring certain elect souls close to his Cross with ineffable love by making use of the contradictions of life, the opposition of men, humiliations which arise from the moral misery of the world. In this way he purifies the souls of his saints, he makes them capable of grasping the message of the Cross, of making it their own and living it with intense generosity. This drawing near to the Cross of Christ is a gift which touches upon the mysterious workings of divine grace and sometimes troubles the outlook of those who think in earthly terms. And yet, in truth, Christ always proclaims his mercy through these very souls, whom he transforms into lofty witnesses to charity because in their trials they have known how to "find refuge in Him", and were able to "give with joy", as we have sung in the psalm.

A deep love of Christ and an authentic love for the poor and the needy is the message that Virginia repeats in this circumstance to the city of Genoa as it is today. . . .

Genoa, a city dedicated to the Madonna, the Madonna della Guardia, whom the Genoese salute as they come and go on their sea voyages; truly a city of the Madonna, because Virginia Centurione wished Mary to be declared and proclaimed Queen of this city. . . .

To the Madonna I entrust the spiritual daughters of Virginia Centurione, those of the Genoese community, the sisters of Our Lady of the Refuge of Mount Calvary, whom you call "Brignoline", those of the community of Rome, the Daughters of Mount Calvary and the fraternities that are active in India, Africa and Latin America. I entrust to the Virgin Mary their joy at this celebration, but also their spirit of charity, their generous devotion to the humble and to the poor, to the education of the young, to the apostolate.

I do this following a statement of Virginia Centurione Bracelli which seems to me worthy of quotation because it is a sign of her trust in God: "To place myself", she said, "in and for all things, in the hands of the One who created me, and who will help me more than I can possibly imagine" (cf. Office of Readings).

So be it for all of us. Amen.[2]

[2] *L'Osservatore Romano*, October 7, 1985, pp. 5, 8.

Blessed Diego Luis de San Vitores Alonso

Missionary, Martyr

b. November 13, 1627, Burgos,
Spain
d. April 2, 1672, on the shore
of Tumon, Guam

Beatified October 6, 1985

Who has ever heard of the Marianas, that group of islands in Micronesia which includes many small islands and a few large ones such as Guam, Saipan, and Rota? From 1565 until 1898, the Spaniards ruled there, and one Spaniard worked successfully as a missionary on those islands and suffered a martyr's death there on April 2, 1672: Diego Luis de San Vitores Alonso.[1] In order to give the Marianas their own patron and intercessor, on October 6, 1985, Pope John Paul II beatified this ardently zealous missionary who lived his entire priestly life according to the biblical watchword *Evangelizare pauperibus misit me* [He sent me to preach good news to the poor] (Lk 4:18).

Diego Luis de San Vitores was born on November 13, 1627, in the Spanish city of Burgos. Since his father belonged to the Spanish nobility and was in the service of the king of Spain, the family had to change its place of residence often; first, from Burgos to Madrid, in the first years of Diego's childhood (1631); then, to

[1] P. Molinari, "Tre nuovi beati della Compagnia de Gesù", in *La Civiltà Cattolica* 136 (1985): 373–79.

Guadix, near Granada (1635); and, finally, back again to Madrid (1638).

For two years Diego was a pupil in the *Colegio Imperial* in Madrid, which was entrusted to the Jesuits. Then, at a very young age, he began his novitiate with the Jesuits, in Villarejo de Fuentes, near Cuenca. At the end of the two-year novitiate, he was not yet sixteen years old, and so he had to spend a third year as a novice before being admitted to vows in the Society. From 1644 to 1646, the young Jesuit cleric studied philosophy and then, from 1646 to 1650, theology. On December 23, 1651, he was ordained a priest.

After completing his third year of probation and after teaching in Oropesa (Toledo), then in Madrid and Alcalá in the years 1653 to 1660, Padre Diego Luis de San Vitores was finally allowed to fulfill his childhood dream and go to the missions. He was not sent to China, though, as he had hoped, but via Mexico to Manila in the Philippines and then to the Mariana Islands. On June 16, 1668, he landed on the island of Guam with five companions, among them four priests.

In less than a year the heralds of the faith had won 6,055 people for the Christian faith on Guam alone, which made 13,289 inhabitants in all, counting those who were baptized on ten other small islands. Now, however, they began to meet with stubborn resistance from the pagans and from a few enemies of the Spanish rulers on the islands. In 1670 blood was spilled for the first time. One of the finest coworkers of Father Diego de San Vitores, Father Luis de Medina, was murdered on January 29, 1670. The successful mission continued to make progress, nevertheless, under the protection of the Spanish military and reinforced by new missionaries. In 1671 the number of the baptized had already reached thirty thousand. The pastoral care of the new Christians was conducted from five churches on various islands. In this evangelization of the Marianas, the driving force was always Father Diego Luis de San Vitores, with his courage and tenacity, with his whole-hearted dedication to this missionary work, and with his ardent zeal for souls. While performing his duties, he moved constantly from one island to another. While looking for a Christian who had fallen away from the faith and whom he was trying to win back, he was attacked on April 2, 1672, by this man who, in a horrible rage, pierced him through with a spear out of hatred for the Christian faith. The heroic missionary died on the shore of Tumon, not far from Agaña, Guam.

Pope John Paul II dedicated the following character study to this herald and martyr of the faith at the beatification in Saint Peter's Basilica in Rome on October 6, 1985:

Diego Luis de San Vitores Alonso, although he was very young, heard deep within himself a voice which attracted and compelled him. He felt attracted to Christ, the eternal envoy of the Father for the salvation of man, who impelled him to go to distant lands as an instrument of his salvific mission. The words of the Savior in the synagogue of Nazareth resounded in Diego's ears: "*Evangelizare pauperibus misit me*" (Lk 4:18; Is 61:1). Jesus stands at the door and knocks; each time his voice made itself clearer and more insistent in the generous heart of the youth who opened himself to God and decided to enter the Society of Jesus, renouncing a brilliant future which his personal gifts and the social position of his family would have procured for him.

In prayer and recollection his soul contemplated "Jesus who went about all the cities and villages . . . preaching the gospel of the kingdom" (Mt 9:35), and asked the Lord for the grace not to be "deaf to his call, but ready and diligent to do his most holy will" (St Ignatius of Loyola, *Spiritual Exercises*, 91). The young religious knocked at the door of his superiors so that they would send him to the Eastern missions to preach the Good News of Christ to the peoples who otherwise would not know him.

After a long and exhausting journey to the East by way of Mexico he reached the Philippines, where he remained for five years before being sent to the Mariana Islands. In June 1668 Father De San Vitores and his Jesuit companions reached the archipelago and established on the island of Guam the centre of their missionary activity.

His apostolic zeal and complete dedication to those people in need of spiritual and human promotion characterized the years of this exemplary missionary, who, in imitation of the words of the Master "greater love has no man than this, that a man lay down his life for his friends" (Jn 15:13), shed his blood in sacrifice, while asking God to forgive those responsible for his death.

The life of this new Blessed was characterized by a total availability to go wherever the Lord called him. He speaks in real and urgent tones to the missionaries of today about the open and ready attitude to respond to the demands of the mandate: "Go into all the world and preach the Gospel to the whole creation" (Mk 16:15).

You young people who are listening to me, or who will receive this message: open your heart to the Lord who stands at the door and knocks (cf. Rev 3:20). Be generous like the young Diego who, abandoning everything made himself a pilgrim and missionary in distant lands to give testimony of the love of God to men.[2]

---

[2] *L'Osservatore Romano*, October 21, 1985, p. 6.

Blessed Francisco Garate Aranguren

Jesuit lay brother

b. February 3, 1857, Azpeitia,
  Basque Provinces
d. September 9, 1929,
  Deusto-Bilbao

Beatified October 6, 1985

A blessed about whom there is really nothing to report, except that as a lay brother in the Society of Jesus he fulfilled his assignments—first, ten years serving as infirmarian; then, forty-two years as doorkeeper—in a truly exemplary fashion and thereby attained the goal of perfection and sanctity, a compatriot of Saint Ignatius of Loyola, the lay brother Francisco Garate Aranguren[1] was raised to the honors of the altar when Pope John Paul II beatified him with two other Jesuits on October 6, 1985.

Brother Francisco Garate was originally from a farmstead in the immediate vicinity of Loyola Castle in the parish of Azpeitia (Guipúzcoa, Basque Provinces, Spain). He was born there on February 3, 1857. At the age of seventeen he entered the Jesuits and began his novitiate, which, at that time, because of the military conflicts in the Basque Provinces, was located in the village of Poyanne, in France. In 1876 he took religious vows as a lay brother. For ten years, conscientiously, with the utmost patience,

---

[1] T. Toni, *El Siervo de Dios, Francisco Garate* (Bilbao, 1942); F. Baumann, "Garate, Francisco", in *Bibliotheca Sanctorum* 6:33–34.

meekness, and kindness, he fulfilled his delicate responsibilities as infirmarian in the three Jesuit colleges in La Guardia, on the Spanish-Portuguese border. Then, from 1887 until his death, on September 9, 1929, he was doorkeeper at the Jesuit University in Deusto-Bilbao; there his virtues aroused the admiration of all who met him. He was a perfect imitator of Saint Alfons Rodríguez, who likewise as a Jesuit lay brother had held the job of porter.

Brother Francisco Garate was always amiable, patient, and untiring as he went about his duties. One day he was asked by the Jesuit Cardinal Boetto how, with such a demanding job, he could maintain such peace and equanimity. He answered, "To the extent that it is possible for me to do everything well, I do it. Our Lord does the rest. With his help everything becomes easy and beautiful, because we have a good Lord."

The *laudatio* for this simple religious, which Pope John Paul II gave at his beatification, is as follows:

The message of sanctity which *Brother Francisco Garate Aranguren* gave us is simple and clear, as was the simplicity of his religious life offered in the porter's office of the university centre of Deusto. From his youth Francisco opened his heart wide to Christ who knocked at his door inviting him to be his faithful follower, his friend. Like the Virgin Mary whom he loved tenderly as a mother, he responded with generosity and confidence without limit to the call of grace.

Brother Garate lived his religious consecration as a radical openness to God, to whose service and glory he was consecrated (cf. *Lumen Gentium*, 44), and from whom he received inspiration and strength to give witness of a great generosity to all. This is attested to by the many persons who passed through the entrance of the university of Deusto attended by the one whom they affectionately called "Brother Kindness"—students, professors, employees, parents of the young residents, people of every class and social condition who saw in Brother Garate the welcoming and pleasant attitude of the one who keeps his heart anchored in God.

He gives us a real and concrete testimony of the value of the interior life as the soul of every apostolate as well as of religious consecration. In effect, when a person hands himself over to God and centres his whole life in him, one does not have to wait for apostolic fruits. From the entrance of a house of studies this Jesuit coadjutor made the goodness of God present by means of the evangelizing force of his quiet and humble service.

² *L'Osservatore Romano*, October 21, 1985, p. 7.

Blessed [Saint]
José María Rubio
y Peralta

Priest, Jesuit

b. July 22, 1864, Dalías, Spain
d. May 2, 1929, Aranjuez

Beatified October 6, 1985
[Canonized May 4, 2003]

An outstanding Spanish preacher and confessor from the Society of Jesus in the last decades of the nineteenth century and the early decades of the twentieth was raised to the honors of the altar on October 6, 1985, in the person of the priest and religious José María Rubio y Peralta.[1]

This blessed was born on July 22, 1864, the son of good Catholic parents, farmers, who handed on the gift of life to twelve children in Dalías, Almería, Spain. After a happy childhood, the youngster began middle school in 1875 in Almería. Since he had clearly discerned at an early age his vocation to the priesthood, he continued his studies from 1876 on at the minor seminary of the diocese of Almería and then entered the major seminary in Granada in 1879, where he studied philosophy for two years, theology for four years, and then canon law for two more years. In 1886 he went to Madrid to complete his studies with a licentiate in theology (1887) and a doctorate in canon law. On September 24, 1887, he was ordained a priest in Madrid. At that time he

[1] C. M. Staehlin, *El Padre Rubio: Vida del Apostol de Madrid*, 2d ed. (Madrid, 1953); *Un Predicatore senza stile: P. Giuseppe Maria Rubio SJ* (Rome, 1957).

already felt a strong inclination to join the Jesuit order, but various circumstances prevented this for nineteen years.

After the newly ordained priest had been appointed assistant pastor in Chinchón for a short time (until 1889), he became pastoral administrator in Estremera, but then in 1890 he was called to Madrid to serve as a professor of metaphysics, Latin, and pastoral theology at the major seminary and also as examiner and notary in the diocesan tribunal.

In 1905, Father Rubio Peralta made a pilgrimage to the Holy Land. In the following year, he was finally able to enter the Society of Jesus, in Granada. There he took his vows on October 12, 1908. After a year of further study and after an assignment in the Jesuit residence in Seville, Father Rubio Peralta still had to go through the so-called Third Probation, in 1910, in Manresa. Finally, based at the Jesuit residence in Madrid until his death, which took place on May 2, 1929, he was able to dedicate himself to a grace-filled and extraordinarily effective pastoral ministry, especially as a preacher and confessor.

So much for the curriculum vitae of this exemplary priest, who had a tremendous love for the Holy Eucharist and for the Sacred Heart of Jesus. In his eighteen years of pastoral activity in Madrid and beyond, he distinguished himself to such an extent that the bishop of Madrid at that time called him the apostle of the Spanish capital. From the early morning hours on, long lines of penitents stood outside his confessional. His many sermons, which were plain and simple and free of any sort of emotional exuberance, struck the hearts of his listeners in much the same way as once the plain preaching of Saint John Mary Vianney, the Curé of Ars, had done.

Father Rubio Peralta was also, first and foremost, a retreat master much in demand for people of every age and occupation. He was untiring in his efforts to promote the work of the *Marías de los Sagrarios* [2] and of the *Caballeros y las Señoras de la Guardia de Honor* [the Knights and Ladies of the Honor Guard]. With great courage and ardent zeal for souls, he made his way even into the districts inhabited by the poorest and most abandoned people in Madrid, and he contributed much to the religious and moral improvement of the people there. In the final years of his life, the pastoral ministry of Father Rubio Peralta was strongly supported by numerous extraordinary occurrences, which earned him the title of "miracle worker". His death on May 2, 1929, in Aranjuez, was, in the eyes of many believers, that of a saint.

Pope John Paul II confirmed this at the beatification on October 6, 1985:

> José María Rubio y Peralta . . . was born in Dalias (Almería) and exercised his apostolate for the most part in the capital of Spain, being known as "the apostle of Madrid". . . . His life as a faithful follower of Christ teaches us that it is the docile and humble

[2] An association of lay women and religious, founded by Blessed Bishop Manuel Gonzalez, who dedicate themselves to making reparation to the Heart of Jesus by spiritually accompanying our Lord in a tabernacle where he is abandoned.— TRANS. (Courtesy of the Carmelite Monastery in Philadelphia.)

attitude to the action of God which makes the Christian progress on the path of perfection and converts him into an effective instrument of salvation.

Everyone knew how Father Rubio exercised a great apostolic activity from the confessional and the pulpit. His exquisite touch as a director of souls helped him come up with the correct advice, the right word, the fitting penance, at times demanding, which during his years of patient and quiet labour were forming apostles, men and women of every social class who, in many cases came to be his collaborators in the works of assistance and charity inspired and directed by him. He was a former of committed laity to whom he liked to repeat his well-known remark: "You only have to throw yourself into it!", inspiring them to make themselves present as Christians in the poor and marginalized areas on the outskirts of Madrid at the very beginning of the era [the turn of the century] when schools were created, people cared for the sick, the aged, and the unemployed.

His untiring relationship with Christ, particularly in the sacrament of the Eucharist and his devotion to the Sacred Heart, drew him into the intimacy of the Lord and his very attitudes (cf. Phil 2:5ff.). In the exemplary path of his life this shining son of St Ignatius presents himself as an authentic *alter Christus* to the man of today, a priest who sees his neighbour as coming from God and who possesses for [that reason] the virtue of communicating to others something of what has been reserved to those who live in Christ.[3]

---

[3] *L'Osservatore Romano*, October 21, 1985, pp. 6–7.

Blessed
Titus Brandsma

Carmelite Priest, Professor,
Editor, Martyr

b. January 23, 1881,
  Bolswaard, Netherlands
d. July 26, 1942,
  Dachau concentration camp

Beatified November 3, 1985

A priest-journalist and martyr[1] from the Netherlands, "for whom the heavens opened over Dachau", as the publication *La Civiltà Cattolica* put it in the title of a biography of this heroic witness to the faith, was raised to the honors of the altar on November 3, 1985, by Pope John Paul II. He truly deserved it, for he was not only a priest, a journalist, and a martyr; he was also an exemplary, saintly Carmelite.

On February 23, 1881, he was born in Bolswaard, near Bolsward in the province of Friesland, in the Netherlands. After attending the secondary school of the Franciscans in Megen, he entered the Carmelites in 1898 and was ordained a priest in 1905. Further studies followed, from 1906 to 1909, at the Pontifical Gregorian University in Rome, where he graduated with a doctorate in philosophy. Then for fifteen years Father Titus Brandsma taught at the Carmelite house of studies in Oss. On the side, he developed an extraordinarily intensive apostolate: he founded a

---

[1] F. Vallainc, *Un giornalista martire: Padre Tito Brandsma* (Milan, 1985); A. Scurani, "Per lui il cielo si chiuse su Dachau", in *La Civiltà Cattolica* 137 (1986): 15–29.

Marian periodical and was editor-in-chief of a local newspaper; he established a Catholic public library and a scientific society; he used his influence to set up a monument to the Sacred Heart of Jesus on a public square; he organized various exhibitions and a congress on the missions. In addition, he made arrangements for the translation of the works of Saint Teresa of Avila into the Dutch language. Truly, it was an unusual and many-sided apostolate that this dynamic monk carried on.

In 1923, Father Titus Brandsma was appointed professor of philosophy and of the history of mystical theology at the Catholic University of Nijmegen. He founded there an institute for the mysticism of the Netherlands and collected more than sixteen thousand photocopies of manuscripts containing mystical and spiritual treatises from the Middle Ages; he organized three congresses on spirituality in the Low Countries; and besides this he was rector of the Catholic University of Nijmegen during the years 1932 and 1933.

In the city where Saint Peter Canisius was born, Father Titus Brandsma did apostolic work beyond academia as well, especially in the ecumenical field, but likewise for the cause of the foreign missions and for the pastoral care of non-Catholics who wanted to convert. He also worked during this time to promote the language and culture of his native province of Friesland. Furthermore, he was an editor of the Dutch Catholic Encyclopedia and chaplain for Catholic journalists.

This indefatigable laborer for the kingdom of God was, despite poor health, always in good spirits. He displayed a great sense of humor in dealing with his fellowmen; he was extremely good-hearted, and there were no limits to his willingness to help those who asked for assistance. Amid all this activity, Father Titus Brandsma always remained a man of unshakeable faith and deep spirituality.

This clever, learned, and multi-talented man of the Church discerned very early on the dangerous character of National Socialism, which had come to power in Germany. As early as 1934, in conferences, in articles that he penned, and in courses that he organized at the university, he demonstrated that he was an opponent to be taken seriously. When the German troops occupied Holland in May 1940, Father Titus Brandsma immediately proved himself to be a fearless, courageous defender of the Catholic Church and her institutions, above all, the Catholic school. As chaplain for Catholic journalists, he strove successfully to keep any sort of Nazi propaganda out of the Catholic newspapers. In December 1941, after repeated attempts by the occupation forces to put pressure on the Catholic press and Catholic journalists, he wrote a letter to the publishers and editors-in-chief of the Catholic newspapers and periodicals, urging them to resist the Nazi propaganda with all their might—whatever the cost. The consequences were not long in coming: on January 19, 1942, Father Brandsma was arrested by the Gestapo and taken to the prison in Scheveningen. In a series of interrogations there, the courageous priest boldly and clearly defended the Church's position with regard to National Socialism.

From March to April 1942, Father Titus Brandsma was detained in the concentration camp at Amersfoort. There he helped his fellow prisoners, to the extent that he was able, encouraging them to persevere, hearing their confessions, comforting them, and setting an example of serenity and cheerfulness. Witnesses have testified that Father Titus Brandsma made a profound impression upon all the inmates.

After a brief incarceration in the prisons of Scheveningen and Cleve, Father Titus Brandsma was finally brought to the concentration camp at Dachau. There he was forced to perform hard labor and was often subjected to cruel and demeaning mistreatment. After only a month, Father Brandsma's strength was completely spent. He was brought to the infirmary of the concentration camp. There, on July 26, 1942, he received a lethal injection of carbolic acid. His body was reduced to ashes.

The death of the Carmelite priest Father Brandsma left a very deep impression on the Netherlands. The reputation of this heroic witness to the faith grew much greater still after the war, with the publication of the writings that he had composed while imprisoned. Blessed Titus Brandsma is the author of the following works: *Godsbegrip* (Nijmegen 1932); *Carmelite Mysticism* (Chicago, 1936; Dublin, 1985); *Mijn cel en dagorde van een gevangene* (Tilburg, 1944); *Het laatste geschrift* (Tilburg, 1944); *De groote heilige Teresia van Jesus* (Utrecht, 1946); *God . . . anders dan vroeger* (Nijmegen, 1969); *Jardín cercado* (Gaudete, 1978); *Ejercícios bíblicos con María para llegar a Jesús* (Nijmegen, 1978); *Geert Groote: zijn keer naar de Heer* (Nijmegen, 1982); *Mystiek leven: Een bloemlezing* (Nijmegen, 1985).

At the beatification of Father Titus Brandsma on November 3, 1985, in the Basilica of Saint Peter in Rome, Pope John Paul II gave the following gripping homily:

> *"The souls of the righteous are in the hand of God"* (Wis 3:1). The Church listens to the word of God today, 3 November, the Sunday after the solemnity of All Saints and after the day commemorating all the faithful departed.
>
> *The Church* listens to *this word on the day* that she raises *to the glories of the altar Titus Brandsma*, son of the Netherlands and a religious of the Carmelite Order.
>
> Once again, a man who passed through the torments of a concentration camp—in this case, Dachau—is raised to the glories of the altar. A man who *"was punished"*, in the words of today's liturgy (Wis 3:4).
>
> And precisely in the midst of this "punishment", in the midst of a concentration camp, which remains the shameful blot upon this century, *God found Titus Brandsma worthy of himself* (cf. Wis 3:5). . . .
>
> Titus Brandsma suffered torments: *in the sight of men he was punished.* . . .
>
> The ex-deportees of the concentration camps know very well what a human Calvary were those places of affliction.
>
> *Places of great trial for men and women.*

The trial of physical force, mercilessly pushed to the extreme of complete annihilation.

The trial of moral force. . . .

The concentration camps were organized according to the programme of disdain for man, *according to the programme of hate.*

Through what trials of conscience, of character, of heart must have passed a disciple of Christ who recalled his words concerning the *love of one's enemies!*

Not to answer hate with hate, but with love. This is perhaps one of the greatest trials of man's moral strength.

From this trial Titus Brandsma emerged victorious. In the midst of the onslaughts of hatred, he was able to love—everybody, including his tormentors. "They too are children of the good God", he said, "and who knows whether something remains in them."

Of course, such heroism is not something that can be improvised. Father Titus spent his whole life bringing it to maturity, from the earliest experiences of his infancy, lived in a deeply Christian family, in his beloved Friesland. From the words and example of his parents, from the teachings he heard in the village church, from the charitable activities which he experienced in the parish community, he learned to know and to practise Christ's fundamental commandment of love for everyone, not excluding one's very enemies.

This was an experience that marked him deeply, in such a way as to give direction to his whole life. Father Brandsma's activities during his life were surprisingly many and varied. But if we wished to seek their inspiration and driving force we would find it here: in the commandment of love taken to its utmost consequences.

Father Brandsma was principally a professor of philosophy and of the history of mysticism at the Catholic University of Nijmegen. In this post he expended the best of his human and professional energies, watching over the intellectual training of a vast number of students. But he did not stop at passing on to them abstract notions remote from the practical problems of their lives. Father Titus loved his students, and for this reason he felt impelled to share with them the values that inspired and sustained his own life. Thus there developed between teacher and pupil a dialogue that expanded and embraced not only the perennial great questions but also the questions posed by the events of a period over which the Nazi ideology was casting ever darker shadows.

But the students were only a small part of the much greater national scene. The heart of Father Titus could not remain indifferent to the many brethren who were outside the academic institutions and who also wanted an enlightening word. For their sake he became a journalist. For many years he worked on newspapers and periodicals, expressing in hundreds of articles the treasures of his mind and sensibility. Here too his work was not simply professional: many colleagues found in him a discreet confidant, a wise counselor and a sincere friend, always ready to share sorrows and inspire hope.

No barrier was able to stop the impulse of charity which animated the great Carmelite. Again, it is love that explains the commitment with which he promoted the ecumenical movement, maintaining an attitude of constant fidelity towards the Church, and one of complete fairness towards those belonging to other confessions. Struck by such a luminous witness of evangelical consistency, a Protestant pastor said of him: "Our dear brother in Christ, Titus Brandsma, is truly a *mysterium gratiae* [mystery of grace]!"

A singularly penetrating judgment, this! In the life of Father Brandsma what above all kindles our admiration is precisely this unfolding, in an ever more manifest way, of the grace of Christ. Here lies the secret of the vast radiation of his activity and the source of the ever fresh wave of his charity. For that matter, Father Titus was himself fully aware of the fact that he owed everything to grace, that is, to the divine life that was working in him, flowing into his soul from the inexhaustible wellspring of the Saviour. The words of Christ: "Apart from me you can do nothing" (Jn 15:5) constituted for him the directing principle of his daily choices.

For this reason he prayed intensely. "Prayer is life, not an oasis in the desert of life", he said. A professor of the history of mysticism, he strove to live the discipline that he taught, every moment of his life. "We must not place in our hearts a division between God and the world, but we must rather look at the world while always having God in the background", he said.

From this profound union with God there arose in the soul of Father Brandsma a constant mood of optimism, which endeared him to those who had the good fortune to know him, and which never left him: it even accompanied him into the hell of the Nazi camp. Until the very end he remained a source of support and hope for the other prisoners: for everyone he had a smile, an understanding word, a kind gesture. The very nurse who, on 26 July of 1942, injected him with deadly poison, later testified that she always retained the vivid memory of the face of that priest who "had compassion for me".

And today we too see the face of Father Titus Brandsma before us, and we contemplate his luminous smile in the glory of God. He speaks to the faithful of his land, the Netherlands, and to all the faithful of the world, reaffirming his lifelong conviction: "Although neo-paganism no longer desires love, love will win back to us the hearts of the pagans. The practice of life will always make it a victorious force which will conquer and hold fast men's hearts."

When we listen to the biography of Titus Brandsma, when we fix our minds upon the *apostolic zeal* of this servant of God, and then upon *his martyr's death*, the words of today's liturgy acquire a particular eloquence: God tested him . . .

Like *gold in the furnace* he tried him, and like a *sacrificial burnt offering* he accepted him (cf. Wis 3:5–6).[2]

---

[2] *L'Osservatore Romano*, November 18, 1985, p. 3.

Blessed
Maria Teresa of Jesus
Gerhardinger

Teacher, Foundress

b. June 20, 1797, Stadtamhof,
   Regensburg
d. May 9, 1879, Munich

Beatified November 17, 1985

A highly meritorious foundress, a descendant of the Bavarian people, was given to the Church of Bavaria as a new blessed in the person of Karolina Gerhardinger[1] (born June 20, 1797, in Regensburg-Stadtamhof), who as a nun took the name Maria Teresa of Jesus. On November 17, 1985, she was raised by Pope John Paul II to the honors of the altar.

The only child of a respectable riverboat captain and his wife, she received her education in the school of the Canonesses of Notre Dame[2] in Stadtamhof. At this school, which was taken away from the canonesses in 1809 in the course of the [third wave of] secularization,[3] Karolina Gerhardinger worked as a teacher from

---

[1] M. L. Ziegler, "Mutter Theresia von Jesus Gerhardinger", in G. Schwaiger, *Bavaria Sancta* (Regensburg, 1973), 3:441–50; E. H. Ritter, *Zeugen des Glaubens* (Regensburg, 1989), pp. 173–78.

[2] From the late Middle Ages on, canonesses were consecrated women who followed a rule that was canonical (cf. "canons regular") rather than monastic. They lived a strictly cloistered life, chanted the Divine Office, and devoted themselves to education and to charitable works for women.— TRANS.

[3] The fierce Enlightenment polemic against monasticism, brought into Catholic countries with freedom of the press, led to the closing and disbanding of many

the age of fifteen on. "She not only distinguished herself by her methodical skill and great pedagogical ability; she also assimilated the thought of her saintly spiritual director Georg Michael Wittmann (d. March 8, 1833), then cathedral rector and later the bishop of Regensburg, who expected that a good education and a Christian upbringing for girls would result in moral renewal and also in an improvement of the economic situation of the Bavarian people" (E. H. Ritter).

After the death of Bishop Wittmann, whom the young teacher had helped very much, his friend Franz Sebastian Job, chaplain of the imperial court in Vienna, took a special interest in her. He made it possible for her to open a school in his hometown, Neunburg vorm Wald, and to begin the first cloistered community of the Association of the Poor School Sisters of Notre Dame with two of her former pupils. In 1834 Karolina Gerhardinger received from King Ludwig I the charter authorizing her to found a convent, which the bishop of Regensburg, Franz X. Schwäbl (d. 1841), approved. In 1835 Karolina Gerhardinger, who now went by the name Mother Maria Teresa of Jesus, took her vows in religion. The young community grew very quickly, so that in 1837 the foundress asked permission from the archbishop of Munich, Lothar Anselm von Gebsattel (d. 1846), to found a motherhouse in his archdiocese. He put at her disposal the former Poor Clares convent on the green in Munich. Ten years later, the young community of nuns, the Poor School Sisters of Notre Dame, already had fifty-two houses in Bavaria. The foundation of other houses in Württemberg, Baden, Westphalia, Silesia, Bohemia, Austria, and England followed.

In 1847, Mother Maria Teresa Gerhardinger traveled with five of her sisters to the United States, where they staunchly supported the Bohemian-born, German-speaking Bishop John Nepomucene

---

religious communities, both contemplative and active, in German-speaking lands. There were three waves, 1760–1777, especially in Bavaria; 1780–1792, especially in Austria; and 1798–1805, again in Bavaria and in Switzerland.— TRANS.

Neumann (d. 1860, canonized 1977) by founding schools, as well as a motherhouse in Baltimore.

In 1848, Mother Maria Teresa Gerhardinger returned to Munich and was principally engaged in obtaining ecclesiastical recognition of her congregation. After severe trials, she obtained papal approval for her religious community in 1854, and she was appointed general superior for life. In this office, she was very strict with herself but full of motherly concern for her fellow sisters. She had a decided talent for forming and training teachers and providing them with continuing education. She created various types of schools and founded the first nursery schools and the first schools for home economics in Bavaria. Mother Maria Teresa was, however, not only extremely effective in educational matters, but also a woman who earnestly strove for perfection and sanctity: an example worthy of imitation for her fellow sisters and pupils because her whole life was directed toward the love of God and love of neighbor. She drew strength for her sacrificial work from daily reception of Holy Communion, from the cultivation of a keen devotion to our Lord in the Blessed Sacrament, and from her unbounded confidence in the intercession of the Mother of God.

At her beatification, the chief Shepherd of the Church said the following about this foundress, whose congregation, upon her death on May 9, 1879, in Munich, already numbered more than three thousand sisters in three hundred locations throughout the world:

> "You are the light of the world" (Mt 5:14). Christ says these words of the Gospel in a special way today to our new Blessed, *Mother Teresa of Jesus Gerhardinger*. Through beatification the Church raises the light of her holy life and work to the lampstand, so that from there it can shine before all men. In Mother Teresa she honours both a gifted educator and the extraordinary work of Christian education which continues to this very day in many countries and continents through the Congrega-

tion of the Poor School Sisters of Notre Dame which she founded.

When Caroline Gerhardinger was only twelve years old, she began to prepare willingly for her vocation as a teacher and, when she later founded her teaching order, she was meeting a great need of her time which she understood as a special call from God. Political and social upheavals had caused a great lack of education and faith, the moral decline of family life, and, most of all, the neglect of youth. These demanded new methods for a deep-seated education and Christian renewal, especially among the rural peoples and the simpler and poorer classes. With Bishop Wittmann, her spiritual director, she was convinced that wives and mothers best ensure the morality of cities and nations; Blessed Maria Teresa of Jesus devoted herself and her sisters mainly to the task of Christian education of girls, thus, through the training of good mothers and wives, to effect the moral strengthening of families and the improvement of society.

Caroline Gerhardinger understood her profession as an educator as a mandate to be, in the spirit of Christ, "salt of the earth" for others (cf. Mt 5:13). Her social response is basically a Christian apostolate which finds its fullest expression in the total self-offering in religious life. Finally, she also founded her Order "to honour God" and for the "salvation of souls". Therefore, her sisters were not only to give instruction in their schools, but to educate "to a living reverence for God . . . and a Christian life".

The secret of the great fruitfulness of Mother Teresa's deeds and work in education was, in addition to her professional excellence, most of all the strength of her own spiritual life: an unshakeable trust in God and a glowing love for Christ and the poor. Sacred Scripture, the Eucharist and prayer were her source of inner strength. She spent long hours before the tabernacle in the quiet of the night, seeking to know God's will and asking for the strength to fulfil it. She chose Mary as a model for herself and her sisters, and dedicated the congregation to her. They were to live and act like Mary, orienting their entire lives to God and bearing Christ into the world.

Maria Teresa of Jesus, a simple but determined and courageous religious, accomplished great things for mankind and the kingdom of God. In the founding of her order she showed herself a "strong woman" who did not shy away from sacrifice or difficulties of any kind in order to fulfil this work, which she always referred to as "God's work". Her order of teachers was a pioneering influence in the development of education in countless European countries and in America. The spiritual heritage of the new Blessed lives on today in some 7,500 School Sisters in Europe, North and Latin America, Asia, Oceania and Africa. Her ideal of education is as real and valuable in the secularized society of today as it was before. May Blessed Mother Teresa of Jesus Gerhardinger continue to be a shining example and intercessor, not only for the sisters of her own congregation, but for all Christian educators as well.[4]

To this homily of the Pope we should add the sermon preached on the day after the beatification, on November 18, 1985, in the Roman Basilica of Santa Maria Maggiore, by Cardinal Friedrich Wetter of Munich, in whose archdiocese the motherhouse of the spiritual daughters of Blessed Maria Teresa Gerhardinger is located:

It was in the year 1810. The father gave the thirteen-year-old Karolina her wish. The shipbuilder Willibald Gerhardinger took his daughter with him on the boat trip down the Danube from Regensburg toward Vienna. Along the way, the riverboat was caught in an eddy. It listed dangerously, and the frightened passengers were screaming. Karolina, however, stood fearlessly by her father. Tradition has it that she said, "My father is at the helm; he knows what he's doing."

[4] *L'Osservatore Romano*, November 25, 1985, p. 3.

"My father is at the helm; he knows what he's doing." This statement of the thirteen-year-old girl, applied to our Father in heaven, gives us a glimpse into the innermost secret of our new blessed, Maria Theresia. Just as the child on the Danube entrusted herself to her father, so too did she entrust herself over the course of almost eighty-two years of life to her Father in heaven. To him she commended the wheel of her little skiff; he could do whatever he willed with her life. This made her life very simple and very great. God stood at the wheel and guided the little skiff of her life through all the difficulties and dangers, just as her father had steered the riverboat through the eddy on that memorable trip down the Danube.

God prepared her in her youth for the great work that he had planned for her. He arranged that Karolina would be trained as a teacher, at the request of the cathedral rector, and later bishop of Regensburg, Georg Michael Wittmann, and that she would raise the standards at the school in her birthplace, Stadtamhof, and make it a model school. During those years God awakened in her a vocation to religious life.

Now came the first disappointment, though. When she was not far from her destination and was ready, together with a cloistered community, to take charge of the school in her home-town of Stadtamhof bei Regensburg, she received from the magistrate a brusque refusal, despite her great accomplishments.

The Father stood at the helm, however, and continued to help her. In 1833 she began to lead a cloistered life, with two companions, in Neunburg vorm Wald. The bitter poverty that awaited them there did not discourage her, because the love of God had filled her heart with love for young people. She saw the many children and adolescents who were exposed to religious neglect and moral degeneration. She wanted to come to their assistance in their need. She was chiefly concerned about raising and educating girls: "For the girls of today are the wives and mothers of tomorrow!" So, trusting in God, she began her work, which she did not view as *her* work, at any rate, but rather as *God's* work. She understood that she herself was only an instrument in God's hand.

This hopeful beginning was overshadowed, however, by the death of her bishop, who had originally had the idea of founding a congregation and who had stood by her since her childhood as a fatherly friend. One year later, Wittmann's friend Job died, the Vienna court chaplain who had assumed the direction of the young community of nuns after the death of the bishop. Thus Blessed Maria Theresia lost both of her most important assistants during the difficult foundational period. To make matters worse, hateful remarks could be heard in Neunburg itself: "Those one-and-a-half nuns can go back to where they came from", the people were saying.

Yet the Father was at the helm; God continued to help. In King Ludwig I of Bavaria she found a patron. He received her in an audience. Previously, however, Maria Theresia Gerhardinger had gone into a church to pray. She became so deeply immersed in prayer that she forgot about the time and arrived late for the audience. The king nevertheless gave her a cordial reception and offered her assistance, because he recognized the greatness of her work and its usefulness for his entire kingdom. "This woman knows what she is doing, and what she is doing is on a grand scale", he later said of her. She also received episcopal approbation for her new religious community. Karolina made her perpetual profession as a nun, took the name of Maria Theresia of Jesus, and consecrated her life entirely to God for ever.

Despite the hostility of the provincial diet toward religious life, despite the calumnies and the vile gossip, despite the bitter poverty, God blessed her foundation. The new religious family grew. Affiliates were started. Sister Maria Theresia had to look around for a larger motherhouse. Already in 1839 she had founded a community in the Au district of Munich. King Ludwig I gave her the former Poor Clare convent near Saint James on the Green in Munich. In 1843, ten years after the first foundation in Neunburg vorm Wald, she was able to move to the convent in Munich, which then became the generalate and motherhouse of the Poor School Sisters of Notre Dame.

Four years later, she received a call for help from the United States. No one cared about the children of the German settlers; they were in danger of running wild. "Providence calls", was the answer of the blessed. She herself brought the first five sisters across the ocean. She was deeply shaken when she saw the misery of the German emigrants, especially that of the children and adolescents. The sisters did not always receive a welcome, however; they also met with resistance, even from bishops. Maria Theresia did not give up until she had gained a foothold. The Lord consoled her in the midst of disappointments and hardships with a profound experience of God, of which she said, in her characteristically reticent way, "Something is happening to me; the Lord has drawn me to himself."

After more than a year's absence, the blessed returned to Munich. The work continued to flourish. She founded affiliates in Westphalia, Silesia, Baden, Austria, Hungary, and England. Despite the evident blessings upon her work, Mother Maria Theresia again encountered difficulties. She came into conflict with the archbishop of Munich, Count Karl August of Reisach (1800–1869), later Cardinal Reisach, of the Roman Curia. It concerned the structure of the new foundation. The archbishop did not want all of the affiliates to report to the motherhouse in Munich. He did not want such extensive authority to be granted to a woman, namely, the general superior. As the archbishop pictured it, a motherhouse should be erected in each diocese served by the School Sisters. That would fragment the congregation. Maria Theresia, however, found bishops to intercede for her community in Rome.

Eventually, there was a reconciliation with Archbishop Reisach. In 1845 the foundation of Blessed Maria Theresia received the approbation of the Apostolic See; the rule was approved provisionally in 1859, definitively in 1865. These years of conflict were extremely difficult for her. She said afterward,

"The period of suffering that just ended has added twenty years to my age."

Now she had reached her destination. The tribulations from within had been overcome. But it was not very long before the tribulations from without started again. In connection with the First Vatican Council, there was a new outbreak of hostility toward the Church. During the *Kulturkampf*, she had to watch while the houses she had founded in Prussia, Baden, Westphalia, and Silesia were abolished. Yet the foundress remained strong.

Where did she get this strength? From her unshakeable trust in God: "The Father stands at the helm; he knows what he is doing." And he knows better than we human beings do. Therefore she wanted only one thing, to do his will, even when that was difficult. "In the Name of God! The Lord does not send more than we can bear, and to take up that cross is the vocation of Christians on earth", she wrote in one of her letters. Another time she said, "Burdens taken up for God become blessings through him." For God's sake she carried heavy burdens. Thus her life became a blessing for countless people, especially for young girls.

And where did she get this indestructible confidence? From her undivided love of God. The ideal that she held up to her sisters she also lived as an example for them. "Our perfection consists, in my estimation, in the love of God. . . . Let us give to God our whole heart; after all, it belongs to him! . . . Let us love him above all else!"

Her loving heart knew also about the mystery and the blessing of suffering. Did not God redeem the world through the suffering of his Son? "All of God's works walk a path full of suffering." This saying of hers is written on her tombstone on the Green in Munich. But she went on to say, "But that makes them that much more steadfast, and they flourish more gloriously." This saying was fulfilled in her and in her life's work. When the blessed placed her life back in God's hands on May 9, 1879, her congregation was flourishing in eastern and western

Europe and in North America. They had begun as a threesome in 1833. At her death, forty-six years later, there were more than twenty-five hundred sisters ready to carry on the work of their foundress and spiritual mother into the future.

"The Father stands at the helm; he knows what he is doing." Blessed Maria Theresia did not try to take the wheel from God's hand. Rather, she entrusted herself to God and allowed him to guide her. Daily, loving dedication to God led her to human greatness and Christian perfection.[5]

---

[5] *L'Osservatore Romano*, November 25, 1985, p. 3.

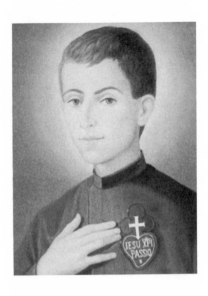

Blessed
Pio of Saint Aloysius
Campidelli

Passionist brother

b. April 29, 1868, Trebbio, Italy
d. November 2, 1889, Casale,
    Italy

Beatified November 17, 1985

A young seminarian and member of the Passionist order who died on the way to the priesthood, Blessed Pio of Saint Aloysius Campidelli[1] was raised to the honors of the altar by Pope John Paul II on November 17, 1985.

The life story of this new blessed is short—it lasted only twenty-one years—and quickly told. It demonstrates impressively, though, how candidates for the priesthood ought to prepare themselves for this sacred calling.

On April 29, 1868, Luigi was born in Trebbio, the fourth of six sons of pious, industrious farmers, Giuseppe and Filomena (née Belpani) Campidelli, and on the same day he was baptized in the parish church of Poggio Berni (diocese of Rimini) with the names Luigi (Aloysius), Nazareno, and Francesco.

Luigi was a sickly child, yet very devout; he always set a good example at the school of the assistant pastor, Father A. Bertozzi, and while serving at the altar and performing other little chores in the church. Luigi received his First Holy Communion on June 9,

---

[1] St[efano] A. Battistelli, *Un fiore di Passione nella generosa Romagna* (Rome, 1936).

1878. It was for him the beginning of a strong and lasting union with Jesus and the awakening of his vocation to the priesthood and religious life. His yearning to consecrate himself in this way took concrete form during the parish mission preached in Poggio Berni by the Passionist Fathers in October 1880. Luigi was admitted to this order at the Passionist Monastery Santa Maria di Casale (Sant'Arcangelo di Romagna) on May 27, 1882, and he was clothed with the habit as Brother Pio of Saint Aloysius.

During his novitiate, Brother Pio had as his novice master Father Michael of the Mother of God, who, during his own novitiate and years of formation, had had Saint Gabriel of the Sorrowful Mother as a classmate. On January 20, 1883, the Passionist novitiate was transferred to Sant'Eutizio, near Soriano (Viterbo). Here the new novice master, Father Vitale, eventually wrote the following about the novice Brother Pio in the record of those who had made their religious profession: "May it please God that all the novices follow in the footsteps of their good classmate Brother Pio; then the novice master could sleep peacefully."

On July 24, 1883, Brother Pio returned to Santa Maria di Casale, where, on April 30, 1884, he made his temporary religious profession with the three vows of poverty, chastity, and obedience and the special vow of the Passionists, always to meditate on the sufferings of Christ. From then on he devoted himself conscientiously to his studies in theology, until he fell seriously ill. He strove in every respect to make progress, both in his studies and also in the spiritual life, and especially to be very faithful to the rule. On May 13, 1886, the young monk in formation began to keep a written record of sacrifices and prayers that he planned to offer to the Blessed Mother as a spiritual bouquet at the hour of his death. From this it is evident how seriously and zealously the young religious was striving for perfection, whole-heartedly intent upon becoming an exemplary religious priest in the Passionist Order. On December 17, 1887, Brother Pio received the four minor orders in Rimini, yet because of the many sayings of the Church Fathers, which he had read, about the unspeakably exalted dignity of the priesthood, he felt, from then on, totally unworthy to desire it. While preparing for ordination to the sub-diaconate, in July 1889, Brother Pio became gravely ill. Immediately, he was willing to offer up his life to God for the Church, for the pope, for his religious order, for the conversion of sinners, and, in particular, for his beloved homeland, Romagna. On November 2, 1889, Brother Pio died, after an ecstasy that had lasted almost an hour. No doubt the words of the Book of Wisdom (4:13) apply to him as well: "Being perfected in a short time, he fulfilled long years; for his soul was pleasing to the Lord, therefore he took him quickly from the midst of wickedness."

At the beatification on November 17, 1985, Pope John Paul II said, about this young man who was perfected in such a short time:

> In the international year of youth, Pio Campidelli, Brother Pio of St Aloysius, is raised to the glory of the altars. This young man, like savoury salt, gave his life for his land, for his people. He offered his life for the Church, the Pope, the conversion of sinners, for his Romagna.
>
> Brother Pio found the fundamental value of his religious life in the very gift of himself. This essential trait of his interior physiognomy was especially evident to others at the moment of his death when, "fully aware of his imminent consummation, he continued daily to offer to fulfil his sacrifice perfectly in order to conform himself to the will of God; he offered it for the Church . . . and in particular for the good of his beloved Romagna" (Canonical Process). Only at that moment did the peculiar note of his virtue express itself, which revealed the style of his entire spiritual experience.
>
> From childhood on, Pio Campidelli had felt an attraction to prayer, liturgy and religious instruction and, sustained by the good example of his family, he maintained it enthusiastically, showing it with expressions typical of innocent childhood, such as devotion to Our Lady, the Blessed Sacrament, and the Cruci-

fied. Having entered the Congregation of the Passionists, he found there a favourable climate for the development of his predominant desire to live in union with God in his very own internal intimacy, and to prepare himself to involve others in this passionate experience through the exercise of the priestly ministry. He was not able, however, to attain the priesthood because God called him to himself at the age of twenty-one. In the special vow of the Passionists to continue the memory of the passion, death and resurrection of Jesus, Pio learned how totally to involve his own life, thereby realizing the mission of the specific vocation of his religious family. He came from a poor family, his health was always frail, his intelligence average; yet he never considered his poverty and limitations as a misfortune, nor was he frustrated by them. He nevertheless fulfilled his greatest potential because he "sought wisdom in prayer . . . from his youth he followed her steps . . . and found there much instruction" (cf. Sir 51:13–16).

Thus Brother Pio was true "salt of the earth" for those who knew him while he was alive and continues to be "salt" for those who draw near to the luminous testimony of his example.[2]

---

[2] *L'Osservatore Romano*, November 25, 1985, p. 3.

Blessed [Saint] Rafqa (Rebecca) Ar-Rayyes

Religious

b. 1832, Himlaya, Lebanon
*d. March 23, 1914, Ad Dahr,
    Lebanon*

Beatified November 17, 1985
[Canonized June 10, 2001]

This chapter deals with a nun from Lebanon whose beatification on November 17, 1985, was a special concern of Pope John Paul II, so as to offer consolation and encouragement to the suffering Christian population of that sorely tried country in the Near East.

This Lebanese blessed[1] was born in 1832 in the village of Himlaya and was baptized with the name Butrusiyyah (Petra, the feminine form of Peter). At the age of seven, she lost her mother; her father married a second time. When she was fourteen years old, her father and stepmother wanted to marry her off, but they could not agree in the choice of a husband. As a result, a family feud started, which the girl tried to escape by running away from home. Butrusiyyah wanted to become a nun and asked to be admitted to Saint Mary of Deliverance, a convent belonging to the Mariamette Sisters, near the village of Bikfayya. Her father and stepmother attempted to remove the girl from the convent by force, but they were not successful. The girl began her novitiate. Then the candidate, who, upon receiving the habit, had taken the

---

[1] P. Sfair, "Rebecca Ar-Rayyes", in *Bibliotheca Sanctorum* 11:66–67.

name of Sister Anissa (= Agnes), was transferred to Ghazir. There she made her religious profession and remained for seven years as cook in the seminary. In 1860, a few months before the catastrophic invasion of the [Muslim] Druzes, she was sent to Deir El-Qamar. During the massacre by the Druzes, Sister Anissa was able to save her own life and that of many children. She made her way to Gebail and then to Maad.

The Mariamette Sisters were dependent upon the Jesuits, and when the latter were driven out of Lebanon, the community of nuns was dissolved. Yet Sister Anissa was determined to remain true to the ideal of religious life, and so she joined the Baladita Order of nuns, who led a very strict contemplative life. Here Sister Anissa received the new religious name of Rafqa—Rebecca.

After a year had passed since her entrance into the convent of Saint Simon El-Qarn, Sister Rebecca asked the Lord to test her fidelity by sending her a sickness. Her prayer was answered in a remarkable way: She was afflicted by various illnesses and, finally, became completely disabled and blind. She bore everything with impressive patience and in complete union with the crucified Lord and the Mother of Sorrows. Sister Rebecca died on March 23, 1914, in the odor of sanctity.

At her beatification on November 17, 1985, in Saint Peter's Basilica in Rome, the Pope said:

[The] origin [of Blessed Rafqa (Rebecca)] makes us immediately turn our eyes and hearts to the dear land of Lebanon, of which the Bible has given us such beautiful images. Today that image is accompanied by a profound heartache because of the immense suffering which afflicts the unfortunate peoples of that country. That is why—and with what fervor—a prayer rises from my heart to the new Blessed. I ask her to intercede before God for her noble homeland, beset by so many torments. May the inhabitants of Lebanon find in the example of this strong woman, who suffered so much and never caused others to suffer, the encouragement to go forward on the path of pardon, reconciliation and peace.

Blessed Rafqa of Himlaya was truly "salt of the earth and light of the world", a mission that is incumbent upon all the disciples of Christ. Having inherited the many rich ecclesiastical and monastic traditions of Lebanon, the new Blessed left to her country and to the Church in return the mysterious flavour of an existence totally impregnated by the spirit of Christ the Redeemer. She is indeed like a light "on a mountain top". One could also apply to her the beautiful verse from psalm 92: "The just flourishes like the palm tree, like a cedar of Lebanon shall he grow!"

Having first entered the *Mariamette Sisters* and taken the name of Sister Anissa, that is Agnes, she was given the task, after a brief preparation, of giving elementary instruction and religious education to the young girls of her homeland. In these delicate tasks she showed a diligence and mildness which profoundly affected her students and their families. The children were instinctively drawn to her. During the persecution of 1860 she saved many of them. It is told how a child of Deir-el-Qamar escaped death by taking shelter under the beloved sister's mantle.

The year 1871 marked a turning point in the life of Sister Anissa. Her beloved Congregation of the Mariamettes was dissolved. She then knocked on the door of the Lebanese Maronite Order, and made her solemn profession in that community on 25 August 1873, taking the name of Sister Rafqa, or Rebecca, which was the name of her own mother. Still enjoying good health in her fifties. Sister Rafqa, mysteriously moved by the Holy Spirit, asked for the grace to be visited by suffering. Far from being the victim of a morbid taste for pain, she experienced a mystical longing for conformity to the suffering of Christ. From 1885 until her death in 1914 she suffered daily from severe pain in her head and eyes; this progressively led to complete helplessness and total blindness. Her most frequent prayer was: "In union with your suffering, Jesus!"

Admirable Sister Rafqa, humble and authentic replica of Christ crucified, we thank you. If you did not add anything to the unique and superabundant redemption of the Lord Jesus, you left us an unsettling witness of a mysterious and painful cooperation in the application of the fruits of that redemption. May the disciples of Christ, wherever they are today, and your Lebanese compatriots so tried by ten years of conflict, find in your life of suffering and glory the evangelical courage to sacrifice, hope, pardon, love![2]

[2] *L'Osservatore Romano*, November 25, 1985, pp. 3–4.

Blessed Alphonsa of the Immaculate Conception Anna Muttathupadathu

Poor Clare

b. *August 19, 1910, Arpukara, Kerala, India*

d. *July 28, 1946, Bharananganam, Kerala*

Beatified February 8, 1986

The Indian Poor Clare Alphonsa of the Immaculate Conception[1] was raised to the honors of the altar on February 8, 1986, in Kottayam, together with the priest Kuriakose Elias Chavara, by Pope John Paul II during his pastoral visit to India. This was a great joy for all the Catholics in the entire Indian subcontinent but especially for the many Catholics of the Indian province of Kerala, particularly because the nun's beatification took place only forty years after her death on July 28, 1946.

Anna Muttathupadathu, as Sister Alphonsa was called after her baptism in the Syro-Malabar rite, was born on August 19, 1910, in Arpukara, Kerala, India. As a small child she lost her parents. She was raised by her grandmother and an aunt on her mother's side. At a very early age, she sensed a call to the consecrated religious state, and in 1927 she entered the Poor Clare convent at Bharananganam. In 1931 she consecrated herself to God by temporary profession, and in 1936 she took her perpetual vows. From then on, she took quite seriously her fidelity to what she had promised in making vows of poverty, chastity, and obedience.

---

[1] G. D'Ascola, "Muttathupadam, Anna Alfonsa", in *Bibliotheca Sanctorum* I:949–50.

At first, Sister Alphonsa was assigned to teach, but she had to give up this sort of professional work for health reasons. Therefore, other duties were given to her that were more in keeping with her frail health. In performing them, she proved to be rather quiet but extremely kind to her sisters in community. She experienced much suffering, however, as a result of hostilities and the sacrifices that were demanded of her. In 1945 she became seriously ill and had a premonition: "I feel that the Lord has destined me to be a victim and a sacrifice of atonement through suffering. It is true: one day when I had nothing to endure, it was for me a wasted day!"

More and more, Alphonsa became a victim soul dedicated to reparation. At her death—it was on July 28, 1946—with all who knew her she left the impression of a truly saintly religious. This reputation continued to grow after her death. Eventually, there were thousands upon thousands who made pilgrimages to her grave—not only Catholics, but also Muslims and Hindus. Her reputation for sanctity finally had become so great that in 1955 the process of beatification was begun with an inquiry in Kerala and then was continued in Rome. Based on the determination of her heroic virtues (1983) and on the miracle that took place through the intercession of Sister Alphonsa (1985), Pope John Paul II was able to proceed with the beatification of this Poor Clare nun on February 8, 1986, in Kottayam, during his journey through India. He said:

The Church throughout the world rejoices with the Church in India as *Father Kuriakose Elias Chavara* and *Sister Alphonsa of the Immaculate Conception* are *raised to the ranks of the Blessed* in the great Communion of Saints. This man and this woman, both members of the Syro-Malabar Church here in Kerala, advanced to great heights of holiness through their wholehearted cooperation with the grace of God. Each possessed an ardent love of God, yet each followed a distinct spiritual path.

Next, the Pope described the life of Father Kuriakose Elias Chavara. Then he went on to talk about Sister Alphonsa:

Sister Alphonsa of the Immaculate Conception, born a century after Father Kuriakose Elias, would gladly have served the Lord with similar apostolic projects. And indeed, she possessed a personal devotion to Father Kuriakose from early in her religious life. But the path to holiness for Sister Alphonsa was clearly a different one. It was *the way of the Cross, the way of sickness and suffering.*

Already at a very young age, Sister Alphonsa desired *to serve the Lord as a religious*, but it was not without enduring trials that she was finally able to pursue this goal. When it became possible, she joined the Franciscan Clarist Congregation [the Poor Clare community]. Throughout her life, which was a brief thirty-six years, she continually gave thanks to God for the joy and privilege of her religious vocation, for the grace of her vows of chastity, poverty and obedience.

From early in her life, Sister Alphonsa experienced great *suffering*. With the passing of the years, the heavenly Father gave her an ever fuller *share in the Passion* of his beloved Son. We recall how she experienced not only physical pain of great intensity, but also the spiritual suffering of being misunderstood and misjudged by others. But she constantly accepted all her sufferings with serenity and trust in God, being firmly convinced that they would purify her motives, help her to overcome all selfishness, and unite her more closely with her beloved divine Spouse. She wrote to her spiritual director: "Dear Father, as my good Lord Jesus loves me so very much, I sincerely desire to remain on this sick bed and suffer not only this, but anything else besides, even to the end of the world. I feel now that God has intended my life to be an oblation, a sacrifice of suffering" (20 November 1944). She came to love suffering because *she loved the suffering Christ*. She learned to love the Cross through her love of the crucified Lord.

Sister Alphonsa knew that by her sufferings she shared in the Church's apostolate; she found joy in them by offering them all to Christ. In this way, she seemed to have made her own the words of Saint Paul: "*I rejoice in my sufferings* for your sake, and in my flesh I complete what is lacking in Christ's afflictions for the sake of his body, that is, the Church" (Col 1:24). She was endowed by God with an affectionate and happy disposition, with the ability to take delight in ordinary and simple things. The weight of human suffering, even the misunderstanding or jealousy of others, could not extinguish *the joy of the Lord* which filled her heart. In a letter written shortly before she died, at a time of intense physical and mental suffering, she said: "I have given myself up completely to Jesus. Let him please himself in his dealings with me. My only desire in this world is to suffer for love of God and to rejoice in doing it" (February 1946).

Both Father Kuriakose and Sister Alphonsa bear witness to the beauty and greatness of *the religious vocation.* . . . [W]ithin the great family of the Church, God our Father calls some of you to follow Christ still more closely and to dedicate your lives with *a special consecration* through the profession of chastity, poverty and obedience. You, the religious of the Church, bear *public witness to the Gospel* and to the primacy of the love of God. By a permanent commitment and lifelong fidelity to your vows, you seek to grow in union with Christ and to contribute in a unique way to the life and mission of the Church. And what a vital contribution is yours!

In *a rich variety of forms*, you live to the full your evangelical consecration. Some of you have heard the Lord's personal call to the *contemplative life* where, though hidden from the world, you offer your lives and prayers for the sake of all humanity. Others have been called to an active *apostolic life*, where you serve in teaching, health care, parochial work, retreats, works of charity and many forms of pastoral activity.

No matter how you serve, dear brothers and sisters in Christ, never doubt *the value of your consecrated life.* Whether your service resembles great apostolic endeavors of Father Kuriakose, or takes the form of hidden suffering like Sister Alphonsa, whatever it may be, it is *important in the life of the Church.* . . . Even when you feel discouraged or weighed down by personal failures or sin, trust even more in the love of God for you. Turn to him for mercy, forgiveness and love. For as Saint Paul says in the same reading: "the Lord helps us in our weakness" (Rom 8:26). It is in him that we find our strength, our courage and our joy.

Without the vital contribution of men and women religious, the charity of the Church would be lessened, her fruitfulness would be diminished. Thus, I pray that the beatification of these two exemplary religious of India will give you renewed zeal for your precious vocation.[2]

[2] *L'Osservatore Romano*, February 17, 1986, pp. 6–7.

Blessed
Kuriakose Elias Chavara

Priest, Founder

b. *February 10, 1805,*
   Kainakary, India
d. *January 3, 1871,*
   Koonammavu, India

Beatified February 8, 1986

Together with the Indian Poor Clare nun Alphonsa of the Immaculate Conception, who belonged to the Syro-Malabar Rite, on February 8, 1986, Pope John Paul II also beatified in Kottayam in India a highly meritorious priest of the same Syro-Malabar Rite, Kuriakose Elias Chavara.[1]

Kuriakose [Cyriacus] Chavara was born on February 10, 1805, in Kainakary (Alleppey, India) and baptized in the Syro-Malabar Rite. After receiving elementary education in his hometown, Kuriakose went to Pallipuram for his studies in the humanities and in theology. Father Thomas Palackal played a decisive role in his education. In November 1829, Kuriakose received holy orders from Bishop Maurillo Stabellini, O.C.D., the apostolic vicar of Malabar. On May 11, 1841, the young priest, together with his teacher Father Thomas Palackal and Father Thomas Porukara, founded the Congregation of the Servants of Mary Immaculate. The members of the congregation made a serious commitment to

[1] W. Herbstrith, *Begegnung mit Indien und einem seiner grossen christlichen Pioniere* (Trier, 1969), pp. 167–231; L. Beccaro, *Piccola Biografia del servo di Dio P. Ciriaco Elia Chavara* (Rome, 1974).

lead a religious life, while remaining open to opportunities to carry on a missionary apostolate.

When Father Thomas Palackal (1841) and Father Thomas Porukara (1849) died, Father Kuriakose Chavara was recognized as the leader of the young religious community. On December 6, 1855, it transformed itself into a Third Order of Discalced Carmelites and assumed the name Congregation of the Servants of Mary Immaculate of Carmel. Father Kuriakose was the first to make his profession with perpetual vows, and he now took the religious name of Kuriakose Elias of the Holy Family. Then he received the vows of ten other priests, whose superior he was from then on as prior of his institute. In 1861 the institute was joined (aggregated) to the Order of Discalced Carmelites.

As the director of his congregation, Father Kuriakose Elias displayed extraordinary talents in forming the members of this religious community; they were quite serious about their consecration to God. Father Kuriakose Elias developed for his congregation a spirituality strongly centered on the Eucharist, which also included a childlike devotion to Mary. Furthermore, the religious community became remarkable for its intense spirit of prayer and mortification, as well as its great sensitivity to new methods of evangelization.

A particularly zealous preaching apostolate, above all, in giving retreats, and prudent individual spiritual direction were the areas in which Father Kuriakose most distinguished himself. His efforts were actively supported by the apostolic vicar of Verapoly and by the missionaries from the Order of Discalced Carmelites. We should mention here especially Father Leopold Beccaro, who from 1864 was the spiritual director and confessor of Father Kuriakose and of his novices. Together with Father Leopold Beccaro, Father Kuriakose Elias founded a convent of the Third Order of Discalced Carmelites in Koonammavu in 1866. From it developed two branches of the Discalced Carmelite Sisters, namely, the Malabar branch, which became the flourishing Congregation of the Mother of Carmel, and the Latin-rite branch, which was called the Congregation of the Theresian Sisters of Verapoly.

Particularly significant were the efforts of Father Kuriakose in response to the disorders caused by the intrusion of the Chaldean metropolitan Thomas Rochos, who succeeded in drawing a large percentage of the parishes over to his side and creating a painful schism. At that time, the apostolic vicar, B. Baccinelli, delegated Father Kuriakose Elias to be his general vicar for the Malabar Catholics. In that position, Father Kuriakose Elias worked untiringly to restore the unity that had been lost; he prayed and preached and strove with all his might, and with extraordinary prudence, to undo the consequences of the schism. Then, when the intrusive metropolitan went away again and his former secretary came from Baghdad to India as the new metropolitan, Father Kuriakose Elias succeeded in convincing him to give up the office he had arrogated and to convert to Catholicism. With all his many-faceted activity, Father Kuriakose still found time to compose spiritual works in prose and poetry in the Malayalam language. Most of these writings were published only after his death; some, however, on pastoral and liturgical themes, he was able to have printed himself.

Father Kuriakose Elias Chavara, a Syro-Malabar priest endowed with great charity, matured in the course of years to become an outstanding figure in the Church of India. He died rich in merits, after a short illness, on January 3, 1871, in Koonammavu, surrounded by his spiritual sons, his noble spiritual director Father Beccaro, and the general vicar.

At the beatification on February 8, 1986, in Kottayam in India, Pope John Paul II said the following about Kuriakose Elias Chavara:

[F]or nearly all of his sixty-five years of earthly life he laboured generously for the renewal and enrichment of the Christian life. His deep love for Christ filled him with *apostolic zeal* and made him especially careful to promote *the unity of the Church*. With great generosity he collaborated with others, especially brother priests and religious, in the work of salvation.

In cooperation with Fathers Thomas Palackal and Thomas Porukara, Father Kuriakose founded *an Indian religious congregation for men*, now known as the Carmelites of Mary Immaculate. Later, with the help of an Italian missionary, Father Leopold Beccaro, he started *an Indian religious congregation for women*, the Congregation of the Mother of Carmel. These congregations grew and flourished, and religious vocations became better understood and appreciated. Through the common efforts of the members of new religious families, his hopes and works were multiplied many times over.

Father Kuriakose's life, and the lives of these new religious, were dedicated to the service of the Syro-Malabar Church. Under his leadership or inspiration, a good number of *apostolic initiatives* were undertaken: the establishment of seminaries for the education and formation of the clergy, the introduction of annual retreats, a publishing house for Catholic works, a house to care for the destitute and dying, schools for general education and programs for the training of catechumens. He contributed to the Syro-Malabar liturgy and spread devotion to the Holy Eucharist and the Holy Family. In particular, he dedicated himself to encouraging and counseling Christian families, convinced as he was of the fundamental role of the family in the life of society and the Church.

But no apostolic cause was dearer to the heart of this great man of faith than that of the *unity and harmony within* the Church. It was as if he had always before his mind the prayer of Jesus, on the night before his Sacrifice on the Cross: "*That they may all be one*; even as you, Father, are in me, and I in you, that they also may be in us" (Jn 17:21). Today the Church solemnly recalls with love and gratitude all his efforts to resist threats of disunity and to encourage the clergy and faithful to maintain unity with the See of Peter and the universal Church. His success in this, as in all his many undertakings, was undoubtedly due to the *intense charity and prayer* which characterized his daily life, his close *communion with Christ* and *his love for the Church* as the visible Body of Christ on earth.[2]

---

[2] *L'Osservatore Romano*, February 17, 1986, p. 6.

Blessed
Antoine Chevrier

Secular priest
Founder of the Prado

b. April 16, 1825, Lyons, France
d. October 2, 1879, Lyons

Beatified October 4, 1986

Le Prêtre ou le véritable disciple de Notre Seigneur Jésus Christ (The priest, or the true disciple of our Lord Jesus Christ) is the title of a remarkable book written by the French priest Antoine Chevrier. Even more remarkable is the life of this priest, who was beatified on October 4, 1986, in Lyons, because in it he showed concretely and impressively what a priest is—the genuine disciple of Jesus Christ—and what he ought to be: unselfish and poor, so as to be present for the poor unreservedly and to give them a living example of the good news of Christ and to proclaim it to them. For love of the poor, he founded in 1857 the institution called *La Providence du Prado* and in 1859 the Congregation of the Priests of the Prado and the Franciscan Sisters of the Prado. Through the members of these communities, the saintly diocesan priest of Lyons continues his exemplary work up to the present day as a living example of what priests ought to be.

Antoine Chevrier[1] was born on April 16, 1825, in Lyons, into a family of modest means and spent his entire life in this French city

[1] J. F. Six, *Un prêtre: Le Père Chevrier: Jalons pour une histoire spirituelle du XIX siècle* (Paris, 1966).

until he was called to his heavenly home on October 2, 1879. He wanted to become a missionary and thought of entering a missionary society. That did not come about. Yet he maintained this missionary spirit, to which he had committed himself at his priestly ordination on May 25, 1850. For this reason, the newly ordained priest accepted a position others had refused: that of vicar (assistant pastor) at the parish of Saint André in the poor working-class district of Lyons. For seven years he did pastoral work here. Then came the momentous Christmas of 1856: in an unprecedented and profound way he took to heart his meditation on the mystery of the Nativity that Christmas Eve. He comprehended in a singular way the purpose and tender significance of the poverty of the Divine Infant in the crib. From then on the insight would not let him go.

In 1857 he accepted the assignment of serving as chaplain for the City of the Child Jesus, a foundation for instructing poor, abandoned children in Lyons. Soon Father Chevrier had to resign from the position because he discovered that its founders were concerned about social programs and not interested, as he was, in the evangelization of these people.

Assisted by Brother Pierre Louat, who devoted himself to the boys, and by Sisters Amalie and Maria, who took care of the girls, Antoine Chevrier decided to acquire a dance hall called the Prado that was located in the vicinity of Saint Andrew's parish. At this location the noble priest was now able to establish an institution dedicated to preparing children for their First Holy Communion. All the other programs of the blessed, too, which he started in order to evangelize the marginalized, the poor, or the unemployed, crystallized around the word "Prado", just like the communities that he founded. He attended to the needs of the children and of the poor and founded a school from which the first priests of the Prado eventually came and, likewise, the first sisters.

Antoine Chevrier was among the first men in France in the second half of the nineteenth century to become aware of and concerned about the loss of faith in the ranks of laborers and, generally, in the lower classes of society. For this reason, he insisted on a contemporary formation for priests, who should be "poor among the poor", so as to draw near to them again.

It is moving to hear how Pope John Paul II, in his homily at the beatification of Father Antoine Chevrier in Lyons on October 4, 1986, elaborated on the significance of this new blessed precisely from this perspective. We really ought to bring to our readers' attention the Pope's long homily in its entirety. Let us at least reprint the most important passages here:

> "*I thank thee, Father,* Lord of heaven and earth, that thou hast hidden these things from the wise and understanding and hast revealed them to babes" (Mt 11:25).
>
> These words were first pronounced by *Jesus of Nazareth,* a son of Israel, descendant of David, Son of God: they marked a *fundamental turning-point* in the history of God's revelation to man, in the history of religion, in the spiritual history of humanity. . . .
>
> [W]e are moved when we discover these words of Christ anew today. They take on a new relevance, because *we have before our eyes* the figure of a priest who was closely linked to this city in the Church of the nineteenth century, *Father Antoine Chevrier.* I have the privilege today of proclaiming him *blessed* at Lyons, among you, and I am truly happy at this.
>
> Today, the universal Church celebrates the feast of *St Francis of Assisi:* he too found his joy in following Christ in the greatest poverty and humility; in the thirteenth century, he helped his contemporaries rediscover the Gospel. Father Chevrier was a fervent admirer of the poor man of Assisi and belonged to the Third Order of St Francis. In the room where he died, there is a small statue of St Francis, and likewise a small statue of *St Jean-Marie Vianney,* whom he went to consult at Ars in 1857, when, as a young priest, he was asking himself how to follow the way of poverty which the mystery of the Crib suggested to him. . . .

These three saints [Francis of Assisi, Jean-Marie Vianney, the Curé of Ars, and Antoine Chevrier] have in common the fact that they belong to those "little ones", those "poor", "gentle and humble of heart", in whom the Father of heaven has found the fullness of his joy, and to whom Christ has revealed the unfathomable mystery of God. . . .

With Jesus, therefore, we too proclaim the praise of God for the marvellous figures of these three saints. They were all filled with the same passionate love for God, and they lived in a similar state of poverty, though each according to his own charism. Saint Francis of Assisi, a deacon, with his companions, awakened the hearts of the people of the Italian cities to the love of Christ. The Curé of Ars, alone with God in his country church, aroused the consciences of his parishioners and of innumerable crowds, by offering them the forgiveness of God. Father Chevrier, a diocesan priest in an urban setting, along with his confrères was the apostle of the poorest working class districts of the outskirts of Lyons at the time of the birth of large-scale industrialization. It was this missionary concern that urged him also to seek holiness by adopting a radical Gospel life-style.

Let us take a special look at Antoine Chevrier: he is one of those "little ones" who cannot be compared with the "wise" and the "learned" of his own day or of other centuries. He constitutes *a class of his own*, with a greatness that is wholly evangelical. His *greatness* shows itself in what one can call his lowliness or poverty. Living humbly, with the poorest of means, he is the witness of the hidden mystery of God, a *witness of the love that God* bears for the masses of "little ones" who are like him. He was their servant, their apostle.

For them, he was the "priest according to the Gospel"—to use the first title of his collected exhortations on "the true disciple of Jesus Christ". He is an incomparable guide for the many *priests present here*, beginning with those of [the] *Prado* [which] he founded. But all the *lay Christians* who make up this assembly will likewise find a great light in him, because he shows to each of the baptized how to proclaim the Good News to the poor, and how to make Jesus Christ present through one's own existence.

An *apostle*—yes, this is what Father Chevrier wanted to be when he was preparing for the priesthood. "Jesus Christ is the one sent by the Father; the priest is *the one sent by Jesus Christ*." The poor themselves enlivened his desire to evangelize them, but *it was Jesus Christ who "took hold of him"*. He was particularly affected by his meditation before the Crib at Christmas 1856. From then on, he always sought to know Jesus Christ better, to become his disciple, to be conformed to him, in order to proclaim him better to the poor. . . .

The apostle, then, is a person *"taken hold of by Christ Jesus"*.

The apostle has absolute confidence that, becoming like Christ in death, he will attain the resurrection from the dead (cf. Phil 3:11).

He is thus the man of *eschatological hope* that finds expression in the hope of each day, in a programme of daily living, through the ministry of salvation which he exercises for others.

Father Chevrier put all his efforts into pursuing this knowledge of Jesus Christ, in order to "grasp" Christ better, just as he himself had been grasped. He meditated unceasingly on the Gospel: he wrote thousands of pages of commentaries, to help his friends to become true disciples in their turn. He even sought to reproduce the life of Christ in his own life. "We must represent Jesus Christ in the poverty of his crib, Jesus Christ suffering in his passion, Jesus Christ letting himself be eaten in the holy Eucharist" (*Le véritable disciple*, Prado, Éditions Librairie, Lyons 1968, p. 101; hereafter cited as *V.D.*). And again: "The knowledge of Jesus Christ is the key to everything. To know God and his Christ: this is the whole man, the whole priest, the whole saint" (Letter to his seminarians, 1875). Here is the prayer that crowns his meditation: "O Word! O Christ! How beautiful you are! How great you are! . . . Make me know you and love you. You are my Lord, and my one and only Master" (*V.D.*, p. 108). . . .

Henceforward, Father Chevrier is completely available for the work of Christ: "To know Jesus Christ, to work for Jesus Christ, to die for Jesus Christ" (Letters, p. 89). "Lord, if you need a poor man, . . . a fool, here I am . . . to do your will. I am yours. *Tuus sum ego*" (*V.D.*, p. 122). . . .

Father Chevrier let himself be fully *absorbed* by the service of others. His brothers were first of all *the poor*, those whom the Lord led him to meet in the flooded district of La Guillotière in 1856, those who were homeless. They were the children of the city of the Child Jesus, whom he came to know through Camille Rambaud, a layman. It was these children whom he gathered together, along with other older ones, in the room of the Prado; they had no schooling and no instruction in the faith, and were unable to follow the preparation for first communion. They were sometimes abandoned, often despised and exploited; as he said, they became "machines for work, made to enrich their masters" (Sermons, Ms. III, p. 12). There were all kinds of miserable and marginal people, who felt that "they had nothing, knew nothing, were worth nothing". The sick and the sinners, too, were among these poor.

Why was Father Chevrier especially drawn to those whom he called, in the manner of the Gospel, "the poor"? He had a clear consciousness of their human misery, and he saw at the same time the gulf that separated them from the Church. He felt for them the love and the tenderness of Christ Jesus. Through him, it was Christ himself who seemed to say to his contemporaries: "*Come* to me, all you who labour and are heavy laden, and I will give you rest. *Take* my yoke upon you, and learn from me; for I am gentle and lowly in heart, and you will *find* rest [for your soul]. Yes, my yoke is easy, and my burden is light" (Mt 11:28–30). . . . Truly, the Lord gave him a special charism to make himself the neighbour of the poor. And, through him, Christ made this city and France of the nineteenth century hear the beatitudes anew: "Blessed are the poor in spirit . . . blessed are those who hunger and thirst for righteousness . . . blessed are the merciful" (Mt 5:3, 6, 7)!

Certainly, every milieu must be evangelized: the rich as well as the poor, the learned as well as the ignorant. No one may be the object of a lack of understanding, or of negligence, or even less, of scorn on the part of the Church. In one sense, all men are God's poor. But in the conditions in which Father Chevrier lived, the service of the poor was a necessary witness, and it remains so today wherever we encounter poverty. He is one of the many apostles who have realized throughout history what we call *the preferential option for the poor.*

Father Chevrier looks at them with the eyes of the Gospel, respecting them and loving them in faith. He finds Christ in the poor and, at the same time, he finds the poor in Christ. He does not idealize them, for he knows their limitations and their weaknesses; he knows, however, that they have often lacked love and justice. He has a sense of the dignity of each person, rich or poor. He desires the good of each one of them, their salvation. . . . His respect impels him to make himself the equal of the poor, to live in the midst of them, like Christ; sometimes to work like them; to die with them. He hopes that in this way the poor will understand that they are not abandoned by God, who loves them as a Father (cf. *V.D.*, p. 63). As for himself, this is his experience: "It is in poverty that the priest finds his strength, his power, his freedom" (*V.D.*, p. 519). The dream is to form poor priests who will go to the poor.

Today, let us ask Blessed Antoine Chevrier to teach us ever more to have respect and evangelical concern for the poor. Dear brothers and sisters, *you know who these poor are in our world today.* They are all those who lack bread, but also those without employment, without responsibilities, without consideration for their dignity, and also those who are without God. It is no longer only the world of the working class that is affected, but many other milieux too. In an excessively consumerist civilization, there are, paradoxically, the "new poor" who do not have the "social minimum". There is the multitude of those who suffer from unemployment, young people who cannot find work, or mature persons who have lost their jobs. . . .

Father Chevrier wished to liberate the poor from *religious ignorance*. At the Prado, he wanted to provide the young people with both education (what we would today call literacy) and instruction in the faith that would permit them to partake of the Eucharist. For this task, he sought and created a team of men and women. "My whole desire would be to prepare good catechists for the Church and to form an association of priests working for this end" (Letter to his seminarians, 1877). They would go everywhere "to show Jesus Christ", as witnesses preaching through their simple and carefully prepared catechesis, but also through their life. He himself dedicated a great deal of his time to this, with means that were poor but appropriate, giving a concrete commentary to each word of the Gospel, and also the rosary, and the Way of the Cross. He used to say: "The catechesis of man is the great mission of the priest today" (Letters, p. 70).

The poor therefore have a right to the totality of the Gospel. The Church respects the consciences of those who do not share her faith, but she has the mission to bear witness to God's love for them.

Today, dear brothers and sisters, the religious context is no longer that of the epoch of Father Chevrier. It is marked by doubt, scepticism, unbelief, indeed atheism, and a claim for the widest freedom. The need for a clear and ardent presentation of the faith—of the totality of the faith—becomes all the more obvious. *Religious ignorance is spreading in a disturbing manner.* I know that many catechists are aware of this, and dedicate their time and their talents, at Lyons and elsewhere in France, to provide a remedy to this situation. The appeal made by Father Antoine Chevrier ought to stimulate us and keep us in a state of mission: do you not hear him exclaim, "How beautiful it is to know how to speak of God!" (Letter, 1873). . . .

And you, Father Antoine Chevrier, lead us in the path of the Gospel. You are blessed! Your figure rises up and shines in brightness of the eight beatitudes of Jesus. This city of Lyons will call you blessed, for it venerated you from the very day of your death. The Church too venerates in you the "little one" whom Jesus extolled more than the wise and the learned, the priest, the apostle, the servant of the poor. Like Paul, who was seized by Christ, you lived *forgetting what lay behind you*, orientated wholly towards what lay ahead. Yes, you are totally turned towards the future, towards the great future of all the peoples in God. You ran towards the goal, to receive the prize that God calls us to receive in heaven above, in Christ Jesus. *It is the prize of love. It is Love!*[2]

[2] *L'Osservatore Romano*, October 20, 1986, pp. 3–5.

Blessed
Teresa Maria
of the Cross
Manetti

Foundress

b. March 2, 1846,
  Campi Bisenzio, Italy
d. April 23, 1910,
  Campi Bisenzio

Beatified October 19, 1986

On World Mission Sunday, October 19, 1986, Pope John Paul II traveled to Florence and there raised a child of a suburb of that city to the honors of the altar by beatifying Teresa Maria of the Cross Manetti, who was born on March 2, 1846, in Campi Bisenzio (San Martino).

Teresa Adelaide Manetti[1] received a strict Christian upbringing from her parents. As she matured, the girl displayed an exceptional talent for organization; already at the age of eighteen Teresa gathered other girls around to live in community and to work together looking after children. Out of this group, which had a special devotion to Saint Teresa of Avila and took its inspiration from her writings, developed the Institute of the Third Order Carmelite Sisters of Saint Teresa. This community spread quickly and received papal approval from Pope Saint Pius X in 1904. That same year the foundress was elected general superior of the community of nuns, but she headed it for only six more years, because cancer ravaged her physical strength, and she died on April 23, 1910.

---

[1] Stanislao di S. Teresa: *La venerabile Teresa Maria della Croce*, 2d ed. (Florence, 1968).

Sister Teresa Maria of the Cross (*a Cruce*, as she was called in her religious community), for all her activities, was a very contemplative woman endowed by God with mystical graces and charisms. She was greatly devoted to prayer, and the adoration of the Lord Jesus in the Holy Eucharist was a particular concern of hers. Yet she was also a realistic and practical woman who applied herself energetically to the service of the poor and the suffering with a very special love. She showed a particular preference for the little ones, the scorned, and the despised, especially for orphaned children.

In the homily at the beatification in Florence, Pope John Paul II gave a particularly beautiful description of the qualities that made up the characteristic sanctity of this woman religious:

> The Church which has centuries of life in Florence wishes to renew her missionary *awareness* and her missionary *willingness*, as she participates in the elevation of one of her venerable daughters to the glories of the altar: *the Servant of God Sister Teresa Maria of the Cross*. This is both the essential and the proper reason for missionary awareness and willingness: *the Church always carries within her the call to holiness* (*Lumen Gentium*, 39ff.), and so continues in her salvific mission.
>
> What does today's *liturgy tell us about holiness*? What does it say to us about the holiness of this Servant of God, who was one of your fellow citizens?
>
> *Holiness* is that "lifting up" of one's eyes "to the hills", of which the Responsorial Psalm speaks (cf. Ps 121[120]:1): it is intimacy with the Father who is in heaven; intimacy through Christ in the Holy Spirit.
>
> In this intimacy *man lives*, aware of his path, which has its limits and its difficulties—*man who looks to God with confidence.*
>
> Holiness is the awareness of being "watched over", watched over by God. The saint knows very well his frailty, the precariousness of his existence, of his capacities. Yet he is not frightened. *He feels secure in spite of all this.*

He trusts in the fact that God "*will not let his foot be moved*, that he will watch over him, keeping him from all evil" (cf. Ps 121[120]:3–5, 7–8).

Even though they note much darkness in themselves, the saints are conscious of being *made for Truth. For God-Truth. Thus they give even more room to this Truth* in their lives. Whence comes the security that makes them stand out: where others vacillate, they stand firm. Where others doubt, they see the truth.

What does the liturgy say to us today with regard to the holiness of the Servant of God Teresa Maria of the Cross?

Holiness sometimes means keeping one's hands raised to God in prayer even while a battle rages all around, while the struggle between good and evil continues.

The effort of contemplation and prayer seems at first glance an estrangement from the battles of life. It seems a renunciation of struggle. Nevertheless, those who see it in this way do not know the *power of prayer. . . .*

Teresa Maria was a great woman of action; still, from the days of her adolescence she had the grace of understanding this power of prayer. She was especially conscious of it during *eucharistic adoration*, which was the wellspring of her strength and joy, as well as of her fervent devotion to the Blessed Virgin Mary.

From a very early age this Servant of God experienced a *unity* between her taste for prayer and the need to *respond to the Love* with which she felt herself loved by Christ. This desire to do good was immediately translated into action. Before the age of twenty, she gathered around her, as a community, a group of young women in order to assist poor and abandoned girls.

Despite difficulties and sufferings, the undertaking was soon established and—under the sign of Carmelite spirituality—became, after only a few years, a Religious Institute of Pontifical jurisdiction, recognized by Pope Pius X in 1904. The Sisters of Teresa Maria then began to spread to other lands as well, such as Lebanon and the Holy Land.

Teresa Maria lived in exemplary fashion the exhortations of St Paul which we have read in the liturgy: "from childhood" *she let herself be convinced by the truth of the Word of God*; she built upon it and *"remained steady"* in it. With the passing years she strengthened her interior "steadfastness" and vigour and was able to "teach", convincing and correcting her spiritual daughters and forming them in justice and all good works—up to this day, and into the future.

A particularly evident characteristic of Teresa Maria was her joy. A woman of maternal tenderness and exceptional balance, her *wise words*, her very gaze and bearing were capable of infusing so much light, comfort and hope in everyone. She was constantly sought out by people of every class and condition, people who would even wait for hours just to be received by her in her little convent on the bank of the Bisenzio, in order to listen to her words of faith which transfigured suffering and restored peace.

However, Teresa Maria's joy was not the illusory joy of this world. She paid a *high price* for that joy, and she paid it gladly, *impelled by love for Christ and souls*. She suffered much: from criticism all the way to calumny; from the martyrdom of a malignant tumour that devoured her with frightful suffering to the anguish of a "dark night" of faith which tried her in the deepest fibres of her spirit. But in all this she perfectly *abandoned herself into the hands of God*, knowing how to live in peace and almost seeming to repeat the words of Paul: "I am overjoyed in every affliction" (cf. II Cor 7:4).

This is the joy which the new Blessed teaches us: a joy which is *truth, fullness* and *fruitfulness*, and which opens us to *divine life*.

Today we have great need of this joy. *It is the joy that comes to us from the Cross*, from that Cross which she added to her name as a religious. In Florence, that Holy Cross also gives its name to a square, which is at once a monument of history, art, culture and faith.[2]

[2] *L'Osservatore Romano*, November 17, 1986, pp. 12–13.

Three Martyrs
from the Carmel of Saint Joseph
in Guadalajara

Three nuns who belonged to the same Carmelite convent and were murdered on the same day, July 24, 1936, at the same place, out of hatred for the Catholic faith,[1] were beatified on the same day, March 29, 1987, by Pope John Paul II. They are here portrayed together.

Left to right:
Blessed Teresa of the Child Jesus
Blessed María Pilar of Saint Francis
Blessed María Angeles of Saint Joseph

[1] Guido Roascio, "Calendario in ricordo delle tre Carmelitane Scalze di Guadalajara", in *Messaggero del S. Bambino Gesù di Praga* (Arenzano Genua, 1987).

Blessed María Pilar of Saint Francis Borgia (Jacoba) Martínez García

Carmelite, Martyr

b. December 30, 1877,
Tarazona, Spain
d. July 24, 1936,
Guadalajara, Spain

Beatified March 29, 1987

Born on December 30, 1877, in Tarazona (Guadalajara, Spain), this new blessed was baptized Jacoba on the same day. She had an older sister who entered the Carmel in Guadalajara and made her final profession there on October 12, 1898, when Jacoba was twenty-one years old. The beautiful ceremony had a contagious effect on the like-minded younger sister. She too entered the Carmel of Saint Joseph in Guadalajara and received together with the habit the religious name of Sister María Pilar of Saint Francis Borgia. On October 15, 1899, she made her profession. Besides the good example of her older sister, this Carmelite, who was destined by God to become a martyr, also had the example of her priest brother, who likewise took very seriously his consecration to God and his vocation as a pastor in Torrellas (1887–1891) and then in Corella (1891–1898). During her childhood and youth, Jacoba had spent many months with him.

In the Carmelite convent, Sister María Pilar always manifested a strong faith and a eucharistic piety. She devotedly carried out her duties as sacristan and portress. Her love for Christ is evident in a resolution she made during a retreat in the year 1930: "United with Jesus, I want to do everything for love of him." In 1933 she wrote the following lines: "Why am I a Carmelite? So that, completely united with God, I might become a great saint. Therefore I want to renounce everything that God demands of me. Therefore, O my Jesus, I want to love thee to the utmost and to strive for the most intimate union with thee. Nothing should have a place in my heart besides thee, O my Bridegroom."

Then, during the Spanish Civil War, when the time of persecution began, Sister María Pilar said to her sisters in community, "If they carry us off to be martyred, let us go singing, together with our Carmelite sisters, the Martyrs of Compiègne, with the song on our lips: 'Heart of Jesus, reign!'" During the first bombardments of Guadalajara, she offered herself to God as a sacrifice for the benefit of the order.

When Guadalajara fell into the hands of soldiers of the Red militia, on July 22, 1936, the Discalced Carmelites had to leave their cloister in civilian garb and take refuge in the houses of acquaintances. On the afternoon of July 24, 1936, while Sister María Pilar, together with two other sisters from her convent, Sister María Angeles of Saint Joseph and Sister María Teresa of the Child Jesus, was looking for other, safer lodgings so as to save their lives, a woman soldier from the militia came down the street toward them and recognized that the three women were nuns from the Carmel. She immediately incited her comrades to shoot at the three. The first nun to be fatally shot was Sister María de los Angeles. The second was Sister María Pilar, who fell to the ground seriously wounded; she was brought to the Red Cross Hospital, where shortly afterward she ended her life, after repeatedly commending her enemies to the mercy of God. The third nun, who likewise died a martyr's death, was Sister Teresa of the Child Jesus. She also resisted sinful propositions that she would have to give in to if she wanted to save her life. Near the cemetery, then, she was shot. She died shouting, *"Viva Cristo Rey!"*—"Long live Christ the King!"

Blessed
Teresa of the Child
Jesus (Eusebia) García y
García

Carmelite, Martyr

b. March 5, 1909,
 Mochales, Spain
d. July 24, 1936,
 Guadalajara

Beatified March 29, 1987

Eusebia García y García, who was born on March 5, 1909, in
Mochales (Guadalajara, Spain), was brought at the age of seven to
Sigüenza to live with a maternal uncle who likewise would die as
a martyr during the Spanish Civil War: Canon Florencio García.
The priest arranged for his niece Eusebia to be educated by the
Ursuline nuns. When she had completed her schooling, she was
filled with enthusiasm after reading *The Story of a Soul*, by Saint
Thérèse of the Child Jesus, and she wanted to enter a Carmelite
convent, too. After a two-year preparation for religious life under
the direction of her saintly priest uncle, Eusebia entered the Carmel of Saint Joseph in Guadalajara on May 2, 1925. When
she received the habit, on November 4, 1925, she took the religious name Teresa of the Child Jesus and Saint John of the
Cross. She made her first profession on November 7, 1926. The
goal that she set for herself as a religious was: "I will sing of thy
steadfast love, O Lord, for ever" [Ps 89:1]. Her motto was: "Love
is repaid with love." She declared that it was her duty to want to
be "a little ant of love". Therefore she chose the ejaculatory prayer
"Sola cum Christo solo" [Alone with Christ alone] as a source of
encouragement.

On March 6, 1930, Sister Teresa of the Child Jesus was permitted to make perpetual profession, so as to consecrate herself entirely and forever to Christ Jesus. From then on, with extraordinary dedication, she made great strides along the path to perfection. She desired to do everything in keeping with the three virtues that were especially dear to her: charity, fidelity, and humility; she also practiced renunciation of everything to which she (being quite versatile and musically gifted) still had any attachment.

As the threat of the Revolution and its campaign against the Church increased, she took up with ever-greater intensity the battle cry *"Viva Cristo Rey!"* Ultimately she set her yearning heart quite openly on martyrdom, for she said often, "If only I could repeat this cry, 'Long live Christ the King!' on the guillotine!" Indeed, she could, and she did, when, on July 24, 1936, a bullet took her life.

Blessed
María Angeles of
Saint Joseph (Marciana)
Valtiera Tordesillas

Carmelite, Martyr

b. *March 6, 1905,*
   Getafe, Spain
d. *July 24, 1936,*
   Guadalajara

Beatified March 29, 1987

The third of the company of martyrs from the Carmel of Guadalajara, with the secular name of Marciana Valtiera Tordesillas, was born on March 6, 1905, in Getafe (Madrid) in the vicinity of Cerro de los Angeles, the tenth child of a family that produced four religious vocations, of whom two were destined for martyrdom, namely, Marciana and her brother Celestino, who belonged to the Piarist Fathers.

In a family with so many children, Marciana was raised mainly by her much older sister Marcellina, who later entered the Sisters of the Immaculate Conception.

Marciana, too, dreamed at a very early age about entering the Carmel, having read *The Story of a Soul*, by Saint Thérèse of the Child Jesus. She prepared for the total consecration in the Carmelite convent by volunteer work in her parish, then by collaborating in the Saint Vincent de Paul conferences and promoting the foreign missions. She also became a zealous coworker with the Servant of God Juan Vicente Zengotita in propagating the Children of Mary, of which she herself had become a member on March 29, 1924.

On July 14, 1929, she was allowed to enter the Carmel in

Guadalajara, and at the clothing ceremony on January 19, 1930, she received the name of Sister María de los Angeles de San José. She made her first profession on January 21, 1931, and solemn profession on January 21, 1934. In the six years that she belonged to the Carmel, she proved to be a cheerful, modest, industrious, adaptable sister who faithfully and conscientiously took the little routine things very seriously and, moreover, demonstrated an extraordinary maturity. She was happy to have the privilege of participating, through her daily sacrifices, in the Paschal Mystery of Jesus Christ for the conversion of sinners. As early as her novitiate, she, too, longed for martyrdom, and she declared openly to her sisters in religion that the grace of martyrdom could be obtained "through particular fidelity in the little things". Only a few hours before her martyrdom, when she could not yet have had any idea about the events to come, she told her prioress how much she longed for the opportunity to shed her blood for Christ. On July 24, 1936, it had reached that point. As the first of the three Discalced Carmelites of Guadalajara who suffered martyrdom, she died, struck by a bullet, at the age of thirty-one.

(A strange coincidence: July 24, the day on which these three Carmelites witnessed to Christ with their blood, is observed on the Carmelite calendar as the memorial of the sixteen Blessed Martyrs from the Carmel of Compiègne.)

Immediately after the martyrdom took place, the bodies of the three murdered sisters were brought into the convent. At their common grave there were soon miraculous answers to prayers. Especially since their beatification, many believers come to the Carmelite church in Guadalajara in order to beg the three martyred sisters, at their tomb, to intercede at the throne of God.

Pope John Paul II, at the beatification on March 29, 1987, said the following about the three blessed Carmelite sisters:

"Though I walk in dark valleys, I fear nothing, because you are with me" (Ps 23:4).

The three daughters of Carmel could have addressed these

words to the Good Shepherd when the hour came for them to give their lives for their faith in the divine Bridegroom of their souls. Yes, "I fear nothing", not even death. Love is greater than death and "you are with me." You, the Bridegroom on the cross! You, Christ, my strength!

This following of the Master, which should bring us to imitate him even to giving up our lives for love of him, has been an almost constant call in early times and always, for Christians to give this supreme witness of love—martyrdom—before everyone, especially before their persecutors. Thus, the Church has kept as a precious heritage through the centuries the words of Christ who said, "The disciple is not greater than the master" (Mt 10:24), and "if they have persecuted me, so will they persecute you also" (Jn 15:20).

In this way we see that martyrdom—the ultimate witness in defense of the faith—is considered by the Church as a very eminent gift and as the supreme test of love, through which a Christian follows the very footsteps of Jesus, who freely accepted suffering and death for the salvation of the world. Although martyrdom is a gift given by God to a certain few, nevertheless everyone—indeed, all of us—should be ready to profess Christ publicly, most of all in times of trial, which the Church never lacks, not even today. In honouring her martyrs, the Church recognizes them simultaneously as a sign of her fidelity to Jesus Christ until death, and as an illustrious sign of her great desire for forgiveness and peace, for harmony and mutual understanding and respect.

Undoubtedly, the three Carmelite martyrs kept in mind, as we know from their testimonies, those words written by their Holy Mother and Doctor of the Church, Teresa of Jesus: "the true religious . . . should not turn his back on the desire to die for him and undergo martyrdom" (*The Way of Perfection*, 12, 2).

In the life and martyrdom of Sister Maria Pilar of St Francis Borgia, Sister Maria Angeles of St Joseph and Sister Teresa of the Child Jesus, some lessons stand out before the Church, lessons which we should avail ourselves of:

— the great importance which the Christian home environment has for the formation and maturation in the faith of its members;

— the treasure which contemplative religious life is for the Church; it is developed in the total following of the praying Christ and is an eminent sign of future heavenly glory;

— the inheritance left to the Church by anyone of her children who dies for his faith, bearing on his lips a word of forgiveness and love for those who persecute them because they do not understand;

— the message of peace and reconciliation of every Christian martyrdom, as a seed of mutual understanding, never as a sowing of hatred and grudges;

— and a call to constant heroism in Christian life, as a courageous witness to faith, without cowardly compliance or relativism.

From this day on, the Church honors the martyrs from the Carmel of Guadalajara, thanks them for their witness, and asks them to intercede with the Lord that our lives, too, with each passing day, will bear more clearly the sign of Christ, who died on the Cross.[1]

---

[1] *L'Osservatore Romano*, April 6, 1987, pp. 1–2.

Blessed
Marcelo Spinola y
Maestre

Lawyer, Priest,
Archbishop, Cardinal

b. *January 14, 1835,*
   Isla de San Fernando, Spain
d. *January 19, 1906,*
   Seville

Beatified March 29, 1987

On March 29, 1987, Pope John Paul gave the Spaniards a new blessed when he raised Archbishop Marcelo Spinola y Maestre[1] to the honors of the altar.

Marcelo, born on January 14, 1835, in San Fernando (province of Cádiz, in Spain), was the firstborn son of Count Spinola y Maestre. The gifted youth studied jurisprudence, earned a doctorate in law, and then practiced as an attorney; in his profession he demonstrated a great love toward the poor, to whom he offered legal counsel free of charge. The reward for this willingness to help the poor was the grace of a calling to the priesthood, granted to him as a late vocation. He entered the seminary in Seville and was ordained a priest in 1864.

The young priest proved his ability as a chaplain in Sanlúcar de Barrameda and as pastor of Saint Lawrence Church in Seville; he demonstrated his exemplary pastoral zeal especially in administering the sacrament of penance. In 1879, Marcelo Spinola became a cathedral canon and, in 1881, auxiliary bishop of Seville. Then he

---

[1] J. M. Javierre, *Don Marcelo de Sevilla* (Barcelona, 1963).

was appointed chief shepherd of three episcopal sees in rapid succession: first, of Coria in 1884; then, of Málaga in 1886; and, finally, of Seville in 1896. On December 11, 1905, Pope Saint Pius X elevated him to the dignity of cardinal.

In all three dioceses this Spanish bishop showed an extraordinary devotion to prayer, much love for the poor, and a spirit of penance. Furthermore, this bishop was remarkable for his dedication in fulfilling his duties as chief pastor. In doing so, he was always modest and humble and, despite all the worries, cheerful, too. He initiated various programs to deepen the faith of the people in his diocese; he built orphanages and schools. In the diocese of Coria he founded a congregation of nuns, the Handmaids of the Divine Heart (*Schiave Concezioniste del Divino Cuore*).

Archbishop Spinola y Maestre was, above all, an effective and zealous preacher of the word of God and a valiant promoter of ecclesiastical policies who fought successfully to keep Sunday a day of rest and to maintain a harmonious relationship between Church and state. Whenever catastrophe struck, he spontaneously showed his paternal kindness and willingness to assist the needy. He was—in a word—an exemplary, holy bishop. The Pope confirmed this at the beatification of the cardinal, who died on January 19, 1906, in Seville, with the following remarks:

Today we also raise to the glory of the altars Cardinal Marcelo Spinola y Maestre, who was Bishop of Coria, in Malaga, and later Archbishop of Seville. This is a suitable opportunity to thank the Lord for the witness of holiness of those whom "the Holy Spirit has set as guardians and shepherds of the Church of God, which he acquired with his blood" (Acts 20:28).

Contemplating the life of this pastor of the Church, I want to point out above all his confidence in the Lord, which was the motto of his episcopate: "I can do all things in him" (Phil 4:13). Supported by this confidence, he was able to shine in those virtues, which constitute the glory and crown of a bishop:

— the heroism and the dedication and total fulfillment of his episcopal duties;

— his love and devoted service to the poor, in poverty and austerity;

— his concern for the formation of the humblest of his flock, which led him to found the Congregation of the "Handmaids of the Divine Heart" for the apostolate of the education of youth;

— his ecclesial independence, over and above divisions and parties; he made himself a bearer of peace and understanding, as well as a defender of the Church's freedom in the fulfilment of her sacred mission;

— all of this was nourished by a burning love of Jesus Christ, and clothed with a deep personal humility.

We who are pastors of the Church should see in the new Blessed an example, a consolation and a hope in the exercise of the ministry that has been entrusted to us. In this connection, the faithful rejoice to see the sublime holiness of one of their dedicated pastors become a reality.[2]

---

[2] *L'Osservatore Romano*, April 6, 1987, pp. 1–2.

Blessed Emmanuel Domingo y Sol

Priest,
Theology Professor,
Founder

b. *April 1, 1836,*
 Tortosa, Spain
d. *January 25, 1909,*
 Tortosa

Beatified March 29, 1987

In Blessed Emmanuel Domingo y Sol[1] we find a priest who, in Spain during the late nineteenth century, dedicated himself with great zeal to the proper education and formation of priests according to the Divine Heart of Jesus.

Born in Tortosa, Spain, on April 1, 1836, the eleventh of twelve children, he first received his training and schooling at home from a good tutor. Then, in October 1851, he went to the diocesan seminary in his hometown, where the aptitudes, conduct, and virtues of the young Emmanuel soon elicited universal admiration. On July 9, 1860, he was ordained a priest. From then on he dedicated himself with a special predilection to religious instruction and preaching. Once he became pastor of Aldés, he became ardent with zeal for the salvation of the souls in his parish and spared no effort to be of use to all and to help everyone.

At the request of his bishop, he enrolled in the University of Valencia and earned an additional licentiate in theology. In 1864, he became a professor of religion; then, in 1865, professor of

[1] A. G. Torres Sánchez, *Vida del Siervo di Dios Manuel Domingo y Sol* (Tortosa, 1937).

theology in Tortosa. Besides his professorate he became involved in many ecclesiastical projects, both in the city itself and also around the diocese. He worked with youth and continued to provide them with a solid religious instruction; he waged campaigns in the press and promoted the distribution of good literature; he acted as spiritual director for many individuals and effectively defended the rights of workers. The concern that was nearest and dearest to his heart, however, was the education and formation of good, zealous priests. For this purpose he founded in 1881 the Fraternity of Diocesan Priests of the Heart of Jesus, a congregation for the training of diocesan priests after the Heart of Jesus. The members of this fraternity were to work first and foremost in the administration of major seminaries. In 1892, he founded in Rome the Spanish College, dedicated to Saint Joseph, for the education of young clerics who complete their studies in the Eternal City, preparing to work in the pastoral ministry in Spain according to the mind of the Church.

To this extremely zealous priest, who died on January 25, 1909, in Tortosa, Pope John Paul II dedicated the following *laudatio* during the beatification ceremony at Saint Peter's in Rome on March 29, 1987:

> The last in this glorious group of new Blessed[s] is a priest of the diocese of Tortosa, Manuel Domingo y Sol, to whom the Church has rightly given the title "the holy apostle of priestly vocations".[2] In effect, when we present him today to the Church as an example, we point out in particular his intense apostolate in favour of vocations to the consecrated life and especially to the priesthood, to which he devoted the greatest concerns of his ministry and life.
>
> This beatification provides priests with motivation to be aware of the importance and fundamental value of this apostolate. The Church needs more priests. Yet at the same time it

[2] *Decr. super virtutibus*, May 4, 1970, *Acta Apostolicae Sedis*, 63 (1971), p. 156.

belongs to the priestly mission—since priests participate in the solicitude of the whole Church—to seek out from among the faithful young and mature candidates who, answering generously the call of Christ, "come, follow me", may be accompanied and formed as worthy ministers who will also teach others (cf. 2 Tim 2:2).

Thus, the formation of future priests, which the new Blessed called "the key of the harvest", that is, the promotion, support and care for vocations, remains even today the favourite and necessary apostolate of the Church and her Pastors. As Mosén Sol—as the new Blessed was popularly called in his dear land [of Catalonia]—himself tells us, "among the works of zeal, there is none as great and rendering as much glory to God as the contribution in giving more and good priests to the Church." It is also suitable to point out especially the new Blessed's apostolate with youth, in which he placed great hopes for the Christian future of nations, and which continues to be a major concern of the Church today.

The whole apostolic ministry of Don Manuel has a source from which he drew the strength and the meaning of his effective activity: his Eucharistic and reparatory spirit, which expresses his spirituality. This is the precious heritage which he left to his Fraternity of Diocesan Worker[3] Priests of the Heart of Jesus, founded as an authentic priestly fraternity, both in its lifestyle, as well as in its manner of work, for the greater sanctification of its members and the greater glory of God.

Today, as we venerate these two pastors, one a bishop and cardinal and the other a priest, I am pleased to single out the fact that both have distinguished themselves in having placed the root and the foundation of their intense ministry in a deep priestly interior life, which is the heart of every apostolate. The two Blessed[s] have distinguished themselves by their ardent and

[3] The actual title of the foundation is The Congregation of Diocesan Priest Workers. The translation "worker priests", however, has been left as in *L'Osservatore Romano*.—TRANS.

intimate love for Jesus Christ in the Eucharist and for the Sacred Heart of Jesus. How grateful we priests of today should be for this example and how we should imitate them in our apostolic life! [4]

[4] *L'Osservatore Romano*, April 6, 1987, p. 2.

Blessed [Saint] Teresa de Jesus de los Andes (Juana Fernández Solar)

Discalced Carmelite

b. *July 13, 1900,*
   Santiago de Chile
d. *April 12, 1920,*
   Los Andes, Chile

Beatified April 3, 1987
[Canonized March 21, 1993]

There is not much to report about the life of that young Chilean woman whom Pope John Paul II raised to the honors of the altar on April 3, 1987, during his pastoral visit to this Latin American land, at a ceremony in O'Higgins Park in Santiago de Chile. Juana Fernández Solar,[1] born on July 13, 1900, in Santiago de Chile, was the daughter of good Catholic parents who were concerned about doing good deeds in that city. The girl grew up in a disciplined environment and was a happy youngster with great enthusiasm for the beauty of nature and for sports. Above all, however, from early childhood Juana was enthusiastic about Christ and filled with tender love for the Virgin Mother of God. She set a good example for the children of her age, imitated her parents in doing much good for others, and volunteered to work for the Church as a catechist. As she did so, it probably dawned on her that the lack of zealous priests was a lamentable deficiency that hindered the building up of God's kingdom in Chile; she also became more and more aware of the plight of many young people who could not

[1] P. Caraffa, "Fernandez Solar, Giovanna Teresa di Gesù", in *Bibliotheca Sanctorum* 1:484.

control their drives and passions and fell into depravity. Thus she sensed within her a longing, which became ever stronger, to become a victim soul and to make reparation for the priests and for the conversion of sinners. This longing then took concrete form as a calling to enter the Carmelite convent and to lead there a hidden life of reparation.

So, at the age of nineteen, Juana left her home and parents for the city of Los Andes and entered the Carmel there belonging to the Discalced Carmelites. The Lord very soon took her at her word that she wanted to be a victim soul and to make reparation for priests and for the conversion of sinners. While still a novice, she was to offer her young life as a sacrifice. This she did when, on April 12, 1920, after a remarkable life of atonement, she died in Los Andes. Quite soon afterward, people began to admire the novice who had attained perfection so swiftly, who had delivered herself over to God in a genuine spirit of sacrifice and reparation. On March 20, 1947, the diocesan investigation was begun. Because of outward circumstances, the process for her beatification was not opened in Rome until 1976. From then on, however, it proceeded rapidly, so that on April 3, 1987, the Pope was able to undertake the beatification. On that occasion he said the following:

"There are three things that last: faith, hope, and love; and the greatest of these is love" (1 Cor 12:13). These words of St Paul, with which he culminates his "Hymn to Charity", resound with new tones in this Eucharistic Celebration.

Yes, "the greatest of these is love." Such are the words brought to life by Sister Teresa of Los Andes, whom today I have the grace and joy to proclaim Blessed. Today, my dear brothers and sisters of Santiago and of all Chile, is a great day in the life of your Church and nation.

A most beloved daughter of the Chilean Church, Sr Teresa is raised to the glory of the altar in the country that gave her birth. In her, God's pilgrim people find a guide in their journey towards the heavenly Jerusalem. . . .

Moved by faith, hope and love, we walk as pilgrims towards God who is Love, and our souls are filled with joy as we discover that this spiritual pilgrimage has its crown in glory, to which Christ Our Lord wants to lead all of us. . . .

Sister Teresa of Los Andes, a young Chilean girl, symbol of the faith and goodness of this people; a Discalced Carmelite, captivated by the heavenly Kingdom in the springtime of her life; the first fruits of the holiness of the Teresian Carmelites in Latin America.

In her brief autobiographical writings, she has left us the witness of a simple and attainable holiness, centred on the core of the Gospel: love, suffer, pray and serve.

The secret of her life completely directed towards holiness is summarized in familiarity with Christ, as a friend who is constantly present, and with the Virgin Mary, a close and loving Mother.

Ever since she was a child, Teresa of Los Andes experienced the grace of communion with Christ, which developed within her with the charm of her youth, full of vitality and cheerfulness, never lacking a sense of healthy amusement and play, and contact with nature, just as a true daughter of her time. She was a happy and dynamic young girl, open to God. And God made Christian love blossom in her, an open love, profoundly sensitive to the problems of her country and the aspirations of the Church.

The secret of her perfection could be none other than love: a great love for Christ, who fascinates her and moves her to consecrate herself to him forever, and to participate in the mystery of his passion and resurrection. At the same time she feels a filial love for the Virgin Mary, who draws her to imitate her virtues.

For her, *God is infinite joy*. This is the new hymn of Christian love which rises spontaneously from the soul of this young Chilean girl, in whose glorified face we can sense the grace of her transformation in Christ, in virtue of an understanding, serving, humble and patient love, a love which does not destroy human values, but rather elevates and transfigures them.

Yes, as Teresa of Los Andes says: "Jesus is our infinite happiness." That is why this new Blessed is a model of the Gospel life for the young people of Chile. Teresa, who heroically practiced the Christian virtues, spent the years of her adolescence and youth in the normal environment of a young girl of her time; in her daily life, she showed her piety in collaborating with the Church as a catechist, at school, with her friends, in the works of mercy, and in the times of rest and recreation. Her exemplary life evidenced a Christian humanism with the unmistakable seal of a lively intelligence, an agile delicacy, and the creative capacity typical of the Chilean people. In her we see an expression of the soul and character of your country as well as the perennial youth of Christ's Gospel which enthused and attracted Sister Teresa of Los Andes.

Today, the Church proclaims Sister Teresa of Los Andes Blessed, and from this day on, venerates and invokes her with this title.

Blessed, joyful, happy is the person who has made the evangelical beatitudes the centre of his life, and who has lived them with heroic intensity.

In this way our new Blessed, having put the beatitudes into practice, incarnated in her life the *most perfect example of holiness, which is Christ himself.*

In effect, Teresa of Los Andes irradiates the joy of those who are poor in spirit, meek and humble of heart, of those who suffer in silence, for this is how God purifies and sanctifies his chosen ones. She hungers and thirsts for justice, she loves God intensely and wants him to be loved and known by all. In her complete immolation, God made her have compassion for priests and for the conversion of sinners; peaceful and reconciling, she sows understanding and dialogue all around her. Above all, her life reflects the beatitude of purity of heart. In effect, she surrendered her life totally to Christ and Jesus opened her eyes to the contemplation of his mysteries.

What is more, God allowed her here on earth to experience

the joy and happiness of union with God in the service of our neighbour.

This is her message: only in God can one find happiness; God alone is infinite joy. . . .

This is a joyous day for the Chilean nation, for Sister Teresa of Los Andes has been raised to the honours of the altar; it seems as if she is giving us a message of life, the words she learned from her father and teacher, St John of the Cross: "Where there is no love, put love, and you find love."

Here on earth there are three things that last: faith, hope and love.

They lead us towards eternity, to eternal salvation in God the Father, Son and Holy Spirit. *To union with God who is love.*

That is why: *the greatest of these is love.*[2]

[2] *L'Osservatore Romano*, May 4, 1987, p. 8.

Blessed [Saint] Edith Stein (Teresa Benedicta of the Cross)

Convert, Carmelite, Martyr

b. October 12, 1891, Breslau, Silesia

d. August 9, 1942, Auschwitz concentration camp

Beatified May 1, 1987
[Canonized October 11, 1998]

Edith Stein: In Search of God is the title of one of many books[1] about the Jewish woman, a philosopher, who became a nun in the only religious order ever founded in Israel, namely, the Carmelites, and then became a martyr in the concentration camp at Auschwitz-Birkenau, together with millions who belonged to the Jewish people. One could also modify the book title just mentioned to read "Edith Stein: In Search of the Messiah". The

---

[1] Of the many books about Edith Stein, the following are especially noteworthy: Teresia Renata de Spiritu Sancto, O.C.D., *Edith Stein: Schwester Teresia Benedicta a cruce: Philosophin und Karmelitin: Ein Lebensbild, gewonnen aus Erinnerungen und Briefen*, 7th ed. (Nuremburg, 1954); Maria Baptista a Spiritu Sancto, O.C.D., *Edith Stein* (Kaldenkirchen, 1962); Willehardt Eckert, O.P., *Edith Stein: Der Opfergang einer grossen Jüdin und Deutschen* (Freiburg im Breisgau, 1959); Maria Bienias, *Das Lebensopfer der Karmelitin Edith Stein* (Stuttgart, 1961); Hilda Graef, *Leben unter dem Kreuz: Eine Studie über Edith Stein* (Frankfurt am Main, 1954); Waltraud Herbstrith, *Edith Stein: A Biography* (San Francisco, Ignatius Press, 1992). The account in this chapter follows very closely—at times word for word—the last-mentioned book; in the foreword to it, the sister of Edith Stein, Frau Doktor Erna Biberstein of New York, called it one of the best biographies. See also F. Holböck, *"Wir haben den Messias gefunden"* (Stein am Rhein, 1987), pp. 76–90.

greatest Son of the Jewish people once said, "He who seeks finds, and to him who knocks it will be opened" (cf. Lk 11:9f.). This would be a good description of the life of this Jewish convert, who was beatified by Pope John Paul II on May 1, 1987, in Cologne [West Germany, and canonized on October 11, 1998, in Saint Peter's Square]. She took seeking and knocking very seriously. That is why she found the Messiah, who by the Cross opened for her the gate to eternal happiness. In solidarity with her Jewish brothers and sisters, however, she wanted as many of them as possible to find the Messiah, too, and, in him, salvation. In the Carmel, this great intercessor prayed urgently for this intention, and by the sacrifice of her life in the concentration camp at Auschwitz-Birkenau she guaranteed infallibly, so to speak, that this prayer would be heard. In this way she became, in keeping with her religious name, *Benedicta a Cruce*—She who is blessed from the Cross.

Edith Stein was born on Yom Kippur, the Jewish Day of Atonement, October 12, 1891, the youngest of eleven children of a strictly observant Jewish family in Breslau. The date acquired deep symbolic meaning throughout the fifty-one years of this Jewish woman's life, as she herself noted in her autobiography *Life in a Jewish Family*. "The highest of all the Jewish festivals is the Day of Atonement, the day on which the High Priest formerly used to enter the Holy of Holies to offer the sacrifice of atonement for himself and for the people; afterwards the 'scapegoat' upon whose head, symbolically, the sins of the people had been laid was driven out into the desert." [2]

Her mother, Frau Auguste Stein, née Courant, lost her husband when he was only forty-eight years old; he died very suddenly while on a business trip. Edith at the time was a little more than two years old.

The courageous mother now had to take charge of the father's timber trade so as to support herself and the children. Yet she also

[2] Edith Stein, *Life in a Jewish Family*, ed. Dr. L. Gelber and Romaeus Leuver, O.C.D. (Washington, D.C.: ICS Publications, 1986), p. 71.

showed an exemplary concern for the proper upbringing of this great crew of children; she especially loved the two youngest, Erna and Edith. She tried to teach them above all to believe in the God of Israel and to worship him correctly through prayer and faithful attendance at the services in the synagogue in Breslau.

Despite this, for the extremely intelligent, temperamental, and precocious Edith, the Jewish faith of her childhood collapsed while she was still very young. She admitted later that, from the age of thirteen until she was twenty-one, she no longer could believe in the existence of a personal God. In her case, though, her naïve childish faith was replaced by a strong and intense search for truth.

After completing secondary school in March 1911, Edith Stein went to the university in her Silesian hometown, Breslau. She aspired to become a teacher, and so she took courses in German, history, and psychology; she wanted to become acquainted with the fundamentals of human existence and the connection between the meaning of life and the essential problem of the soul, the center of the human person. In the lectures and seminars, however, she soon experienced a great disappointment, because there was talk only of a "psychology without a soul". Meanwhile, she acquired a hands-on knowledge of the consequences of modern atheism.

In 1913, she began to study in Göttingen. Very soon she sensed in the lectures of Professor Edmund Husserl, happily enough, a turn toward the truth of existence and an overcoming of subjectivism, because this phenomenologist, who, like Edith Stein, had Jewish origins, was concerned about truth above all else. Unfortunately, he stopped there. Only as he was dying did he press on quite deliberately to the transcendent.

For Edith Stein it was fortunate that in Göttingen she was also able to meet the phenomenologist Max Scheler, whose rediscovery of things Christian presented her with important intellectual challenges to recognize that, in reality, only religion makes man human. In being confronted with the world of Christianity, Edith Stein stumbled upon the primordial need of her heart, the question about the eternal quality that shines in things. She herself wrote, "That was my first contact with a world which until then had been completely unknown to me. The experience did not yet lead me to faith, but it opened up for me a realm of 'phenomena' which I could now no longer pass by blindly." From then on, she could no longer close herself off from the possibility of God's existence.

Meanwhile, the First World War had broken out. Many women students volunteered to serve in the military hospitals. Edith Stein decided to go to the isolation hospital in Mährisch-Weisskirchen, where with great love and willingness to sacrifice she nursed the soldiers from the Austro-Hungarian army who had come down with typhus, dysentery, and cholera.

In 1916, Professor E. Husserl was offered a chair at the University of Freiburg-im-Breisgau. He invited Edith Stein to become his assistant, because in Göttingen he had come to value her intelligence and her cooperative attitude. In that same year Edith Stein graduated *summa cum laude* with a doctorate in philosophy and published her first articles, "Causality in the soul", "Individual and community", and "An analysis of the state".

In 1919, Edith Stein moved back to Breslau to continue her academic projects there. On the side, she made efforts to find a definitive answer to her religious questions.

Then, in the summer of 1921, the "miracle" happened that "put an end to [her] long search for the true faith". At that time she spent a rather long vacation with friends of hers, a married couple named Conrad-Martius, in Bergzabern, a small town in Rhineland-Palatinate. One summer evening she was looking for something to read in the bookcase of her hostess and hit upon the autobiography of the Doctor of the Church and mystic Teresa of Avila. The book enthralled her. She read and read the whole night through. The next morning, when she finally closed the book, she said to herself, "This is the truth!" In this life of a saint she had read and recognized the destiny of her own life. God is not a god of the philosophers and of academics. God is love, and his mysteries are revealed to us, not by the gradual, deductive process of reasoning, but, rather, through faith and loving devotion. After so much searching, Edith Stein happily realized, while reading the autobiography of Saint Teresa of Avila, that the inmost, essential object of the soul is not an unknown quantity, "X", an academic hypothesis to explain psychological phenomena, "but rather something which we human beings can glimpse and sense in prayer and in loving devotion, even though it always remains mysterious": the loving, merciful God, who encounters us in Jesus Christ.

The next day, Edith Stein bought herself a Catholic catechism and a missal. After studying both thoroughly, she went for the first time to a Catholic house of worship, the parish church in the city of Bergzabern. One of the diocesan college of consultors, Father Breitling, happened to be celebrating the Holy Sacrifice of the Mass there. She went to this priest and asked him on the spot for the sacrament of baptism. The sacrament was then scheduled for New Year's Day, 1922. On the same day, she received the Body of the Lord, and from then on she made daily attendance at the liturgy, in which the sacrifice of Christ on the cross is made present sacramentally, the center of her life. On Candlemas Day [the Feast of the Presentation], February 2, 1922, she received in the sacrament of confirmation the seven gifts and the fruits of the Holy Spirit, which include in a special way peace and joy as well. In fact, Edith Stein impressed all her friends from then on with the great, peaceful joy that she radiated as a new convert. The grace of rebirth in the Holy Spirit caused her to hear almost simultaneously the clear call to consecrate her life in the future entirely to God and to follow Saint Teresa into the Carmel. She wrote later, "When I received the sacrament of baptism on New Year's Day, 1922, I thought that this was only the preparation for entering religious life. But a few months later, when for the first time after my baptism I stood face to face with my dear mother, it became clear to me that for the moment she was not up to this new blow. It would not kill her, of course, but it would fill her with such bitterness that I could not have borne the responsibility for causing it."

After her return from Bergzabern to Breslau, Edith Stein had to tell her relatives, especially her mother, about her conversion; she was ready for the worst, even the prospect of being disowned. The Jewish Stein family, having only the folk customs of Silesian Catholicism in view, saw in the Catholic religion nothing more than a sort of superstitious sect. Her brothers and sisters just could not imagine their highly-respected and extremely intelligent sister Edith "groveling on her knees" and "kissing the priests' shoes". The mother's love looked deeper, though; she sensed that her jealous anger was out of place here, that God in some incomprehensible way had laid his hand upon her dearest child. In this situation she could only weep.

The years after Edith Stein's conversion were an especially productive time of "growing into" the Church, both externally and spiritually [cf. Gal 3:27: "For as many of you as were baptized into Christ have put on Christ"]. Still, she wanted to realize as quickly as possible her plan to enter the convent. Her spiritual director, however, the vicar general of the diocese of Speyer, Monsignor Schwind, vetoed her hasty plans to become a nun, especially out of consideration for her Jewish mother, and for the moment he found her a suitable position with the Dominican Sisters in Saint Magdalena in Speyer, who had been looking for a good German teacher. Edith Stein taught now for eight years at the girls' academy and at the teachers' training institute of the Dominican Sisters of Speyer. During this time she was not only a cherished teacher to her pupils, but also a spiritual mother, whose love often supplied what was lacking in the homes of those young people.

In Speyer, Edith Stein lived like a Dominican nun among Dominican sisters; in their community she had found a spiritual home, and she even took the three religious vows privately. While she was in Speyer, the learned Jesuit Father Erich Przywara also encouraged her to take up her scholarly work again and to translate into German the letters of the great English cardinal and convert John Henry Newman and the *Quaestiones disputatae de veritate* [Disputed questions on truth] of Saint Thomas Aquinas. In this work of translating Aquinas, she especially appreciated his honest search for truth, which stopped at nothing and fearlessly consulted even pagan philosophers of antiquity, such as Plato and Aristotle, wherever their natural knowledge pointed toward eternal truth. Under the direction of the Angelic Doctor, the mind of the Jewish convert became more and more open to the "perennial philosophy", which found expression in her work *Endliches und ewiges Sein* [*Finite and Eternal Being*].

In the autumn of 1922, when Edith Stein lost her highly-esteemed spiritual director, Monsignor Schwind, who had died, she found in Archabbot Raphael Walzer, O.S.B., of Beuron a new counselor, whose instructions she followed with a childlike obedience. He, too, refused her permission to enter the Carmel all too quickly, since he was convinced that she was called to accomplish great things in the world.

While Edith Stein sought and found a refuge of prayer and seclusion in Beuron, her intellectual influence began to extend even beyond Germany, for now she was continually invited to lecture as an expert on the problems of modern women.

As a result of Edith Stein's extensive lecturing, her translation of Saint Thomas, and her philosophical debate with phenomenology, she was finally forced to give up teaching school and to take a university position. The Catholic Association of German Scholars (der Katholische Deutsche Akademikerverband) was proud to have in her a Catholic philosopher of importance within its ranks, and it urged her to qualify for a professorship. She applied in Freiburg-im-Breisgau in 1931, but in vain; not only her sex but also her race was an obstacle, since at that time, because of the exacerbated anti-Semitism, the very idea of a Jew, much less a Jewish woman, holding the position of a university lecturer or professor met with vehement objections. Finally, in the spring of 1932, Edith Stein managed to obtain a chair at the Pedagogical Academy in Münster, Westphalia.

Only one year of employment was granted her there. In the midst of her academic work, her soul thirsted to dedicate herself totally to God in religious life, but her spiritual director still refused her permission to do so, pointing out that she could accomplish an incalculable amount of good for the kingdom of God by continuing to give high-level lectures at the education conventions in Salzburg or at conferences sponsored by the Catholic Association of Scholars and the Catholic Women's League.

Besides, in Münster, Edith Stein, with great tact and skill, was bringing many of her Jewish friends to the Catholic faith. In the process, she continued her profound prayer life and ascetical practices and attained an ever-greater interior recollection. So complete was the transformation that a Jewish woman, a childhood friend of hers who had been brought into the Church by her, could say about her, "How Edith had changed! Where once there was ambition, now there was only peace and serenity. Where once there was egotism, now there was only understanding and kindness. With infinite patience she discussed with me personal problems and questions about the faith, philosophical problems, and everything that was on our minds then."

What was particularly on the minds of this Jewish childhood friend and of Edith Stein herself at that time was the ever-increasing anti-Semitism and the beginning of the persecution of the Jews. Edith Stein's eyes were soon opened to the Holocaust that awaited the Jews, and her, too, with them.

Despite her great patriotism as a German woman, Edith Stein had remained proud of her Jewish heritage even after her baptism. As the persecution of the Jews began, she did not think only of herself; she thought about her people and about the many who would be seized by the brutality of racial hatred and perhaps destroyed. She feared especially for her Jewish friends and family in Breslau. Once she confessed to the Jesuit Father Hans Hirschmann, "They do not believe what it means for me to be a daughter of the Chosen People, to belong to Christ not only spiritually, but also as his blood relative."

Soon events in the Third Reich followed one after the other with headlong speed. Once it had come to power, National Socialism made no secret of its hatred for Jews. Many Jews lost their jobs overnight, and in short order there were acts of violence against innocent Jewish people. In this situation, Edith Stein did not want her position on the faculty to jeopardize the Catholic Pedagogical Academy in Münster, which soon might be struggling to stay in existence. After much prayer for discernment as to her future, she decided to give up her work in Münster and to realize her desire to dedicate herself entirely to God as a Carmelite. She received permission to enter the convent, both from Archabbot Raphael Walzer and also from the prioress of the Carmel in Cologne-Lindenthal.

At the age of forty-two, she found herself there in the midst of a group of novices who were twenty years younger and who managed to do everything that the Carmelite Order requires of its sisters much more easily than she could, being a late vocation. But she adjusted humbly and obediently to convent life and rapidly made good progress in Carmelite spirituality.

At the clothing ceremony on April 15, 1934, she received, at her own request, the name Sister Teresia Benedicta a Cruce, Teresa who is blessed from the Cross. In this name she wanted to give expression to her union with the Teresian spirit of the Carmel and her gratitude toward the Benedictine monks of Beuron and toward Archabbot Raphael Walzer for his wise and effective spiritual direction, as well as to her love for Christ's suffering on the Cross, which she embraced as the source of redemption for all mankind, and especially for the Chosen People. She had also had a presentiment that the shadow of the Cross had now fallen with full force not only upon her but upon the entire Jewish people.

Sister Benedicta—as Edith Stein was now called—spent her novitiate year with great zeal and remarkable conscientiousness. As with the other novices, her daily routine alternated between times of prayer and simple household chores. With toil and effort she tried to emulate her sisters in community in cleaning, washing, and mending. Soon, however, the superiors decided that she should apply her literary and academic abilities again as well.

Besides this, she was allowed to send a weekly letter to her sorely-tried mother in Breslau and, within certain limits, to keep in contact with many friends and others from her wide circle of acquaintances who were seeking advice.

On April 21, 1935, Sister Benedicta was allowed to make her first profession. Shortly after she had written the final lines of her great work *Finite and Eternal Being*, she was struck by a very painful blow: on September 14, 1936, on the Feast of the Exaltation of the Cross, while she was in choir attending the ceremony in which the sisters renewed their vows, her aged mother died in Breslau after a terrible agony. The great and constant sorrow of this faithful, courageous Jewish woman, until her death at the age of eighty-seven, was the conversion of her youngest child and her entrance into the convent. In the winter of 1936, Rosa Stein, Sister Benedicta's sister, was able to complete the conversion that she had been planning for so long. In an unfortunate fall on the stairs, Sister Benedicta had broken her wrist and her ankle. So, in the hospital, she was able to give to her blood sister Rosa the final convert instructions and to participate in her baptism.

In the winter of 1937, Sister Benedicta took over the duty of the convent's turn sister (portress), which meant that she had to manage the community's business with the outside world and do a lot of running back and forth. This position, still, gave her many opportunities to help others by performing little acts of kindness and charity.

On April 21, 1938, Sister Benedicta was permitted to take her perpetual vows. The years 1938 to 1942 were for her a time of complete abandonment to the will of God. She had a continual foreboding of the dreadful things that were to come. In the night from the eighth to the ninth of November 1938, during that shameful *Kristallnacht*, the persecution burst in upon the Jews with all its fury. Everywhere synagogues were burning. Every decent German citizen was horrified by the violence, but no one dared to raise a loud protest against it, because it would have been suppressed at once in a bloody, deadly manner.

When news of this deed of shame made its way into the Carmel of Cologne, Sister Benedicta was as though paralyzed with pain; her premonition over the years was now becoming a terrible reality. Deeply shaken, she broke out into a lament: "This is the shadow of the Cross, which is falling on my people. Oh, if they would only come to understand! This is the fulfillment of the curse, which my people called down upon themselves."

With feverish haste, the brothers and sisters of Sister Benedicta now attempted to emigrate with their children to the United States. Only Else and Erna were still able to make the journey and join their brother Arno there. Paul and Frieda were not. The fate of their sister Rosa was also uncertain for the time being. Since Palestine was prohibiting immigration, Mother Teresa Renata, the superior of the Carmel in Cologne, asked the Carmelites in the city of Echt, in nearby Holland, whether they might take Sister Benedicta and her sister Rosa into their convent.

The departure from Cologne on December 31, 1938, was difficult both for Sister Benedicta and also for her sisters in religion. On New Year's Eve, a trusted friend of the Carmel brought Sister Benedicta by automobile across the Dutch border. In a letter to Baroness Bodmann, a friend from her days in Speyer, Sister Benedicta wrote: "On the night of Saint Sylvester I arrived here (at the Carmel in Echt, Holland). It was a difficult decision for us all in the Carmel of Cologne, to separate. But I had the firm conviction that it was the will of God and that in this way worse things could be prevented. . . . Here I have been received with great love. The good sisters made every effort to arrange my journey as soon as possible, and they smoothed the way for me with their prayers."

In another letter, from the end of 1939, Sister Benedicta wrote: "My state of mind, basically, since I have been here, has been gratitude. Grateful that I have the privilege of being here and that the house is the way it is (namely, an oasis of peace). All the while I have a lively sense that we have no fixed abode here. I have no other desire than that the will of God be done to me and through me. It is up to him, how long he lets me stay here and what happens then."

In 1940, Sister Benedicta had the great joy of knowing that her sister Rosa, too, had found security in the Carmel at Echt. After hazardous difficulties, she had succeeded in fleeing via Belgium to Holland. Rosa Stein from then on served the Carmel of Echt as a faithful portress; in doing so she earned the trust of the Carmelites and of the inhabitants of Echt. She would gladly have taken the habit and become an extern member of the Carmelite Order, but the superiors did not dare allow it on account of the situation, which was becoming more and more dangerous for the two Jewish sisters, as the news reports from Luxembourg and Germany indicated; it was reported that the Nazis had begun to dissolve one Carmelite convent after another.

Sister Benedicta prepared herself interiorly for the worst and wrote, "We have bound ourselves to a cloistered existence, but God has not bound himself to leave us forever within the cloister walls. . . . Of course, we can ask to be spared this experience, but only with the sincere and honest intention of adding: Not my will, but thy will be done!"

From the testament that she composed on June 9, 1939, we can see that Sister Benedicta was facing the possibility of her impending martyrdom: "Right now I accept with joy the death that God has planned for me, in complete submission to his most holy will. I ask the Lord that he would be pleased to accept my life and death for his honor and glory, for all the intentions of the Sacred Heart of Jesus and the Immaculate Heart of Mary and of Holy Church, especially for the preservation, sanctification, and perfection of our holy order, namely the Carmel of Cologne and of Echt; in reparation for the unbelief of the Jewish people, and so that the Lord may be received by his own and that his kingdom may come in glory; for the deliverance of Germany and peace in the world; finally, for my relatives, living and deceased, and for everyone whom God has given to me: that not one of them may be lost."

In 1940, when German troops invaded and occupied Holland,

the home of Sister Benedicta, it was soon clear to her that she could no longer stay in Holland without endangering the Carmel in Echt, since the persecution of the Jews had long ago been extended to the occupied territories also.

While in Eastern Europe crematories and gas chambers were already being set up, so as to bring the "Jewish question" to the infamous "Final Solution", the Jews in Holland, among them Sister Benedicta and Rosa Stein, were already receiving one summons after the other from the SS. They, too, were ordered to affix the yellow Star of David to their clothing.

In this situation Sister Benedicta made efforts to obtain a visa to Switzerland, in the hope that she could transfer to the Carmel of Le Pâquier, in the Canton of Fribourg. She tried everything so as to be able to leave Holland legally.

The deportation of non-Christian Jews to the East continued unceasingly in Holland, too, to the horror of the Dutch Christians, who protested loudly against it. This was done in an especially forceful way by the Catholic bishops of Holland in a pastoral letter that was read from pulpits throughout the land on July 26, 1942.

One week after the protest of the Dutch bishops came the real response of the Nazi authorities: in one fell swoop—contrary to the previous promise that the *Christian* Jews would not be disturbed—all Catholic Jews and the Jewish members of monasteries and convents in Holland were arrested.

The second of August 1942 was a Sunday. Sister Benedicta spent it in prayer and in proofreading *The Science of the Cross*, a study of the life and mysticism of Saint John of the Cross, on which she had worked during the last nine months under obedience to her superiors. At five o'clock in the afternoon, the convent bell rang for the hour of contemplation in choir. Suddenly the doorbell rang: two SS officers stood at the gate and demanded that the prioress, Sister Antonia, immediately hand over Sister Benedicta and her sister Rosa Stein. A painful leave-taking followed. The truck that was waiting at the street corner during this surprise attack took on the two Jewish women and sped off on a jolting ride from Echt to Roermond, bringing them with other passengers to the local military headquarters. From there they went to an assembly camp in Amersfoort; the prisoners arrived in the middle of the night. Although their treatment by the SS had been polite thus far, now the Jewish prisoners were driven into the dormitories with blows and clubs.

The prisoners were eventually carried off to the northern part of the country, to the collection camp in Westerbork, where they had to await their fate. Then came the sorrowful trip to the east.

There, the Way of the Cross ended for Sister Benedicta and Rosa Stein in the concentration camp at Auschwitz-Birkenau. Together with millions of Jewish brothers and sisters they had to finish their walk on that Way in the gas chambers of Auschwitz. The date of death for the two sisters was listed as August 9, 1942, on the notarized death certificates; an official gazette in the Netherlands announced in 1950: "No. 44074 Edith Teresia Hedwig Stein, born 12 October 1891 in Breslau, died at Echt, 9 August 1942 O. No. 44075 Rosa Maria Agnes Adelheid Stein, born 13 December 1883 in Lublizitz (Germany), died at Echt 9 August 1942 I."

Sister Benedicta's last scholarly work about the father of her order, John of the Cross—she gave it the highly significant title of *The Science of the Cross*—remained unfinished. And yet she completed it magnificently, not in written words, but in her symbolic total consecration to the crucified and risen Messiah and in putting into action what she had briefly summarized in *The Science of the Cross* in the following formula: "The nuptial union of the soul with God is the goal for which she was created; redeemed by the cross, accomplished on the cross, and for all eternity signed and sealed with the cross."

The homily of John Paul II at the beatification of Edith Stein in Cologne gives a moving description of this new blessed:

"These are the ones who have survived the great period of trial; they have washed their robes and made them white in the blood of the lamb" (Rev 7:14).

Today we greet in profound honour and holy joy a daughter of the Jewish people, rich in wisdom and courage, among these blessed men and women. Having grown up in the strict traditions of Israel, and having lived a life of virtue and self-denial in a religious order, she demonstrated her heroic character on the way to the extermination camp. Unified with our crucified Lord, she gave her life "for genuine peace" and "for the people" (see *Edith Stein, Jüdin, Philosophin, Ordensfrau, Märtyrin*). . . .

Today's beatification marks the realization of a long-outstanding wish on the part of the Archdiocese of Cologne as well as on the part of many individuals and groups within the Church. Seven years ago the members of the German Bishops' Conference sent a unanimous request for this beatification to the Holy See. Numerous bishops from other countries joined them in making this request. As such, we are all greatly gratified that I am able to fulfill this wish today and can present *Sister Teresa Benedicta of the Cross* to the faithful on behalf of the Church as *blessed in the glory of God*. From this moment on we can honour her as a martyr and ask for her intercession at the throne of God. In this I would like to express congratulations to all, most of all to her fellow sisters in the order of Our Lady of Mount Carmel here in Cologne and in Echt, as well as in the entire order. The fact that Jewish brothers and sisters, relatives of Edith Stein's in particular, are present at this liturgical ceremony today fills us with great joy and gratitude.

"O Lord, manifest yourself in the time of our distress and give us courage" (Esther 4:17).

The words of this call for help from the first reading of today's liturgy were spoken by Esther, a daughter of Israel, at the time of the Babylonian captivity. Her prayer, which she directs to the Lord God at a time when her people were exposed to a deadly threat, [is] profoundly moving:

"My Lord, our King, you alone are God. Help me, who am alone and have no help but you, for I am taking my life in my hand . . . you, O Lord, chose Israel from among all peoples . . .

and our fathers from among all their ancestors as a lasting heritage . . . be mindful of us, O Lord. . . . Save us by your power" (Esther 4:17).

Esther's deathly fear arose when, under the influence of the mighty Haman, an archenemy of the Jews, the order for their destruction was given out in all of the Persian Empire. With God's help and by sacrificing her own life Esther rendered a key contribution towards saving her people.

Today's liturgy places this more than two-thousand-year-old prayer for help in the mouth of *Edith Stein*, a servant of God and a daughter of Israel in our century. This prayer became relevant again when here, in the heart of Europe, a new *plan for the destruction of the Jews* was laid out. An insane ideology decided on this plan in the name of a wretched form of racism and carried it out mercilessly.

Extermination camps and *crematoriums* were rapidly built, parallel to the dramatic events of the Second World War. Several million sons and daughters of Israel were killed at these places of horror—from children to the elderly. The enormously powerful machinery of the totalitarian state spared no one and undertook extremely cruel measures against those who had the courage to defend the Jews.

Edith Stein died at the Auschwitz extermination camp, the daughter of a martyred people. Despite the fact that she moved from Cologne to the Dutch Carmelite community in Echt, her protection against the growing persecution of the Jews was only temporary. The Nazi policy of exterminating the Jews was rapidly implemented in Holland, too, after the country had been occupied. Jews who had converted to Christianity were initially left alone. However, when the Catholic bishops in the Netherlands issued a *pastoral letter* in which they sharply protested against the deportation of the Jews, the Nazi rulers reacted by ordering the extermination of Catholic Jews as well. This was the cause of the martyrdom suffered by Sister Teresa Benedicta a Cruce together with her sister, Rosa, who had also sought refuge with the Carmelites in Echt.

On leaving their convent Edith took her sister by the hand and said: "Come, we will go for our people." On the strength of Christ's willingness to sacrifice himself for others she saw in her seeming impotence a way to render a final service to her people. A few years previously she had compared herself with Queen Esther in exile at the Persian court. In one of her letters we read: "I am confident that the Lord has taken my life for all (Jews). I always have to think of Queen Esther who was taken away from her people for the express purpose of standing before the king for her people. I am the very poor, weak and small Esther, but the King who selected me is infinitely great and merciful."

Dear brothers and sisters, the second reading in this special Mass is from Saint Paul's letter to the Galatians. He wrote there: "May I never boast of anything but the cross of our Lord, Jesus Christ. Through it, the world has been crucified to me and I to the world" (Gal 6:14).

During her lifetime, Edith Stein too encountered the secret of the cross that Saint Paul announces to the Christians in this letter.

Edith encountered Christ and this encounter led her step by step into the Carmelite community. In the extermination camp she died as a daughter of Israel "for the glory of the Most Holy Name" and, at the same time, as *Sister Teresa Benedicta of the Cross*, literally, "blessed by the Cross".

Edith Stein's entire life is characterized by an incessant search for truth and is illuminated by the blessing of the cross of Christ. She encountered the cross for the first time in the strongly religious widow of a university friend. Instead of despairing, this woman took strength and hope from the cross of Christ. Later she wrote about this: "It was my first encounter with the cross and the divine strength it gives those who bear it. . . . It was the moment in which my atheism collapsed . . . and Christ shone brightly: Christ in the mystery of the cross." *Her own life and the cross she had to bear were intimately connected with the destiny of the Jewish people.* In a prayer she confessed to the Saviour that she knew that it was his cross that was now being laid on the Jewish people and that those who realized this would have to accept it willingly on behalf of all the others. "I wanted to do it—all he has to do is show me how." At the same time she attains the inner certainty that God has heard her prayer. The more often swastikas were seen on the streets, the higher the cross of Jesus Christ rose up in her life. When she entered the Carmelite order of nuns in Cologne as Sister Teresa Benedicta a Cruce in order to experience the cross of Christ even more profoundly, she knew that she was "married to the Lord in the sign of the cross". On the day of her first vows she felt, in her own words, *"like the bride of the lamb".* She was convinced that her heavenly Groom would introduce her to the profound mysteries of the cross.

Teresa, Blessed by the Cross was the name given in a religious order to a woman who began her spiritual life with the conviction that *God does not exist.* At that time, in her schoolgirl years and when she was at university, her life was not yet filled with the redeeming cross of Christ. However, it was already the object of constant searching on the part of her sharp intellect. As a fifteen-year-old schoolgirl in her home town of Breslau, Edith, who had been raised in a Jewish household, suddenly decided, as she herself put it, "not to pray any more". Despite the fact that she was deeply impressed by the strict devotion of her mother, during her school and university years Edith slips into the intellectual world of atheism. She considers the existence of a personal God to be unworthy of belief.

In the years when she studied psychology, philosophy, history and German at the Universities of Breslau, Göttingen and Freiburg, God didn't play an important role, at least initially. Her thinking was based on a demanding ethical idealism. In keeping with her intellectual abilities, she did not want to accept anything without careful examination, not even the faith of her fathers. She wanted to get to the bottom of things herself. As such, she was engaged in a constant search for the truth. Looking back on this period of intellectual unrest in her life, she saw in it an important phase in a process of spiritual maturation. She said: "My search for the truth was a constant prayer." This is a comforting bit of testimony for those who have a hard time believing in God. The search for truth is, itself, in a very profound sense a search for God.

Under the influence of Edmund Husserl and his phenomenological school of thought the student Edith Stein became increasingly dedicated to the study of philosophy. She gradually learned to "view things free of prejudice and to throw off 'blinkers'". *She came into contact for the first time with Catholic ideas* through a meeting with *Max Scheler* in Göttingen. She described her reaction to this meeting as follows: "The barriers of rationalistic prejudice, something I grew up with without being aware of it, fell and suddenly I was confronted with the world of faith. People I dealt with on a daily basis, people I looked up to in admiration, lived in that world."

Her long struggle for a personal decision to believe in Jesus Christ was not to come to an end until 1921, when she began to read the autobiographical *Life of Saint Teresa of Avila*. She was immediately taken with the book and could not put it down until she had finished it. Edith Stein commented: "When I closed the book I said to myself: 'That is the truth!'" She had read through the night until sunrise. In that night she found truth—not the truth of philosophy, but rather the truth in person, the loving person of God. Edith Stein had sought the truth and found God. She was baptized soon after that and entered the Catholic Church.

For Edith Stein baptism as a Christian was *by no means a break with her Jewish heritage*. Quite on the contrary she said: "I had given up my practice of the Jewish religion as a girl of fourteen. My return to God made me feel Jewish again." She was always mindful of the fact that she was related to Christ "not only in a spiritual sense, but also in blood terms". She suffered profoundly from the pain she caused her mother through her conversion to Catholicism. She continued to accompany her to services in the synagogue and to pray the psalms with her. In reaction to her mother's observation that it was possible for her to be pious in a Jewish sense as well, she answered: "Of course, seeing as it is something I grew up with."

Although becoming a member of the Carmelite Order was Edith Stein's objective from the time of her encounter with the writings of Saint Teresa of Avila, she had to wait more than a decade before Christ showed her the way. In her activity as a teacher and lecturer at schools and in adult education, mostly in Speyer, but also in Münster, she made a continuous effort to combine *science and religion* and to convey them together. In this she only wanted to be a "tool of the Lord". "Those who come to me I would like to lead to him", she said. During this period of her life she already lived like a nun. She took the vows privately and became a great and gifted woman of prayer. From her intensive study of the writings of Saint Thomas Aquinas she learned that it is possible "to approach science from a religious standpoint". She said that it was only thus that she was able to decide to return seriously (after her conversion) to academic work. Despite her respect for scholarship, Edith Stein became increasingly aware that the *essence of being a Christian is not scholarship, but rather love.*

When Edith Stein finally entered the Carmelite Order in Cologne in 1933, this step did not represent an escape from the world or from responsibility for her, but rather a *resolved commitment to the heritage of Christ on the cross.* She said in her first conversation with the prioress there: "It is not human activity that helps us—it is the suffering of Christ. To share in this is my desire." On being registered in the order she expressed the wish to be named "Blessed by the cross". She had the words of Saint John of the Cross printed on the devotional picture presented to her on taking her final vows: *"My only vocation is that of loving more."*

Dear brothers and sisters. We bow today with the entire Church before this great woman whom we from now on may call upon as one of the blessed in God's glory, before this great daughter of Israel, who found the fulfillment of her faith and her vocation for the people of God in Christ the Saviour. In her conviction those who enter the Carmelite Order are not lost to their own—on the contrary they are won for them. It is our *vocation to stand before God for everyone.* After she began seeing the destiny of Israel from the standpoint of the cross, our newly beatified sister let Christ lead her more and more deeply into the mystery of his salvation to be able to bear the multiple pains of mankind in spiritual union with him and to help atone for the outrageous injustices in the world. As "Benedicta a Cruce"—Blessed by the Cross—she wanted to bear the cross with Christ for the salvation of her people, her Church and the world as a whole. She offered herself to God as a "sacrifice for genuine peace" and above all for her threatened and humiliated Jewish people. After she recognized that God had once again laid a heavy hand on his people, she was convinced *"that the destiny of this people was also my destiny"*.

When Sister Teresa Benedicta a Cruce began her last theological work, "The Science of the Cross", at the Carmelite convent in Echt (the work remained incomplete since it was interrupted by her own encounter with the cross) she noted: "When we speak of the *science of the cross* this is not . . . mere theory . . . but rather *vibrant, genuine and effective truth.*" When the deadly threat to the Jewish people gathered like a dark cloud over her as well, she was willing to realize with her own life what she had recognized earlier: "There is a vocation for suffering with Christ and by that means for involvement in his salvation. . . . Christ continues to live and to suffer in his members. The suffering gone through in union with the Lord is *his* suffering, and is a fruitful part of the great plan of salvation."

With her people and "for" her people Sister Teresa Benedicta a Cruce travelled the road to death with her sister Rosa. She did not accept *suffering and death* passively but instead combined these consciously with the *atoning sacrifice of our Saviour Jesus Christ*. A few years earlier she had written in her will: "I will gladly accept the death God chooses for me, in full submission to his holy will. I ask the Lord to accept my suffering and death for his honour and glory, and for all interests . . . of the holy Church." The Lord heard her prayer.

The Church now presents Sister Teresa Benedicta a Cruce to us as a blessed martyr, as an example of a heroic follower of Christ, for us to honour and to emulate. Let us open ourselves up for her message to us as a woman of the spirit and of the mind, who saw in the science of the cross the acme of all wisdom, as a great daughter of the Jewish people, and as a believing Christian in the midst of millions of innocent fellow men made martyrs. She saw the inexorable approach of the cross. She did not flee in fear. Instead, she embraced it in Christian hope with final love and sacrifice and in the mystery of Easter even welcomed it with the salutation, "*ave crux spes unica*". As Cardinal Höffner said in his recent pastoral letter, "Edith Stein is a gift, an invocation and a promise for our time. May she be an intercessor with God for us and for our people and for all people."

. . . *We bow in profound respect before the testimony of the life and death of Edith Stein,* an outstanding daughter of Israel and, at the same time, a daughter of Carmel, Sister Teresa Benedicta a Cruce, a person who embodied a dramatic synthesis of our century in her rich life. Hers was a synthesis of a history full of deep wounds, wounds that still hurt, and for the healing of which responsible men and women have continued to work up to the present day. At the same time, it was a synthesis of the full truth on man, in a heart that remained restless and unsatisfied "until it finally found peace in God".

When we pay a spiritual visit to the place where this great

Jewish woman and Christian experienced martyrdom, the place of horrible events today referred to as "Shoah", we hear the voice of Christ the Messiah and Son of Man, our Lord and Saviour.

As the bearer of the message of God's unfathomable mystery of salvation he said to the woman from Samaria at Jacob's well:

"After all, salvation is from the Jews. Yet an hour is coming, and is already here when authentic worshippers will worship the Father in spirit and truth. Indeed, it is just such worshippers the Father seeks. God is Spirit, and those who worship him must worship in spirit and truth" (Jn 4:22–24).

Blessed be Edith Stein, Sister Teresa Benedicta a Cruce, a true worshipper of God—in spirit and in truth.

She is among the blessed. Amen.[3]

[3] *L'Osservatore Romano*, May 18, 1987, p. 19.

Blessed
Rupert Mayer

Jesuit, Spiritual Director,
Confessor

b. January 23, 1876, Stuttgart
d. November 1, 1945, Munich

Beatified May 3, 1987

After the beatification ceremony for Father Rupert Mayer[1] on the
morning of May 3, 1987, in the Olympia Stadium in Munich,
Pope John Paul II knelt that very afternoon at the grave of the
new blessed in the *Bürgersaal* in the old city in Munich and read
on the tombstone the brief inscription: "P. Rupert Mayer SJ,
23.1.1876—1.11.1945".

These two dates encompass sixty-nine years. Those were years
of a full priestly life in the most difficult times. It was the lifetime
of a man whom the mighty of the so-called Third Reich considered to be a reprehensible lawbreaker whom they wanted to silence. Thousands, however, esteemed him as a true man of God:
they heeded his words, they sought his advice, they asked for his
help in a thousand different concerns. His elevation to the honors
of the altar has been gratefully acknowledged and affirmed with
great joy by countless Catholics in German-speaking territories as
the hard-earned crown of his life, of his untiring charity, of his
striving for truth and justice, as well as of his sorrow and suffering
in the persecuted Church.

---

[1] W. Hergenröder, *P. Rupert Mayer SJ, ein Lebensbild* (Regensburg, 1988).

197

Rupert Mayer was born on January 23, 1876; he was the second of six children of the merchant Rupert Mayer and his wife Emilie, née Wehrle.

In contrast to the good Catholic atmosphere in the loyal, church-going Mayer family, Stuttgart, the capital of the state of Württemberg, was at that time also the home of a sharply anti-Catholic and anti-clerical spirit. Among the faculty of the secondary school that Rupert Mayer attended as a student, there was hostile anti-Catholic sentiment. When Rupert turned sixteen, his father sent him to the school in Ravensburg, where a better spirit prevailed. As a student there he was very talented in sports and music, but otherwise less gifted; through great diligence he completed his high-school studies with distinction and received a diploma in 1894.

In Ravensburg, Rupert Mayer had become acquainted with Jesuit scholastics from Feldkirch, in Vorarlberg, who inspired him with enthusiasm for the Society of Jesus. He now surprised his parents back home with his decision to become a Jesuit; the reason he gave was that this community provided their candidates for the priesthood with the best possible education. His father did not agree at all with his son's plans. Finally, though, father and son settled on the following compromise: if Rupert still wanted to become a Jesuit one year *after* he was ordained a priest, he would then have his father's blessing.

Studies in philosophy and theology followed, starting on October 16, 1894, in Fribourg, Switzerland, and continuing from 1895 to 1896 in Munich and from 1896 to 1898 in Tübingen. Then Rupert Mayer entered the major seminary in Rottenburg. In March 1899, he became a subdeacon and a deacon, and on May 2, 1899, he was ordained a priest by Bishop Paul Wilhelm von Keppler.

The newly ordained priest was given his first pastoral assignment in June 1899 to Spaichingen, a small town with three thousand inhabitants at the foot of the *Dreifaltigkeitsberg* (Trinity Mountain). The parish assistant was very conscious of social issues, and soon he was extremely well-liked in that locality on account of his willing-ness to help the poor and the sick.

The young priest held fast to his decision to become a Jesuit, and Bishop von Keppler gave him permission to do so with the words, "Go, and be a credit to us!" So, on October 1, 1900, he began his novitiate in the Society of Jesus in Tisis-Feldkirch, Vorarlberg, Austria. On October 5, 1901, he was admitted to first vows. Then he was sent for further studies to Valkenburg, Nether-lands. In 1904, Father Rupert Mayer served as assistant to the novice master in Tisis. From 1905 to 1906 he completed the so-called tertiate, the third year of probation, as is the custom among Jesuits. Afterward, Father Mayer, based in Valkenberg, began giv-ing parish missions in Germany, the Netherlands, and Austria, a ministry that lasted until 1911.

It was a decisive step for the rest of his priestly life when Father Rupert Mayer was called to Munich in 1912, at first as a chaplain for the migrant workers who were looking for work and lodgings in the state capital of Bavaria. At that time more than twenty thousand people arrived each year in Munich to work as laborers, as low-level civil servants at the post office or with the railroad, or as domestic servants, but also as adventurers, seeking their fortune in the big city. The chaplain's job was to help these migrants from the rural areas to keep their faith, to guard against immorality, and to make themselves at home in the life of the Church in the big city.

One of Father Rupert Mayer's chief concerns in his pastoral ministry at that time was the endangered family. To address this need he founded in 1913, together with the spiritual director A. Pichlmair and Carl Walterbach, the Sodality of the Holy Family.

When the First World War broke out, Father Mayer volun-teered to serve as a military chaplain. He was assigned first to a field hospital as a non-salaried infirmarian; then, from January 1915 on, as the chaplain of a military division, he was stationed in various theaters of operations. In this capacity Father Mayer dem-onstrated great bravery in many situations, especially when he was seriously wounded in late December 1916, resulting in the amputation of his left leg at the knee and, subsequently, of his left thigh. Count Konrad von Preysing (who was then a cathedral canon in Munich and later became Bishop of Eichstätt and of Berlin) visited the wounded Father Mayer in the sick bay of the Karl-Theodor-Klinik in Munich and afterward wrote: "Father Rupert Mayer's equanimity about the loss of his leg made a deep impression on me then. . . . I was also impressed that he, who was scarcely healed or perhaps had not recovered at all, was already starting his apostolic work again, giving conferences for the nursing sisters there, and so on. For me, the most prominent features of his spiritual condition were a consuming zeal for souls and a great fearlessness, when the kingdom of God was concerned."

Father Rupert Mayer also demonstrated great bravery in the turmoil after the war. Week after week he went to the political meetings of the radical socialists and Communists and, later, of the National Socialists. According to W. Hergenröder, it was "not a penchant for discussion that drew him to such meetings but, rather, his principles as a pastor".

In the preparation and carrying out of the great popular mission in Munich during Advent 1919, Father Rupert Mayer was very much in evidence, as Cardinal-Archbishop Michael von Faulhaber called him "the chief apostle of the 3,600 promoters of the mission". The result was that on November 28, 1921, he was named *Präses*, or spiritual director, of the Marian Men's Confraternity in Munich. The spiritual director's task was to guide its members to a deeper understanding of our Lady, to the daily practice of Marian devotions, and, finally, in their sanctification through apostolic work, undertaken in union with Mary so as to share in the responsibility for bringing about the reign of Christ. He was, in fact, successful to a large extent, above all because, as of January 12, 1922, he was also appointed preacher and confessor in Saint Michael's Church in Munich and therefore had in the Jesuit residence beside Saint Michael's not only a cell to live in, but also a private conference room. People in every sort of spiritual and material need, of both high and low estate, found their way to Father Rupert Mayer. Among the penitents of this Jesuit at that time was also the apostolic nuncio Eugenio Pacelli, who later became Pope Pius XII.

Father Rupert Mayer did not merely wait for people to come to him, however; he went after them and especially sought out the deserving poor. He went after people also by introducing the early "train-station Masses" on August 15, 1925, at the main terminal in Munich, and for ten years he personally celebrated the first Holy Masses at 3:10 and 3:50 A.M. every Sunday, although on the previous Saturday afternoon and evening he had spent five hours in the confessional.

Father Rupert Mayer was also a "man of the pulpit", who often preached up to seventy times in a month. As a preacher, as Father

Father Rupert Mayer, S.J.

J. Sudbrack, S.J., notes,[2] he was "not one of those gifted individuals who have a wealth of language and poetic imagery at their disposal; neither was he one of the great theologians or a profound metaphysician. Detached from his personal presence, the sermons that have been preserved seem folksy, simple, often even naïve. But they inspired people. Father Mayer preached the truth. With him there was no difference between what he said and what he lived. His listeners sensed this. His enemies must have experienced it, too."

His sermons earned for Father Rupert Mayer persecution and imprisonment. On May 15, 1936, he received a first warning by order of the Justice Department of the Third Reich. On April 7 or 8, 1937, he was forbidden to speak anywhere in Germany outside of an ecclesiastical setting. On June 5, 1937, Father Mayer was arrested and held for interrogation until July 23, 1937. On January 5, 1938, he was arrested a second time, because he had resumed his preaching. He was brought as Prisoner No. 9469 to the penitentiary in Landsberg but was released again on May 3, 1938, on the condition that he stop preaching entirely. His third arrest was on November 3, 1939. On December 22–23, 1939, he was taken to the concentration camp in Sachsenhausen, and then, since he was in extreme danger of dying from a serious illness, he was sentenced to internment in the Benedictine monastery in Ettal.

On May 6, 1945, the Americans marched into Ettal and freed Father Rupert Mayer, who then, on the feast of the Ascension of Our Lord, May 10, 1945, began to preach again after a long silence, from the famous Baroque pulpit in the monastery church in Ettal. The crowds who were listening expected a thorough reckoning with the ruined Nazi regime. Father Mayer, however, spoke only about love of enemy and exhorted all to forgive and forget the injustices that they had suffered.

On May 11, 1945, Father Mayer was brought to Munich. He moved back into his old room beside Saint Michael's Church,

[2] J. Sudbrack, S.J., *Pater Rupert Mayer: Zeugnis für Gott—Dienst am Menschen* (Würzburg, 1988).

which to a great extent had been destroyed, and continued his apostolate of prayer, sacrifice, preaching, and hearing confessions. Above all, he reestablished contact with the men of the Marian Men's Sodality and once again served as their spiritual leader, friend, and advisor.

The hardship and misery of the months behind bars, unfortunately, had severely affected the health of the zealous priest. In July and again in September of 1945 Father Rupert Mayer suffered a slight heart attack, followed by a third one on All Saints Day 1945, as he was celebrating Holy Mass—this time it was fatal. The Josefinum hospital in Munich admitted the dying man. On the evening of the feast of All Saints, a priest announced to the faithful who were gathered in the bombed-out church of Saint Michael: "It is not the custom in the Jesuit order to give funeral orations or eulogies. But there is one thing, surely, that I may say in all modesty about our deceased confrère Father Rupert Mayer: 'He did good for all people.' That is the short funeral oration and eulogy for our deceased confrère, the unforgettable Father Rupert Mayer: 'He did good for all people.' That says it all."

He was a fighter, for God and his kingdom. Therefore we can understand his words: "It makes no difference whether we preach, fight, or suffer. The main thing is that it all happens for the kingdom of God." Therefore we can also understand his favorite prayer: "Lord, let it be done to me as you will. I will do as you will. Only help me to understand your will!"

In the homily at the beatification ceremony in Munich, Pope John Paul described Blessed Rupert Mayer strikingly, as follows:

The words of today's Gospel, which were spoken by Jesus Christ when he sent the first Apostles out into the world, appear to assume a new relevance in the life and work of God's servant, Rupert Mayer. Jesus says: "What I am doing is sending you out like sheep among wolves. You must be clever as snakes and innocent as doves!" And then: "Be on your guard with respect to others" (Mt 10:16–17). How significant these words are: *I am sending you out among the people*—and at the same time: *Be on your guard with people*. And why did Jesus warn his disciples about them? "They will drag you into court . . . you will be brought to trial before rulers and kings . . . on my account" (Mt 10:17–18).

When Rupert Mayer decided as a young priest in 1900 to join the Society of Jesus the Jesuits were still officially regarded as "enemies of the Reich" and banned from the country by law. He himself referred to them as "outlawed, exiled and homeless people" since they were not allowed to establish and maintain branches in the Reich. The powerful anti-Catholic incitement and activity against this order, rather than deter him, strengthened him in his resolve to join this maligned Society of Jesus.

Soon called to Munich, Father Mayer found himself increasingly confronted by anti-religious and anti-Church currents, in an atmosphere of mockery and hatred of Christ and the Church, an atmosphere which demanded ever more courage to profess the Catholic faith. The more open and brutal the activities against religion and the Church became in those years, the more determined Father Mayer became in his *defence of the truth of the faith and the rights of the Church.*

In the reading of the Epistle to the Ephesians, we heard the words of the Apostle: "You must put on the armour of God if you are to resist on the evil day; do all that your duty requires, and hold your ground. Stand fast, with the truth as the belt around your waist. . . . In all circumstances hold faith up before you as your shield. . . . Take the helmet of salvation and the sword of the spirit, the word of God!" (Eph 6:13–17). What the Apostle recommends here Rupert Mayer did in excellent fashion. He put on God's armour and never discarded it until his death. Undeterred and unflinching, he fought for God's cause. As an incorruptible witness to the truth he openly opposed the false prophets of those years, always prepared to fight for the Gospel of peace. Equipped with the shield of a deep, unwavering faith, he brandished in his famous sermons the sword of the spirit, the word of God. . . .

"When they hand you over, do not worry . . .", Jesus also said to the Apostles. Rupert Mayer knew that after 1933 his sermons *were monitored by the police*. Nevertheless, he proclaimed the full, the whole, truth. When he was arrested by the Gestapo he stated: "I declare that if I am released, in spite of the fact that I have been banned from preaching, I shall continue to do so on grounds of principle, both in the churches of Munich and in the rest of Bavaria." He could not remain silent, just as St Paul could not, who said: "I am ruined if I do not preach the Gospel!" (1 Cor 9:16).

Willingly Blessed Rupert Mayer suffered *imprisonment and concentration camp* for his principles. On the questionnaire he had to complete in prison he wrote: "I am not at all dissatisfied with my lot. I do not regard it as a blemish but as the crowning glory of my life." And from the Gestapo prison, prior to his transfer to Sachsenhausen concentration camp, he wrote: "When the prison door closed shut and I was alone in my cell where I have already spent so many hours, tears came to my eyes, tears of pleasure at having been chosen to be locked up for the sake of my profession and to look to a most uncertain future." That is not the voice of just a bold individual but of a Christian who is *proud to share the Cross of Jesus Christ*. . . .

In one of his letters to his elderly mother from prison we read: "Now I really have nothing and no one other than God. And that is enough, indeed more than enough. If only people would understand this there would be many more happy people on earth." In the solitude of prison Father Rupert Mayer directed his entire energy *to the deepening of his inner union with God*. In complete devotion to him he sought to transform all his affliction and distress into inner renewal and salvation. As the accused before his judges he experienced the comforting and invigorating closeness of God which Christ had promised to his witnesses: ". . . do not worry about what you will say or how you will say it . . . you yourselves will not be the speakers; the spirit of your Father will be speaking in you" (Mt 10:19–20). . . .

Even in his great oppression Father Rupert Mayer experienced God as his inner strength and as the joyful fulfillment of his life. At the same time he himself, through this deep communion with God in times of great need, was a source of comfort for many, the bringer of new hope and confidence, the *father of the poor* who named him their *fifteenth auxiliary saint.*[3] Just as the people used to throng around Jesus and received help from him, they also came with all their problems to him. Sixty, seventy people a day came to him for help. He received them all with an open heart. He also spent many hours in the confessional, where many came to seek help in their spiritual need.

"We must radiate warmth. People must feel at home in our presence and that the reason for this lies in our union with God." With these words he tells us his intentions in the service of the poor. He wanted to make God's love visible and tangible and to help people understand that God loved them. His goodness and helpfulness carried such force that they could also stand abuse. When he was told about this, he merely replied: "A person who has never been cheated has never done anything good." The folly of his love is part of the folly of the Cross in which the loving God turns to us to draw us all to him.

The principle to which Father Rupert Mayer remained faithful all his life was: "Christ is the essence of life. There are no compromises." What he was he wanted to be totally. His *determination to follow Christ* led him to holiness. In keeping with the motto of his order: "All for the greater glory of God", he was engrossed with God's honour and God's rights. "God has first claim on us", he said. He knew that he was thus fighting also for the rights and dignity of man. Today we hear a great deal about

[3] Catholics in Bavaria and Austria honor *die Vierzehn Nothelfer*, "the Fourteen Holy Helpers of those in need", a group of saints, all but one of them martyrs, beloved for their extraordinary power of intercession.— TRANS.

human rights. In very many countries they are violated. However, no one speaks of God's rights. Yet *human rights* and *God's rights* belong together. Where God and his laws are not respected, man's rights, too, will not be respected. This was clear from the conduct of the Nazi rulers. They ignored God and persecuted his servants. They treated people in an inhumane fashion, in Dachau just outside Munich, and in Auschwitz, just outside of my former diocese of Cracow. It is still true today: God's rights and human rights stand and fall together. Our life is only in order if our relationship with God is in order. That is why Father Rupert Mayer said in the worldwide tribulations of the last war: "The present time is a most serious warning to the peoples of the earth to return to God. They cannot manage without God!" Those words have lost none of their validity. Today still we have to give God his due. Then man will receive his due.

Dear brothers and sisters, the saints and the blessed of the Church are God's message, past and present, to us. Hence they are there for us to *venerate and imitate*. Let us therefore today open our hearts to the message which Rupert Mayer has proclaimed so vividly with his words and deeds. Let us, like him, see in God the essence and source of our life. He had a child's unshakeable trust in God. "Lord, let thy will be done. Let me act in accordance with your will. Only help me to understand your will", was the first verse of his favourite prayer. God our Lord was the source from which, in long hours spent in prayer, during Mass, and in fulfilling his daily duties, he drew the strength for his amazing life's work.[4]

---

[4] *L'Osservatore Romano*, June 1, 1987, p. 2.

Blessed
Andrea [Andrew]
Carlo Ferrari

Priest, Theology Professor,
Bishop, Archbishop,
Cardinal

b. *August 13, 1850, Lalatta di
Pratopiano, Italy*
d. *February 2, 1921, Milan*

Beatified May 10, 1987

The great mother diocese of the Lombardy region, the archdiocese of Milan, has had several times the good fortune—even in the twentieth century—of being led and governed by saintly pastors, successors of its two great bishops, Saint Ambrose and Saint Charles Borromeo. For instance, from 1894 to 1921, a chief pastor stood at the head of the archdiocese of Milan in the person of Archbishop Andrea Carlo Ferrari, who was so exemplary and dynamic that on May 10, 1987, he was raised to the honors of the altar.

Andrea Ferrari[1] was born on August 13, 1850, in Lalatta, a district of Pratopiano in the diocese of Parma, the son of Giuseppe Ferrari and his wife, Maddalena, née Longarini. Starting in 1861, he studied at the minor seminary and then the major seminary of Parma and unwaveringly pursued a priestly vocation, until, on December 19, 1873, he was ordained a priest.

Father Ferrari was actually involved in regular pastoral work only from 1874 to 1875. From autumn 1875 until May 1891 he

---

[1] G. B. Penco and B. Galbiati, *Vita del Cardinal Andrea Carlo Ferrari, archivescovo di Milano* (Milan-Rome, 1926).

served primarily in priestly formation, first as vice rector and secondary schoolteacher at the minor seminary of Parma, then from 1877 on as rector of the major seminary, as well as a professor of dogmatic and moral theology. One result of this teaching activity was his *Summula theologiae dogmaticae generalis ad mentem sancti Thomae* (Little summa of general dogmatic theology according to the thought of Saint Thomas), which appeared in print for the first time in 1885 (3d ed., 1896).

On May 29, 1890, the seminary rector, the Very Reverend Andrea Ferrari, became the bishop of Guastalla; in 1892, the bishop of Como; and then already in 1894, the archbishop of Milan and cardinal protector of the church of Saint Anastasia in Rome. Here he took, in addition to his baptismal name, the name of his great predecessor Charles Borromeo, whom he emulated over the course of twenty-seven years of self-sacrificing service to the large archdiocese. As Saint Charles Borromeo once had done, in March 1895 he began a visitation of the entire archdiocese, which was quite extensive, making his way even into the farthest mountain parishes, and he completed these strenuous rounds five times during his episcopate. During his visitations, as a good shepherd, he strove to do everything possible in the individual parishes to awaken, strengthen, and deepen the religious life and morality of the parishioners. In the years 1902, 1910, and 1914, Cardinal Ferrari held diocesan synods, and in 1906 he even ventured to call a provincial council for the entire ecclesiastical province of Lombardy.

Moreover, Cardinal Ferrari planned various congresses in Milan, such as the Eucharistic Congress of 1895, the Fifteenth Church Music Congress (1897), a congress commemorating the fiftieth anniversary of the dogmatic definition of the Immaculate Conception (1904), a congress commemorating the fiftieth anniversary of Mary's apparitions in Lourdes (1908), the congress for the 300th anniversary of the canonization of Charles Borromeo, and in 1913 the congress commemorating the 1600th anniversary of the Edict of Milan, promulgated by Emperor Constantine.

Archbishop Ferrari demonstrated great openness to the social questions of the day. For instance, in thanksgiving for the social encyclical *Rerum novarum*, he established a chair for economics on the theological faculty of the major seminary, which he entrusted to the famous and saintly university professor Giuseppe Toniolo, of the University of Pisa, and then to Professor Dalmazio Minoretti, later the cardinal-archbishop of Genoa. Besides that, Archbishop Ferrari promoted various social organizations, such as fraternal financial associations, and prompted his clergy to initiate various social programs of a cooperative sort.

The Catholic press was also the object of the vigilant concern of the solicitous chief shepherd. He made efforts to combine the two Catholic newspapers, *L'Osservatore Cattolico* and *La Lega Lombarda*, which were competing with each other, by founding *L'Unione*, later entitled *L'Italia*.

Cardinal Ferrari also promoted the establishment of the Catholic University of Milan and in the last year of his life founded another program for popular and social education, which was then named *Opera Cardinal Ferrari*, after him.

During the anti-Modernist campaigns under Pope Pius X, Cardinal Ferrari, who always stood loyally in solidarity with the magisterial directives of the Holy See, did not escape grievous suspicions about him personally, about his seminary, and about his entire archdiocese. He endured all silently and prayerfully, in the hope that the hour of tribulation would soon be at an end. This occurred only when the new pope, Benedict XV, expressed his complete confidence in him.

But soon afterward a new trial began for this chief pastor who showed such fatherly concern for his archdiocese. The First World War had broken out, with all its suffering and all its misery. Many of the projects started by the archbishop came to a standstill. He devoted special care now to the widows and orphans, families in financial difficulties, soldiers and prisoners of war, and to the search for missing persons. During the war years, Cardinal Ferrari also had to defend himself against suspicions that he was not patriotic enough in his sympathies, on account of the as yet unresolved Roman question.

When Cardinal Ferrari, after a painful illness, was called to his eternal reward, on February 2, 1921, he was able to reckon as the result of his long pastoral ministry the reestablishment of harmony and peace in his archdiocese; the high religious and moral caliber of his diocesan clergy, who had grown to be quite numerous; the contemporary renewal of pastoral methods and their adaptation to the new conditions throughout the archdiocese; and a happy reinvigoration of faith, religious practice, and morality in the people of the diocese.

Pope John Paul II commended this Milanese archbishop at the beatification on May 10, 1987, in Saint Peter's in Rome, emphasizing the following:

> Christ was the "gateway" to holiness for Cardinal Andrea Carlo Ferrari, who, after having been Bishop of Guastalla and of Como, ruled the Archdiocese of Milan for no less than twenty-seven years, following with ardent pastoral fervour in the footsteps of his great predecessors Ambrose and Charles [Borromeo].
>
> Supported by a robust faith and an enlightened zeal, he was able to point out with sure judgement the course to be taken among the new and difficult situations that were emerging in the religious and social context of his time. He was able to see with the eye of the Good Shepherd the pastoral problems that were arising as a result of historical circumstances and to indicate ways of confronting and resolving them. For this reason, he is an example of great relevance to our times.
>
> Knowing that ignorance of the essential principles of the faith and of the moral life exposed the faithful to atheistic and materialistic propaganda, he organized a modern and penetrating form of catechesis. He also renewed the style of pastoral activity. Taking his inspiration from "the Good Shepherd", he never tired of saying with great forcefulness that one should not wait passively for the faithful to come to the Church; rather it

was necessary to go out, as Jesus did, into the streets and city squares, to meet them, speaking their language. Almost four times he made a visitation of the vast Ambrosian diocese, going to the most distant and out-of-the-way places, even on a mule and on foot, where from time immemorial a bishop had not been seen. This was why some people said, when they saw his untiring pastoral activity: "Saint Charles has returned!" (*Positio super virtutibus*, p. 267).

The solicitude of the pastor was expressed also in the promotion of new forms of assistance, adapted to the changing times. The first to benefit from the wonderful flowering of social initiatives were the abandoned children and young people, the workers, the poor.

Thus there matured in the heart of Cardinal Ferrari the project of a Society, which constitutes today a precious heritage of his: the Company of Saint Paul, also called "Opera Cardinale Ferrari". From the original idea of a House of the People, which would accommodate the organizations of the apostolate of the laity and those of the archdiocesan charities, there developed a series of activities inspired by the ingenious and courageous pastoral dynamism of the Archbishop: the "Secretariat of the People", the canteens, the missions for the workers, the children's Home, and the Home for the re-education of those discharged from prison, the great initiatives in Catholic publications, the organization of mass pilgrimages.

The outstanding merit of Cardinal Ferrari was precisely that of perceiving with felicitous intuition the urgency of involving the laity in the life of the ecclesial community, by organizing its power for a more influential Christian presence in society. He was a diligent promoter of the male and female branches of Catholic Action, which developed under his decisive impulse, and from Milan had a beneficial influence on the whole of Italy. He did all in his power for the establishment of the Catholic University, and had the joy of seeing its early beginnings.

But the secret of the tireless apostolic activity of the new

Blessed was his interior life, founded on deep theological convictions, imbued with a tender and filial devotion to Our Lady, centred on Jesus in the Eucharist and on the Cross, expressed in a constant attitude of great goodness towards all, of compassionate solicitude towards the poor, of heroic patience in suffering. On 29 September 1920, in the midst of the agonizing pains of a cancer that was choking him, he wrote in his diary these final words: "May God's will be done always and in all things!" May Cardinal Andrea Carlo Ferrari, whom we now invoke as "Blessed", help us also to do always the will of God, in which our sanctification is to be found.[2]

[2] *L'Osservatore Romano*, May 25, 1987, p. 18.

Blessed
Louis-Zéphyrin
Moreau

Priest, Bishop

b. April 1, 1824, Béçancour,
Quebec, Canada
d. May 24, 1901,
Saint-Hyacinthe

Beatified May 10, 1987

Blessed Louis-Zéphyrin Moreau[1] is a Canadian bishop who was raised to the honors of the altar on May 10, 1987. He was born on April 1, 1824, in Béçancour, in Nicolet parish, Quebec, Canada, the fifth of thirteen children of poor, good Catholic parents.

The pastor of his native village, Abbé Dion, gave him his first instructions in Latin, since the boy's piety and modesty indicated that he could have a vocation to the priesthood. From 1839 on, the boy was able to continue his studies at the seminary in Nicolet. Eventually, he was wearing clerical garb and seemed happy, confident, and well-adjusted in his priestly formation. Then, all at once, his frail health started to cause him trouble. In September 1846, Monsignor Signay ordered young Moreau to put aside his cassock, because of course he would never be able to become a priest on account of his poor health. Yet the candidate for priesthood did not give up. He applied to the bishop's chancery in Quebec for admission as a priestly candidate. But there, too, he was turned down. So, finally, he knocked at the door of Bishop

---

[1] R. Litalien, *Le prêtre québecois à la fin du XIXe siècle: Style de vie et spiritualité d'après Mgr. Louis-Zephyrin Moreau* (Montreal, 1970).

Bourget of Montreal. The ordinary sent him to his co-adjutor, Monsignor Prince, who accepted young Moreau, despite his frail health, as a priestly candidate for the diocese of Montreal. On December 19, 1846, he was ordained a priest.

For the first five years of his priesthood, Father Moreau worked as secretary at the side of Bishop Prince. When the latter was transferred from Montreal to serve as ordinary of the diocese of Saint-Hyacinthe in June 1852, he took young Father Moreau there with him as his closest collaborator. And so the arrangement continued in the following twenty-three years with the three bishops who would govern in succession the recently created diocese of Saint-Hyacinthe in Quebec. They always kept Father Moreau at their side as a trusted coworker, to their great satisfaction—first as secretary and then as cathedral rector; eventually Prelate Louis-Zéphyrin Moreau became the apostolic administrator of the diocese when the see became vacant. When Bishop Charles La Rocque died, however, Father Moreau became his successor on November 19, 1875, and on January 16, 1876, he was consecrated a bishop.

The new chief shepherd of Saint-Hyacinthe was remarkable for his great kindness and charity, so that the people always spoke of him only as "the good Monseigneur Moreau". He was always amiable and modest. He conducted pastoral visitations in his diocese regularly, with great care and precision, and taught his priests that his greatest concern was to have, not only good clergymen, but holy priests in the diocese that was entrusted to him.

He fought against irregularity of any sort, against intolerance and presumption, against bad newspapers, and against secret societies. He founded many pious associations in the parishes of his diocese, brought in the Sisters of Saint Joseph in many localities to teach girls in the schools, and was extraordinarily zealous in promoting vocations to the priesthood and the religious life. One indication of the zeal with which this chief pastor went about his work is his voluminous correspondence, running to fifteen thousand handwritten letters.

During the twenty-five years that he governed the diocese, this bishop watched over Christ's flock, which had been entrusted to him as a truly good shepherd. He died on May 24, 1901, in the seventy-seventh year of his life. Almost all of the priests of the diocese of Saint-Hyacinthe were already of the opinion then that a saint had been called to his eternal reward.

Pope John Paul II eulogized this Canadian bishop at the beatification on May 10, 1987, as follows:

Following the Good Shepherd, Louis-Zéphirin Moreau devoted his life to leading the flock entrusted to him in Saint-Hyacinthe, in Canada. As priest, and then bishop of this young diocese, he knew his sheep. He laboured tirelessly to give them nourishment, "that they might have life, and have it abundantly" (Jn 10:10). In him, the faithful found first of all a man entirely dedicated to God, and then a true intercessor. It is good that the Church honours him today and presents him as a pastoral model.

The "good Bishop Moreau" was able to give his attention daily to every individual. He respected everyone, practised the most concrete charity for the poor whom he received in his home. He loved to visit the parishes and the schools. He was close to the priests whom he consulted, whom he stimulated in their activity, in their spiritual life, in the deepening of their intellectual life, so that they could bring to Christians a catechesis enlightened by a faith understood and lived. The bishop gave proof of a keen spirit of discernment, and one could rely on his clear and courageous word, both in the teaching addressed to all and in the answers given to individuals.

Conscious of the needs of a diocese which was growing, Bishop Moreau multiplied the initiatives for the religious and scholastic training of youth, for the care of the sick, the organization of mutual assistance and also the establishment of new parishes, the training of candidates for the priesthood. In all of these domains, he was daring and would overcome the obstacles with patience.

He sought the cooperation of the religious congregations for numerous tasks. Understanding the great value of the consecrated life, he was able to support foundations that were daring [despite] their poverty. He personally contributed in a profound way to the spiritual animation and to the orientation of the religious institutes founded or newly established in his diocese.

Beyond the confines of Saint-Hyacinthe, Bishop Moreau was recognized as an exemplary ecclesiastic. He analysed with clarity the problems of his time; with a combination of firmness and moderation, he defended the essential principles and values, he worked for unity among Christians, he secured useful forms of mediation. A diligent representative of the Holy See, he remained in full communion with the successor of Peter, whose teaching he presented with care.

In spite of his physical frailty, he lived in great austerity. He could never have undertaken his enormous tasks except by the strength he drew from prayer. He portrays himself when he writes: "We shall do well the great things with which we are entrusted only if we stay intimately united with Our Lord." One could call him the bishop of the Sacred Heart: daily the pastor gave his life for his sheep, for he loved them with the burning love of Christ.[2]

[2] *L'Osservatore Romano*, May 25, 1987.

Blessed
Pierre-François Jamet

Priest, University Rector,
Founder

b. *September 13, 1762,*
   Fresnes, France
d. *January 12, 1845,*
   Caen, France

Beatified May 10, 1987

A priest who remained completely loyal to the Church during the French Revolution and proved to be an excellent guardian of the souls entrusted to him, Blessed Pierre-François Jamet[1] was raised to the honors of the altar on May 10, 1987.

Born on September 13, 1762, in Fresnes (Orne), he completed his secondary schooling at the *collège* in Vire and his studies in philosophy and theology at the University of Caen, where he was ordained a priest on September 22, 1787, shortly before the French Revolution broke out. The young priest refused to take the oath of loyalty to the new civil constitution, yet he remained in the country—despite enormous dangers—and devoted his priestly ministry, to the extent that that was still possible, to the nuns of the Congregation of the Good Savior (*Congrégation du Bon-Sauveur*) in Caen. In 1790 he was designated their chaplain and spiritual director.

In 1805, when the storm of the Revolution was over, Bishop Charles Brault appointed him superior of the community, which consisted of fifteen professed sisters and four novices. He gathered

---

[1] G. A. Simon, *La doctrine spirituelle et les vertus de l'Abbé Pierre-François Jamet* (Caen, 1951).

the dispersed nuns, looked after them in every respect, materially and spiritually, and found new areas for these sisters to work in, especially in the care and instruction of deaf-mutes. For this purpose, Father Jamet developed new methods and further developed the existing sign language. He wrote several books on the instruction of deaf-mutes, for instance, his *Mémoirs sur l'Enseignement des Sourds-Muets* (Caen, 1820–1822).

On November 14, 1822, Father Jamet became rector of the University of Caen. His priestly charity and ministry extended beyond the deaf-mutes to include the mentally handicapped as well. He always devoted special care, nevertheless, to the Sisters of the Good Savior, for whom he was a theologically learned and pious spiritual director, as is demonstrated by his meditations on the mystery of the Most Holy Trinity (*Méditations sur le mystère de la Très Sainte Trinité, à l'usage des religieuses de la Congrégation du Bon-Sauveur*, Caen 1830; 3d ed., 1957).

At the death of Blessed Pierre-François Jamet, on January 12, 1845, the institute of women religious that he had always encouraged with his assistance was so well established that there were already 232 professed sisters in three houses of the congregation of the Community of the Good Savior of Caen. He was rightly called the second founder of this congregation of nuns, which had been founded in 1717 by M. Leroy in Caen.

Pope John Paul II spoke about this French priest at the beatification on May 10, 1987:

Now we turn our attention to the French priest Pierre-François Jamet. He lived the same ardent charity in the many forms of his priestly activity. He impresses us by his courage, by his ability to pursue at once the course of a man of high culture, a faithful priest, a servant of the poor.

He had just been ordained a priest when he was named confessor and spiritual director of the Sisters of Bon-Sauveur. He took all the risks involved in remaining during the French Revolution. He gave an example of firm attachment to the Church and never abandoned the Christians. In secret, he celebrated the sacraments with joy. He clearly discerned the threats confronting faith, but he placed all his confidence in the gifts of God.

A respected university man, the Abbé Jamet at one time had a heavy academic responsibility. A balanced education, a demanding formation on the intellectual as well as on the moral and spiritual levels: such were the concerns which simultaneously guided his activity. In a milieu where rival convictions and loyalties created opposition, the Rector Jamet respected persons, but he assured with firmness the development of the institutions for which he was responsible. Available and dedicated, he was a true servant of humanity as long as he could accomplish his task in conscience.

Pierre-François Jamet never for a moment abandoned the service of the poor. He urges the Sisters of Bon-Sauveur and encourages them to develop their work, becoming their "second founder". We admire his intrepid generosity, his concern not to leave the most handicapped of his brothers without care. He will organize ever better the reception of the mentally ill: he loves them to the point of learning to take care of them, and often he even heals them. A pioneer in assistance to deaf-mutes, he supplies them with a means of expressing themselves, he allows them to rediscover a language, he restores them to dignity. We salute him as an inventor and a builder of charity.

Through the extent of his activity, Pierre-François Jamet witnessed also to what a man can accomplish when the presence of God dwells in him. He was able to say: "My God, I am yours, as you are mine." A pastor, he led his sheep on the paths of life. He drew especially the Sisters of Bon-Sauveur to the following of the Redeemer and into the intimacy of the Holy Trinity. We recognize him when he repeats the prayer of Jesus: "Holy Father, preserve, for the glory of your name, the children whom you have given to me, and may they always be united." [2]

[2] *L'Osservatore Romano*, May 25, 1987, pp. 18–19.

Blessed [Saint] Benedetta Cambiagio Frassinello

Wife, Foundress

b. *October 2, 1791,*
   Langasco, Italy
d. *March 21, 1858,*
   Ronco Pavia, Italy

Beatified May 10, 1987
[Canonized May 19, 2002]

Blessed Benedetta Cambiagio,[1] whose married name was Frassinello, was a wife and widow who became the foundress of a religious congregation and with great love took care of poor girls who were abandoned or at risk. On May 10, 1987, she was raised to the honors of the altar.

She was born on October 2, 1791, in Langasco, Italy, into a Christian family that, to all appearances, was well situated. At her parents' recommendation, the pious girl married an upright young man by the name of Giovanni Battista Frassinello. After two years of marriage, during which the young couple were not blessed with any children, they agreed to live in a so-called Josephite marriage. They took a vow of perpetual chastity and resolved from then on to consecrate their lives completely to God and to charitable works. Since they themselves had not had any children, they took in poor abandoned children, especially girls who were at risk. With her husband's consent, Benedetta established a home

---

[1] L. Traverso, *La serva di Dio Madre Benedetta Cambiagio* (Milan, 1939).

for abandoned and at-risk girls in Pavia in 1826. Several years later, she founded the congregation of the Benedictine Sisters of Divine Providence. The sisters of this community were to provide a loving, Christian education for young people—especially the poor and the abandoned and girls who were at risk—and to establish homes, schools, and workshops for that purpose. She was successful in this work. At the death of Benedetta Cambiagio Frassinello, who meanwhile had been widowed, the congregation she had founded numbered thirty-five houses and two hundred nuns; its constitutions were approved by the Holy See in 1937.

In all the difficulties that she encountered in her charitable work, Blessed Benedetta trusted unswervingly in Divine Providence. She set an example of a life of faith, hope, and love until, on March 21, 1858, at the age of sixty-six, she was called to her eternal reward.

Pope John Paul II said the following about this exemplary woman at the beatification on May 10, 1987:

Jesus was, finally, the "gateway" to holiness for Benedetta Cambiagio, foundress of the Institute of the Benedictine Sisters of Providence. A courageous and enterprising woman, she managed to win to her ideal of total self-giving to Christ even her husband, Giovanni Battista Frassinello, starting together with him a family open to the reception of the young people in need of material support and of moral guidance. This was the beginning of a work which was to do so much good, helping children who were deprived of assistance and training them to be good Christians and generous mothers of families, capable of doing credit to themselves, to society and to the Church.

The difficulties she had to face to put such an apostolic plan into effect were always supported by an intrepid faith, rooted in a profound humility, which she nourished by the daily contemplation of the Crucified. While maintaining a certain simplicity, she rested her activity on strongly theological bases: the Eucharist, source of courage, of light and of constancy; complete abandonment to the "Loving Divine Providence", doing everything only for love of God and the desire to please him. This was the secret of the interior strength which the new Blessed was able to show in the midst of the gravest difficulties. She was able to cope with hostilities which were stirred up against her because she abandoned herself totally to the power of God, convinced that "when God wants something he does not fail to supply the appropriate means".

Blessed Benedetta Cambiagio Frassinello presents herself therefore to all of us as an example of living faith and of courageous hope, translated into an untiring commitment of charity, which, through the simplest and humblest of means, is able to reach the heart and to arouse therein the resolution to live an authentically Christian life.[2]

---

[2] *L'Osservatore Romano*, May 25, 1987, p. 19.

Blessed Karolina Kózka

Martyr of purity

b. *August 2, 1898,*
   Wal-Ruda, Poland
d. *November 18, 1914,*
   Wal-Ruda

Beatified June 10, 1987

With this new blessed, the Polish Pope has given his Polish home-land a counterpart to Saint Maria Goretti from his own people. Allow me to note, incidentally, that similar young girls from German-speaking territories could be mentioned who, after living a chaste, Christian life, fell victim to a debauched individual while courageously defending their purity and virginity.

Karolina Kózka[1] was born on August 2, 1898, in Wal-Ruda, in the diocese of Tarnów, Poland. In this same Polish diocese, which belonged then to Austria-Hungary, Gregor Thomas Ziegler (d. April 15, 1852), later bishop of Linz, in Upper Austria, served as an exemplary chief shepherd from 1822 to 1827.

Karolina Kózka was born into a large farming family—the fourth of eleven children—in which the children received a truly Christian upbringing from their good Catholic parents. The whole social milieu in Galicia at that time also helped young people to mature into genuinely Christian adults. In the case of Karolina Kózka, a zealous priest, Father Ladislaus Mendrala, her

---

[1] Z. Zimowski, "Kózka, Carolina", in *Bibliotheca Sanctorum* 1:720–21.

spiritual director, also played an important role, so that she not only stayed pure and chaste, but also became very active in a many-sided lay apostolate in her parish. Karolina Kózka devoted her free time to her brothers and sisters, but also to the children of neighboring families, giving them religious instruction. She also loved to assist the frail elderly and sick people in the parish.

Exactly six months after receiving the sacrament of confirmation, Karolina had to prove herself, aided by the gift of fortitude, in a mortal conflict: On November 18, 1914—shortly after the start of hostilities in the First World War—she was attacked by a Russian soldier in the woods nearby her home. She was supposed to give in to the lustful desires of the soldier; for religious reasons she put up a strong resistance, but to no avail. She became a martyr while defending her virginity.

Pope John Paul II beatified this brave sixteen-year-old girl, whose heroic courage in defending her purity of heart has never been forgotten in Galicia, on June 10, 1987, in Tarnów, during his second visit to his Polish homeland. During the beatification ceremony he said, among other things:

The saints, is not their mission to . . . confound? Yes, They can have that mission too. Sometimes such a saving confusion is necessary in order to see man in all truth. It is necessary in order to discover, or re-discover the just order of values. It is necessary for us all, old and young. Even if this young daughter of the Church of Tarnow, whom we shall call blessed from today, speaks through her life and death first and foremost to young people. To boys and girls. To men and women.

She speaks of the great dignity of woman: of the dignity of the human person. She speaks of the dignity of the body, even if in this world it is subject to death and corruption, just as her young body was subjected to death by assassination [murder], but this human body carries within itself the seed of immortality, which man is to attain in God, living and eternal, through Christ.

Therefore: the saints exist to give witness to the great dignity of man. To give witness to Christ, crucified and risen "for us and for our salvation", means to give witness at the same time to the dignity which man has before God. To give witness to the vocation which man has in Christ.

Karolina Kozka was conscious of this dignity. Conscious of this vocation.

She lived and matured in this awareness. Finally, with the same awareness, she gave her young life, when it was necessary to give it, to defend her dignity as a woman. To defend the dignity of a Polish peasant girl. "Blessed are the pure in heart, for they shall see God" (cf. Mt 5:8). . . .

The liturgy of today's beatification, especially the responsorial psalm, allows us in a certain sense to read the single moments of this witness, of this martyrdom.

Is it not you, Karolina, speaking thus: "Protect me, O God: I take refuge in you. I said to God: 'You are my Lord'" (Ps 16 [15]:1–2)?

Is it not you expressing yourself through the words of the psalmist? At the moment of a terrible threat from another, a man with the means of overpowering you . . . you took refuge in God. And the cry "You are my God" means: do not let foul arrogance prevail over me, for you are the source of my strength . . . in weakness. You, only Lord of my soul and body: my Creator and Redeemer of my life and death. You, God of my heart, from whom my memory and conscience are not separated.

"I place the Lord ever before me,
he stands at my right hand, I cannot waver.
. . . even at night my heart instructs me" (ibid., v. 8, 7).

Thus speaks the psalmist. And thus speaks Karolina at the moment of the mortal test of faith, of purity and of strength.

Let us follow the tracks of the flight of this girl, who tried to resist the armed aggressor, who sought ways of saving her life and dignity in the woods near her native village.

"You show me the way of life" (cf. ibid., v. 11).

The path of life. On that path of flight, she was struck by the final mortal blow. Karolina did not save her mortal life. She found death. She gave this life, in order to obtain life: with Christ in God.

Indeed it was in Christ, from the moment of the Sacrament of Baptism, which she received in the parish church of Radlow, that her new life began. And then, struck down by the hand of an aggressor, Karolina gave final witness in this world to the life that was in her. . . . Death signifies a new beginning of this life, which is from God, which becomes our part by means of Christ, through his death and resurrection.

So Karolina perished. Her young body remained under the bushes. And the death of a young, innocent girl seems to announce with particular force the truth expressed by the psalmist:

"The Lord is my part of the inheritance.

The Lord is my destiny.

My life is in his hands" (cf. ibid., v. 5).

Yes. Karolina abandoned in the Ruda wood is already safe, is in the hands of God, who is the God of Life. The martyr cries out together with the psalmist: "I will bless the Lord."

Daughter of simple parents, daughter of the land on the Vistula, "star" of your people, today the Church unites herself with that other cry of your soul—and calls you: Blessed!

Christ became your "wisdom, justice, sanctification, redemption" (1 Cor 1:30). He has become your strength.

Let us thank Christ for the power which he manifested in your chaste life and in your death through martyrdom.[2]

---

[2] *L'Osservatore Romano*, July 20, 1987, p. 3.

Blessed
Michal Kozal

Priest, Bishop, Martyr

b. *September 27, 1893,*
    Ligota, near Gnesen, Poland
d. *January 26, 1943,*
    Dachau concentration camp

Beatified June 14, 1987

The many Polish priests who were interned in the concentration camp at Dachau by the devilish system of National Socialism, and in most cases were tortured to death, had a bishop among them who provided them with a shining example of courage and self-sacrifice. He was Bishop Michal Kozal,[1] who was beatified by Pope John Paul II on June 14, 1987, in Warsaw—probably as a representative for all the Polish priests martyred in Dachau (there were more than two thousand of them).

Michal Kozal was born on September 27, 1893, in a little village not far from the cathedral town of Gnesen, one of many children in a poor family of practicing Catholics.

The gifted youngster soon discovered that he had a calling to the priesthood. He arrived at this goal on February 23, 1918, when he received the sacrament of holy orders in the cathedral of Gnesen.

After a short stint in a small parish, where, in addition to the regular pastoral ministry, he worked especially with the youth, in 1923 he became prefect for the students of the Catholic high

---

[1] B. Lewandowski, "Kozal, Michele", in *Bibliotheca Sanctorum* 1:720.

school in Bydgoszcz; then, in 1927, spiritual director at the major seminary in Gnesen; and, finally, the rector there.

On June 12, 1939, Michal Kozal was appointed auxiliary bishop of Włocławek by Pope Pius XII. His grace-filled ministry there lasted only twenty-two months, because the Gestapo had been after him ever since they began their military occupation of his Polish homeland; they finally arrested him on April 3, 1941.

He was incarcerated, first in Włocławek, then in Lad; finally, he was brought to the concentration camp in Dachau, where he died heroically on January 26, 1943, personally putting into action Christ's words: "Greater love has no man than this, that a man lay down his life for his friends." Indeed, while in the concentration camp at Dachau, Bishop Kozal had taken particular care of his sick brother priests, until he himself, physically exhausted, died of typhoid.

All the priests imprisoned with this Polish bishop, and all who became more closely acquainted with him and were able to observe his attitude and way of life, testified to the sanctity of this man of God.

In the cathedral of Włocławek, a monument was erected in 1954 to him and to the 220 priests of this diocese who had to forfeit their lives in Dachau. The most magnificent memorial to this heroic bishop, however, was established by his Polish compatriot Pope John Paul II, who beatified him and raised him to the honor of the altars. In his allocution after the beatification, the Pope described the valiant pastor of souls:

Bishop Michal Kozal, called to episcopal service in the Church of Włocławek on the eve of the last war and the terrible occupation. Then imprisoned and deported to the concentration camp of Dachau. One of many millions! There he was martyred in the odour of sanctity. Today, here in Warsaw, raised as a martyr to the glory of the altars.

His fellow countrymen know the story of his life and of his martyrdom.

Here is a man, but one among those in whom has been manifested the power of Christ "in heaven and on earth". The power of love against the follies of arrogance, of destruction, of contempt and of hate.

This love, revealed to him by Christ, Bishop Kozal received in all the fullness of its demands. He did not draw back even from the most difficult demand: "love your enemies" (Mt 5:44).

May he become yet another patron of our difficult times that are so full of tensions, of enmity and of conflicts. May he, before the generations of today and of tomorrow, be a witness of how great is the power of grace of our Lord Jesus Christ, of him who "loved unto the end".[2]

[2] *L'Osservatore Romano*, August 10, 1987, p. 5.

Blessed
Jurgis (George) Matulaitis
(Matulewicz)

Priest, Religious,
General Superior,
Archbishop

b. *April 13, 1871,*
Liuginé, Lithuania
d. *January 27, 1927,*
Kaunas, Lithuania

Beatified June 28, 1987

As though presenting a gift in honor of the 600th anniversary of the "baptism" or beginning of Christianity in Lithuania (cf. apostolic letter, June 5, 1987), Pope John Paul II gave a new blessed to the sorely-tried Church of Lithuania in the person of Bishop Jurgis (George) Matulaitis (Matulewicz),[1] who died on January 27, 1927, and was beatified on June 28, 1987.

He was born on April 13, 1871, in Liuginé, a Lithuanian village in the parish, or township, of Mariampolé, the last of eight children of a poor Lithuanian farming couple of modest means. At the age of three, the boy lost his father, in 1874, and then his mother when he was ten, in 1881. The financial straits in which the family lived were probably a reason that Jurgis was stricken with tuberculosis of the bone at the age of fifteen. He suffered from it throughout his life; in 1887, for instance, he had to interrupt his secondary schooling, which he had begun in 1882. He recuperated at home and worked for two years on the farm. In

---

[1] V. Cusumano, *Innamorato della Cheisa: Profilo biografico e Diario del Servo di Dio Giorgio Matulaitis* (Milan, 1963).

1889 he continued his studies in Kielce, in Poland. During that time he changed his Lithuanian name, Matulaitis, to the Polish name, Matulewicz. In 1891, the student entered the diocesan seminary of Kielce to study philosophy and theology. In 1893, however, when the seminary was closed by tsarist officials and the students were dispersed to various Polish seminaries, Jurgis Matulewicz went to the seminary of the archdiocese of Warsaw. He remained there until 1895. Then he went to the Roman Catholic Academy in Saint Petersburg. There he was ordained a priest in 1898. The professors at the academy wanted the gifted young priest to travel to western Europe to deepen his knowledge of theology and then to take a professorial chair at the Academy in Saint Petersburg. Matulewicz, however, preferred to begin pastoral ministry in his diocese, Kielce. His work as an assistant priest lasted only two months, though, because the state of his health took a serious turn for the worse. He was sent to Kreuznach, in Germany, to recuperate from tuberculosis of the bone. From there he went to Switzerland, where he completed his study of theology at the University of Fribourg, earning a doctorate in theology on the basis of a dissertation, *Doctrina Russorum de statu justitiae originalis* (The doctrine of the Russians concerning the state of original justice). That same year, Dr. Jurgis Matulewicz returned to the diocese of Kielce and began his pastoral ministry as the assistant priest in Imielo. A few months later, he was appointed professor of Latin and canon law at the diocesan seminary in Kielce; eventually he was named vice rector of the seminary and a member of the cathedral chapter.

The state of his health worsened again seriously. He went this time to Warsaw to recuperate.

During his stay in Warsaw, Dr. Matulewicz devoted himself intensively to social service activities, working together with his friend Marcel Godlewski, a well-known sociologist. Through his initiative at the time, the Association of Christian Workers was founded in Warsaw. In 1907, he began organizing conferences on social issues. At the same time, he did pastoral work in Warsaw among the Lithuanians living there. In 1907, Dr. Matulewicz received a professorship at the Roman Catholic Academy in Saint Petersburg. There he taught sociology at first, then dogmatic theology. In 1908, the additional duties of serving as spiritual director and vice rector of the Academy were assigned to him.

It should be emphasized especially at this point that, in 1909, Professor Matulewicz saved the religious order of Marians from dying out. The order had been forbidden in Russia; at the time it had only one religious house left, located in the native place of Professor Matulewicz, in Mariampolé. In that house lived the last member of the community and the last general superior, Vincent Sekowski. So Professor Matulewicz obtained permission from the Holy See to enter the Marian Order secretly and to take religious vows without completing a novitiate. He then drew up new constitutions. Very quietly, then, the community continued in existence. When the general superior Vincent Sekowski died in 1911, three priests, namely, Professor Matulewicz, Francis Bucys, and John Totoraitis, gathered in the sacristy of a church for a general chapter meeting. Professor Matulewicz was elected the new general superior. He remained in that post until his death in 1927. Under his direction, the Order of Marians flourished again, so much so that at his death it had 319 members. But Professor Matulewicz was not only active in the Marian Order. He also assisted in the difficult births of two communities of women religious: the Sisters of the Poor (better known later by the name Sisters of the Immaculate Conception of the Blessed Virgin Mary) and the Handmaids of Jesus in the Eucharist, so that he is considered to be the founder of both.

At the outbreak of the First World War, in 1914, Professor Matulewicz remained in Poland and stayed in a former Camaldolese monastery in Bielany, near Warsaw. Here he established a novitiate for his order and an orphanage for two hundred orphaned children. At the end of World War I, Professor Matulewicz resettled in Mariampolé, in Lithuania—where he should be called Matulaitis again—and had the members of his order follow him there. His stay in Mariampolé lasted only a short time, however, because in 1918 Pope Benedict XV appointed him bishop of Vilnius. This episcopal see had been vacant since 1907, when Bishop Eduard van Ropp was banished by the tsarist authorities. During the seven years in which Bishop Matulaitis lived and worked in Vilnius, he developed an extremely intensive apostolate. In his efforts to settle differences among Lithuanian, Polish, and Russian nationals, he also managed to make many enemies for himself. At any rate, the years in Vilnius from 1918 to 1925 were very difficult for Bishop Matulaitis. He proved himself, however, to be an exceptionally wise, prudent, and just ordinary.

When the Holy See and Poland entered into a concordat in 1925, Vilnius was elevated to the status of an archdiocese. When that occurred, Bishop Matulaitis did not want to stand in the Vatican's way concerning the appointment to the metropolitan see; rather, he asked twice, on May 1 and June 27, 1925, to be relieved of the administration of the archdiocese of Vilnius. Pope Pius XI accepted his resignation on July 14, 1925. Bishop Matulaitis now wanted to devote himself entirely and exclusively to the direction and development of his religious order. He went to Rome on August 15, 1925, with the intention of establishing there the generalate and the house of studies (Marianum) for his order, but on September 1, 1925, Pius XI appointed him apostolic visitor for the Church of Lithuania. He was charged with restoring and reorganizing its structure, in the manner subsequently determined in the papal bull *Lituanorum gente*, dated April 4, 1926. Henceforth, the Lithuanian ecclesiastical province would consist of the metropolitan see of Kaunas, in addition to nine dioceses and a *praelatura nullius*.[2] Bishop Matulaitis, the apostolic visitor, made efforts to restore relations between the Lithuanian government and the Holy See. He selected suitable candidates for the

[2] A *praelatura nullius* [*dioecesis*] is a specially demarcated territory, distinct from any diocese, which is governed by an ordinary. Such a territory could consist of three or more parishes or of the lands within the jurisdiction of an abbot-ordinary, for example, of Monte Cassino.— TRANS.

episcopal sees in Lithuania and prepared the groundwork for a concordat between Lithuania and the Holy See. Quite unexpectedly, Bishop Matulaitis died on January 27, 1927, in Kaunas, at the age of fifty-six.

It must also be mentioned here, certainly, that there were cordial relations between George Matulaitis and Pope Pius XI. The Pope characterized the Lithuanian bishop even during his lifetime as a "genuinely holy man". To anyone who would listen, Pope Pius XI said repeatedly that he considered Bishop Matulaitis to be the most capable ordinary in that northeastern part of Europe. Pius XI described Bishop Matulaitis as an "unusually close priest-friend" for whom he felt "trust and affection". After all, Achille Ratti, later Pope Pius XI, had been sent to Warsaw in 1918 as apostolic visitator and nuncio and had spent three years there. He not only corresponded regularly with Bishop Matulaitis, but also met with him frequently. "More than once," wrote Pius XI shortly after he was elected the successor of Saint Peter, "We have seen for Ourselves, the wisdom and justice with which You fulfill Your duties as a good shepherd."

Pope John Paul II, too, has a great respect for Bishop Matulaitis; he demonstrated this on the occasion of the 600th anniversary of the "baptism" of Lithuania in his apostolic letter of June 5, 1987. There the Pope wrote, among other things,

> Lithuania's six hundred years of Christian life include countless testimonies to the uninterrupted action of the Holy Spirit, who has adorned your Church with his fruits (cf. Gal 5:22), raising up a multitude of men and women worthy of recognition as true disciples of Christ. I would like to recall with you some of the sons and daughters of Lithuania who have left in the hearts of the people the indelible mark of their virtues and their apostolic zeal.

First of all, Pope John Paul II mentions Saint Casimir, then Bishop Merkelis Giedraitis, "a true apostle of the Tridentine Reform", and also Bishop Motiejus Valancius. Finally, he turns his attention to Bishop Matulaitis, "another most worthy son of the Lithuanian Church and Nation", who is deservedly being raised to the honors of the altar. As

a true "servant and apostle of Jesus Christ" (2 Pet 1:1) he was in Vilnius the far-sighted and caring Pastor of all of his children, even the most remote. Faithful to his episcopal motto, "Conquer Evil with Good", he faced many serious difficulties in the exercise of his ministry, making himself "a slave to all, that he might win the more" (cf. 1 Cor 9:19), and caring only for the good of the Church and for the salvation of souls.

Many pastoral initiatives remain associated with his fruitful ecclesial service, among which I wish to mention the works of lay apostolate and the dissemination of the Church's social teaching, whereby he sought to alert the faithful to their responsibility to restore all things in Christ. We also owe to him the reform of his Congregation of Marian Clerics and the foundation of the Congregation of Sisters of the Immaculate Conception and the Congregation of Handmaids of Jesus in the Eucharist.

Named by Pope Pius XI Apostolic Visitator to Lithuania, this Servant of God worked with prudence and zeal, thus enabling the Pope to establish the Ecclesiastical Province of Lithuania with the Apostolic Constitution *Lituanorum Gente* (4 April 1926). Catholic life experienced a notable revival in the area of catechetics, priestly and religious vocations, Catholic Action activities and various cultural expressions inspired by the Gospel.

The good seed sown so generously by Bishop Matulaitis produced a hundredfold, and the Church experienced a new spring. But he himself wished to become a seed which dies in the earth so as not to remain alone but to bear much fruit (cf. Jn 12:21), and this is evident from this touching invocation which he left as a kind of testament in his spiritual diary, and which I wish to repeat with you today: "Jesus, grant that I may immolate myself for your Church, for the salvation of the souls redeemed by your Blood, so that I may live with you, work with you, suffer with you, and, as I hope, also die and reign with you." [3]

At the Angelus after the beatification ceremony on June 28, 1987, Pope John Paul II said:

This morning the Church of Rome, together with the sister Churches of Europe, was spiritually united, with a solemn concelebration in St Peter's Basilica, to the Bishops of Lithuania who are celebrating today at Vilnius the sixth centenary of the "Baptism" of that Nation.

At the same time I had the joy of raising to the honours of the altars a great son of that people, the Servant of God [George Matulaitis (Matulewicz)], Archbishop and Religious, founder and reformer of religious congregations, animated by a great love for Our Lady Immaculate, an eminent figure of an indefatigable and intrepid pastor.[4]

In the homily at the beatification, the Pope called Blessed George Matulaitis "a pastor full of courage and initiative, capable of facing, with prudence and a spirit of sacrifice, situations of difficulty for the Church." [5]

[3] L'Osservatore Romano, June 29, 1987, p. 2.
[4] L'Osservatore Romano, July 6, 1987, p. 7.
[5] Ibid.

Blessed
Marcel Callo

Martyr

b. December 6, 1921,
Rennes, France
d. March 19, 1945,
concentration camp at
Mauthausen (Upper Austria)

Beatified October 4, 1987

In this French martyr, who was a member of the Young Christian
Workers movement in France; became a victim of Nazi tyranny in
the concentration camp at Mauthausen, Austria (Gusen II); and
was beatified on October 4, 1987, Pope John Paul II gave Catholic
youth throughout the world, and especially in France and Austria,
a splendid example of unshakeable fidelity to the Catholic faith.

Marcel Callo[1] was born into a deeply devout family on December 6, 1921, in the city of Rennes, in western France, the sixth of
nine brothers, of whom one became a priest. For seven years,
young Callo went to his parish church every day in the early
morning to serve at Mass. Therefore, now that he has been beatified, he makes a splendid patron for altar servers in particular.

On October 1, 1934, Marcel began his apprenticeship in a print
shop in the city of Rennes. In his free time, he was an enthusiastic
participant in scouting activities. After completing his apprenticeship, he became a member of the *Jeunesse Ouvrière Chrétienne*

[1] J.-B. Jégo, *Un exemple: Marcel Callo, 1921–1945* (Rennes, 1948). *Marcel Callo, Zeuge
des Glaubens und der Versöhnung: eine Dokumentation von Josef Reding* (Franz Sales-Verlag
Eichstätt, 1991).

(J.O.C. = Young Christian Workers). Within the ranks of the Christian working-class youth, he was active in the lay apostolate from then on. Very soon he became a group leader. As a result of the occupation of his French homeland, however, Marcel was caught up in the National Socialist war machine in March 1943. He was assigned to the *Service du Travail Obligatoire* [compulsory work force] and shipped off to Germany as a laborer, where he had to toil in the Zella-Melhis work camp in Thuringia. There he used his scant free time doing apostolic work in secret among his fellow internees, so as to alleviate their bitter fate far from home.

It was not long before Marcel Callo was accused of being "much too Catholic". On April 19, 1944, he was incarcerated in Gotha. For the young Christian worker, the following five months were extremely bitter, filled with unspeakable physical and spiritual sufferings. Yet he endured everything with Christian heroism and in doing so matured, achieving genuine sanctity.

On October 4, 1944, Marcel Callo was transferred from the prison in Gotha to the concentration camp at Mauthausen in Upper Austria. There the brave young Christian was subjected to deprivations of every sort, to murderously hard labor, and to a strict prohibition of any and all contacts with his native land or his family in Rennes. These unremitting hardships left him physically and emotionally ruined, until death came on March 19, 1945, shortly before the end of the war, and put an end to his earthly life.

On October 4, 1987, Pope John Paul, at the beatification of Marcel Callo, gave the following description of this blessed of the Young Christian Workers:

Yes, in his mercy, the Lord has always given . . . to his people a cohort of saints who proclaim the greatness of man when he permits himself to be seized and led by the Spirit of God.

Marcel Callo, whom I have the joy of declaring Blessed, in the midst of his family, of his diocese of Rennes and of numerous representatives of the J.O.C. and of Scouting, *did not arrive alone* at the point of evangelical perfection. A humble family, deeply Christian, carried him. Scouting, then the J.O.C., took their turn. Nourished by prayer, the sacraments and an apostolic action that reflected the teaching of these movements, he built Church with his brothers, the young Christian workers. It is in the Church that one becomes Christian, and it is with the Church that one builds a new humanity.

Marcel *did not immediately reach* evangelical perfection. Full of talents and of good will, he also knew long struggles against the spirit of the world, against himself, against the weight of things and of people. But, fully open to grace, he let himself be led progressively by the Lord, even until martyrdom.

The trial matured his personal love for Christ. From his prison he wrote to his brother, recently ordained a priest: "Fortunately, he is a *Friend* who does not leave me alone a single instant and knows how to sustain me and console me. During these crushing and painful hours, everything is borne with him. How grateful I am to Christ for having traced for me the path on which I am at this time."

Yes, Marcel met the Cross. First, in France. Then torn from the affection of his family and of a fiancée whom he loved tenderly and chastely—in Germany, where he relaunches the J.O.C. with some friends, several of whom also died witnesses of the Lord Jesus. Chased by the Gestapo, Marcel continued until the end. Like the Lord, he loved his own until the end and his entire life became eucharist.

Having reached the eternal joy of God, he testifies that the Christian faith does not separate earth from heaven. Heaven is prepared on earth in justice and love. When one loves, one is already "Blessed". Colonel Tibodo, who had seen thousands of prisoners die, was present on the morning of 19 March 1945; he testifies insistently and with emotion: Marcel had the appearance of a saint.

The living message left by the Young Christian Worker Marcel Callo concerns all of us.

To the young Christian workers, he shows the extraordinary radiance of those who let themselves be inhabited by Christ and give themselves to the integral liberation of their brothers.

To the Christians of the diocese of Rennes . . . , Marcel Callo recalls the spiritual fruitfulness of Brittany, when she knows how to live the faith of her fathers.

To all of us, laity, religious, priests or bishops, he relaunches the universal call to holiness: a holiness and a spiritual youth which the world needs so much in order to continue to announce the Good News "in good times and in bad"![2]

Blessed Marcel Callo

[2] *L'Osservatore Romano*, October 12, 1987, p. 19.

Blessed Antonia Mesina

Martyr of Purity

b. June 21, 1919, Orgósolo, Sardinia

d. May 17, 1935, in the forest of Orgósolo

Beatified October 4, 1987

At the age of not quite sixteen years, a young girl, Antonia Mesina, experienced the fulfillment of the beatitude: "Be faithful unto death, and I will give you the crown of life" (Rev 2:10). This girl from Sardinia is also one of the company of those who, during the twentieth century, followed the example of Saint Maria Goretti.

On June 21, 1919, she was born, the second child of Agostino Rubanu and his wife, Grazia, née Rubanu, a couple who lived in Orgósolo, diocese of Nuoro, on the island of Sardinia, who welcomed all eight of their children as gifts from God. The large family lived very simply. From 1929 to 1931, Antonia belonged to the Catholic youth group of her home parish, and then, from 1934 until her premature death, she was a member of the Young Women of Catholic Action. On May 17, 1935, while gathering firewood in the forest, she was attacked by a lecher who intended to rape her. When Antonia bravely defended herself, the fiend murdered her. At her burial, two days later, the entire population of the village of Orgósolo accompanied the youthful martyr of purity to her final resting-place. A Passionist priest, Father Fortunato, has described the life of this courageous girl in a book, *Antonia Mesina, uccisa come Santa Maria Goretti* [Antonia Mesina, murdered like Saint Maria Goretti].[1]

When Antonia Mesina was declared blessed on October 4, 1987, Pope John Paul II said:

Rejoice with me . . . , you of the diocese of Nuoro, you inhabitants of Orgósolo and of all Sardegna, for *young Antonia Mesina*, whom we proclaim Blessed today. Her martyrdom is first of all the arrival point of humble and joyous dedication to the life of a large family. It was her constant "yes" to the hidden service in the home that prepared her for a total "yes".

From early childhood—early post-war years—Antonia experienced the severity of her land and the generosity of its people. Guided by her parents, the teacher and the pastor, she courageously opened herself to the *values of life and faith*. Particularly at the school of Young Women of Catholic Action she set down deep human and Christian roots of a desire for purity and of giving.

And at only sixteen years, she found herself living her heroic "yes" to the *beatitude of purity*, defended to the point of supreme sacrifice.

The bundle of wood gathered to make bread in the oven at home, that day in May of 1935, remains on the hills beside her body torn apart by tens and tens of blows with a rock. That day another fire was lit and another bread was prepared for a much larger family.

Blessed because they were "pure of heart", *Marcel* [Callo], *Pierina* [Morosini] and *Antonia* [Mesina] are offered to you, lay faithful, to you, youth, as witnesses of a *love on a journey*, able to see beyond the human, to "see God" (Mt 5:8); they are offered to you as examples of *mature faith*, free of compromises, aware of

---

[1] P. Fortunato, *Antonia Mesina, uccisa come Santa Maria Goretti* (Rome, 1974).

the human and Christian dignity of the person, as a *song of hope* for the new generations which the Spirit continues to call to the radicality of the Gospel.[2]

[2] *L'Osservatore Romano*, October 12, 1987, pp. 19–20.

Blessed
Pierina Morosini

Factory Worker,
Martyr of Purity

b. January 7, 1931,
   Fiobbio di Albino, Italy
d. April 6, 1957,
   Bergamo, Italy

Beatified October 4, 1987

It is evidently a particular concern of the Holy Father, Pope John
Paul II, through beatifications and canonizations, to provide models of courage in the struggle to preserve purity of heart to the
girls and young women of today, who are at such great risk from
the sexual libertinism of our time. And this he did at the beatification on October 4, 1987, when he beatified two girls who suffered
martyrdom while fighting for their purity and virginity: Pierina
(Petrina) Morosini and Antonia Mesina.

Pierina Morosini[1] was born on January 7, 1931, in the village of
Fiobbio, in the municipality of Albino, diocese of Bergamo, in
Italy, the first of nine children of a farming couple of modest
means, Rocco Morosini and Sara, née Noris. At the age of six, on
January 10, 1937, she received the sacrament of confirmation, and
she made her First Holy Communion on June 5, 1938, when she
was seven. Both sacraments had extraordinarily beneficial results
in Pierina's spiritual life.

After completing primary school, she attended a women's trade

---

[1] B. Verzeroli, *Pierina Morosini* (Bergamo, 1960).

school, where she learned to be a clothing cutter and a seamstress. She went on to work in the Honegger textile factory in Albino. With her earnings she provided the support needed by her large family, since her father by then was unable to work. Pierina was a member of the Young Women of Catholic Action and diligently participated in all their activities within the parish. She was particularly involved in promoting vocations to the priesthood and the religious life and in working for the foreign missions.

On April 27, 1947, she made a pilgrimage to Rome and took part in the beatification of Maria Goretti. This journey, the only time in her entire life that she traveled a great distance, must have made a strong impression on Pierina. In the plan of God's providence, she was to have the same lot as Saint Maria Goretti.

Every day, before Pierina went to work at the textile factory, she made a visit to the parish church, attended Mass there, and received Holy Communion. As she walked to church and to the factory, she regularly prayed the Rosary.

On April 4, 1957, in the afternoon, having completed her work, she set out on the way home. On an isolated stretch of road near Monte Misma, she was attacked by a wicked fiend who wanted to have his way with her. Pierina is sure to have resisted with all her might, and he struck her a mortal blow with a rock. Her relatives, who were troubled that Pierina still had not arrived home late that evening, which was not at all like her, looked for her anxiously and then found her, horribly maltreated and unconscious. As quickly as possible, Pierina was brought to the main hospital in Bergamo. She died there two days later, on April 6, 1957, without having recovered consciousness. The surgeon at the hospital, who had tried to save Pierina's life, cried out spontaneously at the moment of her death, "Now we have another Maria Goretti!"

In his homily at the beatification on October 4, 1987, Pope John Paul II said the following about this new blessed:

Rejoice with me and with the whole Church, you brothers and sisters of the diocese of Bergamo, inhabitants of Fiobbio and of

Albino, who came to Rome for the beatification of *Pierina Morosini*.

The roots of her religious spirit are in the midst of you. Having grown up in an environment of an intense *spiritual life incarnate in the family*, Blessed [Pierina] Morosini followed Christ, poor and humble, in the daily care of many people. Having discovered that "she could become holy without entering the convent", she opened herself lovingly to *parish life*, to Catholic Action and to the vocational apostolate. Personal prayer, daily participation at Holy Mass and spiritual direction led her to understand the will of God and the expectations of her brothers, and to bring to maturity the decision to consecrate herself privately to the Lord in the world.

For ten years she lived the difficulties and joys of a *worker in a cotton-mill* of the area, working shifts and always travelling on foot. Her colleagues testify to her fidelity to work, her friendliness joined to reserve, the esteem that she enjoyed as a woman and as a believer.

On her way home, thirty years ago, her martyrdom was consummated, the extreme consequence of her Christian integrity. *Her steps however did not stop*, but continue to mark a luminous path for all those who experience the attraction of evangelical challenges.[2]

---

[2] *L'Osservatore Romano*, October 12, 1987, p. 19.

Blessed
Arnould Jules Nicholas Rèche

Christian Brother

b. *September 2, 1838,*
Landroff, Alsace
d. *October 23, 1890,*
Reims, France

Beatified November 1, 1987

Brother Arnould,[1] a teaching brother in the order of Saint John Baptist de la Salle, was declared blessed and raised to the glory of the altars on the feast of All Saints 1987, in Saint Peter's in Rome. He came into the world on September 2, 1838, the first of nine children of Claude and Anna Rèche, née Clausset, in Landroff, diocese of Metz, and on the same day he was baptized with the name Jules Nicholas. Besides the deep faith and righteousness of his parents, there was little else in that world except poverty. So it remained in the years that followed, during Jules' childhood and youth. Despite everything, he had a happy childhood. When he was old enough to be apprenticed, Jules became a servant of the Grueber family, who grew quite fond of the youth because of his diligence and his tactful behavior. Through his work for the Grueber family, Jules not only earned a living for himself, but also was able to help support his sick mother and the many brothers and sisters in his needy family. On Sundays and holy days, Jules assisted the pastor and served him at the altar. In this he was an

---

[1] A. de Lande, *Frère Arnould, ami des jeunes* (Moulins-les-Metz, 1981).

example of diligence and devotion for the other young boys of that locality. At the age of twenty-one, Jules completed his service with the Grueber family. From 1859 to 1862, he was employed in the construction of a church in Charleville, France; here, too, he gave his fellow workers an excellent example.

One day Jules met teaching brothers who, for the first time since the Revolution, had returned to Charleville. Jules took courses with them on Sundays and holy days in their Oratory. One day he asked the director of the Christian Brothers to admit him also to the evening courses held on workdays, so that he could complete his education. This regular contact with the Christian Brothers eventually inspired Jules with the thought of consecrating himself to God as they did, in the work of educating youth. On November 13, 1862, he began the novitiate and soon after received the religious habit and the religious name Arnould [Arnold]. One year later, in 1863, Brother Arnould was assigned to the Christian Brothers community in Reims to work in the school. In the fourteen years that Brother Arnould spent in Reims, he made such good progress in his cultural, theological, and ascetical formation, that at the age of thirty-nine he was appointed novice master. He held that office for thirteen years, during which he demonstrated marvelous tact and magnanimity in guiding the future religious of his community. Finally, he became the superior of the community of Christian Brothers in Reims, which was dedicated to the Sacred Heart of Jesus. On October 23, 1890, the exemplary teaching brother suffered a serious aneurysm of the brain, which on that same day put an end to his earthly life.

In 1987, Pope John Paul II said the following about Brother Arnould Rèche at his beatification:

Among these disciples of Christ signed with the seal of holiness, I have the joy today [on the Solemnity of All Saints], to declare as blessed Brother Arnould, who allowed himself to be seized by "the Holy Spirit, the Sanctifier, the Unifier"; who said, "it is in the heart of Our Lord above all that one must seek the Holy Spirit on earth."

Holiness took form in him in a way of poverty, in the work which he began at a very early age in order to help his family. Until adulthood, the future De La Salle Brother responded fully to his Christian vocation. He continued his formation in spite of obstacles. He lived his faith intensely and knew how to become a convincing witness of it to those around him. As a poor man, in accepting trials, he was happy to advance with sure step towards the Kingdom of God.

With simplicity, Jules Rèche entered into the state of lay religious life. Once he had become Brother Arnould, he developed his natural gifts as an educator. With sure judgement, he showed himself an example of equilibrium. He invited his pupils to develop their knowledge, at the same time developing good human relations and a demanding spiritual life. His influence is due as much to his professional awareness as to his generous dedication and the profundity of his faith.

His way of being a "pure heart", to whom it is given to "see God" was an austere asceticism, a life of prayer which impressed his brothers, a self-offering in union with the Passion of Christ, his familiarity with the Word of God which nourished him, his happiness in serving God, thanksgiving, which he called a "true prayer of love". According to the testimony of a retreatant, Brother Arnould drew his "tranquillity, prudence, light and silence" from the constant presence of the Holy Spirit within him. Let us invoke him that, as the spiritual master that he was in the last century, he may sustain his brothers today in their life dedicated to education in all its forms. We ask him to help youths become Christian adults, happy to see themselves as children of God in seeking, according to the Beatitudes, justice and peace.[2]

[2] *L'Osservatore Romano*, October 26, 1987, p. 20.

Blessed
Ulrika Franziska Nisch

Servant, Nun

b. September 18, 1882,
Mittelbiberach-Oberdorf,
Baden-Württemberg, Germany
d. May 8, 1913,
Hegne, Bodensee

Beatified November 1, 1987

On All Saints Day in 1987, Pope John Paul II beatified two German nuns, Holy Cross Sister Ulrika Nisch[1] and Ursuline Sister Blandina Merten.

Ulrika Nisch was born an illegitimate child on September 18, 1882, in Mittelbiberach-Oberdorf in Upper Swabia (Baden-Württemberg). Her parents were Ulrich Nisch and Klothilde Dettenrieder. They wanted to get married, but the mother of the bride was against the marriage; the mayor of the village, too, refused to proceed with the formalities of a civil marriage because Ulrich Nisch, a stableman, had no financial means whatsoever to support a family. Now those two stubborn young people wanted to obtain marriage by having a child. During her pregnancy, Klothilde Dettenrieder had much to suffer from her mother and the inhabitants of the village, which probably had an effect on her child. At her baptism in the parish church in Mittelbiberach, the

---

[1] B. Baur, *Kein Mass kennt die Liebe: Das Leben der Dienerin Gottes Schwester Ulrika Nisch von Hegne* (Constance, 1963). Klaus Hemmerle, *Die leise Stimme: Ulrika Nisch, ihr Weg und ihre Botschaft* (Freiburg, 1988).

child received the name Franziska, after her maternal grandmother, as a sign of reconciliation. It was not until one year later that Ulrich Nisch and Klothilde Dettenrieder were able to marry; from then on they lived in Unterstadion. Although both parents worked tirelessly, as did their children later on—of thirteen, only five reached adulthood—the family was always needy. Franziska spent the first years of her life in Mittelbiberach-Oberdorf with her grandmother and with her mother's sister, Gertrud Dettenrieder, who was also her godmother. At a very early age, Fränzi, as she was called, learned how to pray; she also liked to go with the grown-ups to church.

In 1889, Franziska was brought by her parents to Unterstadion to attend school there; she was shy and tended to remain in the background. At home she found it difficult to relate to her parents, particularly because her father was very stern with her. She was allowed to spend her last two years of school in Mittelbiberach-Oberdorf, living with her aunt again. Even after leaving school, she stayed with her aunt and helped out by giving lessons, working in the inn, and especially by taking care of her aunt's two little boys.

In 1898, Franziska was sent to Sauggart to an uncle who ran a general store and a dairy. There Franziska was exploited to the point of exhaustion. She then exchanged that job for one in a household in Biberach that had a bakery, a brewery, and a tavern. When she learned that German girls were paid much higher wages in Switzerland, she applied for a position there, so that she could help her parents and brothers and sisters more. So, in 1901, Franziska became a maidservant in Rohrschach, by Lake Constance, in the household of Josef Vinzenz Morger, the director of the pedagogical institute; her chief duty there was to take care of the four children.

Several times before that, Franziska had expressed the desire to become a nun in a strictly cloistered convent, but her relatives always advised against it, since she could not scrape together the dowry with which a candidate usually entered the convent. Only her former catechist and pastor, Father Joseph Rupf, encouraged her by remarking, "If you have the calling, then you must also go!"

When Franziska came down with erysipelas in the spring of 1904, she was cared for in the hospital in Rohrschach by Holy Cross Sisters from the motherhouse in Ingenbohl. The unselfishness and devotion of the sisters impressed her, and she made a definite decision to become a nun. Her confessor, Father Helg, advised her to enter the newly founded provincial house in Hegne. He arranged for her to be admitted, despite her illegitimate birth and lack of dowry. On October 17, 1904, Franziska went to the provincial house of the Holy Cross Sisters in Hegne, near Constance, north of the island of Reichenau. There the novice mistress asked her what work she would particularly like to have. She answered, "Give me a job where I can make many sacrifices." And so it was, then: she was assigned to work in the kitchen. Amid the pots and pans, from then on for the next nine years, until her death, she would gradually attain sanctity.

So that she could try working on a hospital ward, the candidate was sent on May 5, 1905, to Zell-Weierbach, near Offenburg. There she had to cook for the religious community, take care of the housecleaning by herself, and help out in caring for the sick. In 1906, she was called back to Hegne, where, on April 24, 1906,

Mittelbiberach Castle in Württemberg. In the stables of this castle, the father of Ulrika Nische was employed as a stableman.

she received the habit and was admitted to the novitiate. As her name in religion she received her father's name, Ulrich, and from then on was called Sister Ulrika; again she had to work hard and conscientiously in the convent kitchen. As a novice she set a fine example for the other novices as to how a nun prays, obeys, and unselfishly loves God and her fellow men.

After the novitiate year, Sister Ulrike took her first vows on April 24, 1907. She did so exclaiming, "I have reached the goal. I am so happy!" On the day after her profession, Sister Ulrika was transferred to the hospital in Bühl to take charge of the hospital kitchen there. One year later, she became the second cook at the Saint Vincent House in Baden-Baden. Here she was always an encouraging example for the maids and the apprentice girls, whose work she had to organize.

The religious and ascetical formation of the sisters in Hegne was guided during the years 1900 to 1909 by the spiritual director Adolf Schwarz. He sought to teach the sisters in particular a twofold lesson: love of seclusion and love of humiliations. In both of these, Sister Ulrika was his best student: she loved the obscurity of a hidden life, and "for love of the Savior" she longed for humiliations. Her motto was: "Love knows no measure, so in love and for love we should just suffer everything and work." She was not content with performing her duties conscientiously; she was always ready to help everybody, to encourage all to do good, and, by her example of complete abandonment, to bring them closer to Christ, whom she loved more than anything.

Sister Ulrika found strength for her sacrificial life in prayer. Despite her very heavy physical labor, she experienced no fatigue at prayer. She always knelt upright, with her eyes closed or directed to the tabernacle. It is evident—from the notes that she wrote down under obedience to her confessor—that she led a profound interior life and achieved a genuinely mystical state in the prayer of quiet and in ecstasy; she also experienced mystical espousals and spiritual marriage with Christ. Visions also were granted to her; for instance, at the very beginning of her religious life she saw her guardian angel, and she thought that everybody would eventually see one. Later came additional visions concerning God, the Blessed Virgin, angels, and other saints. She was even permitted to have glimpses into the future.

Because this Holy Cross nun received extraordinary graces, it was also her lot to go through unusual trials: besides humiliations and illness, she suffered spiritual aridity, desolation, and, worst of all, doubts as to whether she was the victim of delusions. At the beginning of 1912, the grace-filled illuminations, visions, and raptures gradually ceased, and instead she suffered more and more from the thought that it had all been just her imagination and the work of the devil, who now appeared to her in the place of her guardian angel and frequently vexed her quite dreadfully; he often tormented her day and night. At the same time, an impenetrable darkness descended upon Sister Ulrika's spirit.

The anxieties and doubts about the faith became horrific. She saw the devil following and pursuing her everywhere, and it appeared that she was to a certain extent delivered over to him. In her great distress on account of the devil, her interior doubts, and spiritual darkness, Sister Ulrika perseveringly had recourse to prayer and obedience to her superior, who looked after her with maternal care. Moreover, witnesses have been correct in emphasizing that the power of God's grace was evident in Sister Ulrika's way of remaining cheerful and kind, despite her sufferings and trials, and accepting everything "for the love of God".

From her notebooks we know that God had already prepared her two years previously, in 1910, for this obsession by Satan. "I saw a striking picture. It was a long, wide corridor, filled with smoke and fog, and it billowed and writhed so, that in my whole life I have never seen anything like it. One cannot possibly imagine it. I noticed that there was always someone beside me. [When receiving Communion,] I asked my Bridegroom, when we were together, what it meant. And he said that I would still have to weather many more storms which the evil fiend was brewing. And then I understood what the whirling smoke meant."

The real confrontation with the devil began in 1912, and by then she had already stopped keeping a notebook of her personal experiences; therefore we learn nothing more from the nun herself about this terrible satanic persecution. All the more valuable, therefore, is the following testimony of Sister Michaela: "In one stroke everything was gone. She never saw her guardian angel beside her any more; the Savior, the Blessed Mother of God, all the many saints with whom she had conversed—all gone. Instead of her guardian angel, the devil came now and tormented her day and night. Many times I found her sitting very sadly in a corner. She had to struggle with awful doubts about the state of her soul."

In early 1912, Sister Ulrika made a retreat in Hegne. When she returned to Baden-Baden, Sister Michaela asked her what she had experienced during the spiritual exercises. Sister Ulrika reported physical and spiritual trials of every kind. She then made a telling remark, which her superior quoted verbatim: "All I would have had to do was to stretch out my arms, then I would have been like the Savior on the cross."

The archabbot of Beuron, Benedict Baur, O.S.B., in his biography *Kein Mass kennt die Liebe* [Love knows no measure], comments as follows on these demonic assaults:

Anyone who has read or heard of the often long, drawn-out sufferings and trials which saintly and highly-favored souls undergo, finds nothing remarkable in the demonic persecutions, the strange spiritual states of interior darkness and desolation, the severe doubts about the faith and the temptations to sadness which the Servant of God suffered. Those are simply the means with which God, who is a jealous God [cf. Ex 34:14, Deut 4:24, etc.], works upon the soul, in order to prepare her for perfect union with him in love."

We owe the concrete details to a report by the superior, Sister Bonaventura, in whom Sister Ulrika placed a special trust:

At the beginning of 1912 the rapture ceased, little by little. A great dryness came over her. She suffered mainly from the trial of wondering whether it had all been her imagination, whether it was all from the Evil One, who then appeared to her, too, and plagued her. One day she came to me and asked what a "lodge" was. I was astonished and asked her what on earth she had to do with the Lodge. Then she said to me, "That One"—as she usually called the devil—"told me that I should go to the Lodge. There I would get clothing and money so that I could leave (the convent)." She suffered horribly from these constant torments. She told me that there were two nasty fellows beside her; the one always harassed her, while the other just looked on. She never saw anything with her bodily eyes; only interiorly. I could swear to everything that I have written.

We find an echo of the devilish temptations and torments in a letter that Sister Ulrika wrote in the late summer of 1912 to Sister Bonaventura, the superior in Baden-Baden: "I often think of what we went through, which no one even suspected. Now it is all over."

Due to fatal tuberculosis of the lungs and larynx, the kitchen nun at the Saint Vincent House in Baden-Baden had to give up her work in July 1912 and return to the provincialate. Now a candidate for death, she was still remarkable especially for her patience in suffering, her unpretentiousness, and her gratitude. On May 8, 1913, she died, "unselfishly, just as she had lived".

Very soon after Sister Ulrika was buried in the convent cemetery in Hegne, people came, at first the sisters of her community, then the faithful from all walks of life, to pray at the grave of this saintly nun with confidence for their various intentions. Many of them receive miraculous answers to their prayers. Sister Ulrika had said shortly before her death, "The good God wants me to die as I have lived. He will do what he pleases, in his own time." It pleased him to arrange things so that this Holy Cross nun, who attained perfection amid the pots and pans, would be the first of her congregation—even before its first general superior, the saintly Swiss nun Maria Theresia Scherer—to be raised to the honors of the altar.

In his homily at the beatification on November 1, 1987, in Saint Peter's Basilica in Rome, the Pope said that Ulrika Nisch was being beatified, "because she fulfilled the conditions of the Beatitudes of the gospel in the thirty-one years of her earthly journey." The Pope then spoke of the poverty of Sister Ulrika Nisch and of her serving in the last place; he referred to the trials of her sickly body and to the "occasional darkness" in her soul. But the love of God found no resistance in her thoughts, feelings and will. Having a pure heart, she was permitted even in this life "to see God" in mystical union [cf. Mt 5:8]. "Completely filled by God, Ulrika Nisch became more and more a vessel of his love which imbued all her external works and made the simplest services for those around her precious. . . . Indeed, she is blessed because she . . . trusted solely in the power of 'immeasurable Love' (cf. Mt 5:5)." [2]

---

[2] Benedict Bauer, O.S.B., *Kein Mass Kennt die Liebe* (Konststanz: Merk, 1969). See also *L'Osservatore Romano*, November 23, 1987, p. 8.

Blessed Blandina Maria Magdalena Merten

Religious

*b. July 10, 1883, Düppenweiler,
Saarland, Germany*
d. May 18, 1918, Trier

Beatified November 1, 1987

In the so-called *Stille Ecke*, or "quiet corner", of Saarland, in the village of Düppenweiler, Maria Magdalena[1] was born on July 10, 1883, to farmer Johann Merten and his wife and was welcomed into a family that already included her siblings Franz and Elise. This child who later became a holy nun, Sister Blandina, whom Pope John Paul II raised to the glory of the altars on November 1, 1987, was remarkable even at a very early age for her piety, kindness, and helpfulness.

From 1889 to 1897, Maria Magdalena attended the primary school of her native village. Not until the age of thirteen, on April 12, 1896, was she allowed to make her First Holy Communion, and a little later, on April 21, 1896, she received the sacrament of confirmation. In the years 1897 to 1899, the exemplary pupil was prepared for teacher-training college by her highly respected teacher Frau Genter, and at the same time the girl's services were enlisted as her assistant in the classroom.

From April 1899 until September 1902, then, Maria Magdalena

---

[1] H. Visarius, *Eine verborgene Gottesbraut* (Trier, 1967).

Merten studied at the women's pedagogical institute in Marienau, near Vallendar. She completed her studies and matriculated with a teacher's certificate.

From November 1902 until April 1908, the young teacher worked in a series of schools—in Oberthal near Sankt Wendel, in Morscheid in Hunsrück, and in Grossrosseln on the Saar River— where she was esteemed and well-liked by all. She also showed special love and concern for poor and sick children.

Together with her older sister, Elise, who until then had kept house for the young teacher, Maria Magdalena entered the Ursuline convent in Calvarienberg, near Ahrweiler, on April 22, 1908. She received the religious name Blandina, while her sister, Elise, was called Blanda. On November 3, 1910, they both made their temporary profession and on November 4, 1913, final profession. At that time Sister Blandina, with the approval of a Jesuit, Father Augustin Merk, took an additional vow, besides those of poverty, chastity, and obedience: the *votum victimae*, declaring her willingness to sacrifice anything and everything for Christ and to become more and more a victim soul. From then on, Sister Blandina had an inner certainty that the Lord had accepted this special vow of hers. The young nun, who was assigned to Saarbrücken in No-

Blandina Merten as a fifteen-year-old girl.

vember 1910 and sent to Trier in 1911, was in fact admitted soon afterward to the school of suffering when she contracted a serious case of tuberculosis.

As of the autumn of 1916, Sister Blandina's illness forced her to take up permanent residence in the infirmary of the Ursuline convent in Trier. Despite her pains, she was always cheerful and resigned to God's will, as is evident from her statement "O holy will of God, I love you above all things, and I would like to live on earth as though nothing existed except God and me. I want to love God more than any creature has ever loved him."

Sister Blandina was completely unselfish. She demanded nothing, never complained, but smiled all the time, happy that she was allowed to suffer for Christ and thus make atonement. Finally, when she had learned that it would only be a few more months until she went home, she rejoiced to share this "good news" with the people who were dearest to her. Despite the unceasing commotion and loud noise in Trier at that time, day and night, because of the war and the frequent attacks from the air, Sister Blandina remained quite calm in her seclusion and abandonment to God's will; she died peacefully in the Lord on May 18, 1918.

In a biography published in Trier in 1967, H. Visarius called Sister Blandina Merten *Eine verborgene Gottesbraut*—a hidden bride of God—and with her beatification on November 1, she was made known throughout the world.

To the German pilgrims who had come to Rome for the beatification of Sister Blandina Merten and Sister Ulrika Nisch, Pope John Paul II spoke on November 2, 1987, and said, among other things:

Our meeting here in the Vatican gives me the welcome opportunity to declare to all of you once more my heart-felt joy over the beatification of two of your fellow citizens, women from your homeland. Sister Ulrika Nisch and Sister Blandina Merten, the one a cook and the other a teacher: both Blessed, because in their life and work they were unreservedly open to the love of

God; because each one gave her heart, which God had filled, as a gift to her neighbors who were seeking and suffering; because they both accepted with confidence the allotted circumstances in which they lived, and which were sometimes hard, and made every effort, to the best of their ability, to make them fruitful for the kingdom of God.

At this point I would like to anticipate one possible misunderstanding: It was not their upbringing in poverty, nor their frail health, nor their employment in little-noticed, lowly tasks that led them to blessedness, but rather the spiritual strength that both of them drew from the wellspring of our faith, with which both Sisters deliberately accepted these adverse conditions and transformed them into a full and worthwhile life. They did not flee from the burdensome restrictions in their lives, but mastered them with God's help through their prayer and willingness to make sacrifices.

In doing so they did not retreat into their interior spiritual world in a self-satisfied way, but rather, following Christ's example, they generously shared with others the riches and treasures that were stored up in their hearts together with God's grace. By coming in contact with them, people who were dejected were encouraged and felt as though they were "in paradise". Here they experienced concretely and tangibly the power of a love that is kindled by God. From the circle of such richly gifted people then came the first witnesses who testified to their experience of genuine, unselfish love in dealing with Sister Ulrika and Sister Blandina. Their judgment was and is the foundation for the Church's declaration. Yes, these two lives have lasting worth in God's sight and an exemplary significance for us all![2]

---

[2] This talk has been translated from the German because it was not published in the English edition of *L'Osservatore Romano*. However, see *L'Osservatore Romano*, November 23, 1987, pp. 7–8, for the Holy Father's beatification homily.—ED.

Blessed George Haydock and Eighty-four Companions

Secular Priest, Martyr

b. circa 1557, Cottam Hall,
   near Preston, Lancashire,
   England
d. February 10, 1584,
   London

Beatified November 22, 1987

According to the Most Rev. John Brewer, Bishop of Lancaster, no picture of George Haydock exists. This window honors him.

Under the cruel queen of England Elizabeth I, countless priests and lay Christians suffered martyrdom for their fidelity to the Catholic faith and for defending the primacy of the successor of Peter in Rome. Fifty-four of these heroes of the faith were beatified in 1886, and an additional nine in 1895; two of the latter group, namely, the Lord Chancellor Thomas More and Bishop John Fisher, were canonized in 1935. Subsequently, in 1929, another one hundred thirty-six English martyrs were beatified. Pope Paul VI then canonized forty of the English martyrs: eleven of those beatified in 1886 and twenty-nine of those beatified in 1929.

Now, in turn, Pope John Paul II, on the feast of Christ the King (November 22) in 1987, raised eighty-five English martyrs to the glory of the altars, among them sixty-three priests (fifty-five diocesan priests and eight religious) and twenty-two laymen.

This new group of blessed English martyrs is headed by the diocesan priest George Haydock.[1] He is preeminent among the eighty-five martyrs because of his spirited defense of papal primacy during his trial and his rejection of the purported hierarchical authority of Queen Elizabeth I; for his courageous stance he then suffered martyrdom. The biography of this valiant priest is probably also the best documented of any of the eighty-five English martyrs. His life and death will be sketched briefly here, followed by a list of the other eighty-four English martyrs (with name, occupation, age, and the year and place of martyrdom). Almost all of these English martyrs gave witness by the shedding of their blood on the basis of a law, passed by the English Parliament in 1585, that was aimed at the priests and the laymen associated with them: men who had been ordained Catholic priests abroad after June 24, 1559, and who had then slipped back into England and taken up residence there were guilty of high treason and were sentenced to death.

George Haydock was born in 1557, in Cottam Hall, near Preston (Lancashire), the youngest child among four brothers and a sister. His parents, Vivian and Ellen (née Westby) Haydock, were a loyal Catholic couple. During the first years of young George's life, the Catholic Queen Mary died (1558), and Queen Elizabeth I took the throne and immediately started persecuting the Catholics. At the age of sixteen or seventeen, the youth was sent by his widowed father to the English college in Douay, France, which his mother's brother-in-law, William Allen (later a cardinal), had founded in 1568 as a seminary for the education of priests for the English mission. Between 1574 and 1603 (the year in which Queen Elizabeth I died), 438 priests loyal to the Pope were sent from Douay to England. One of the priests educated there was George Haydock; he did not spend all of his seminary years in Douay, however, but transferred to the English college in Rome, which was founded in 1579. There he received

<hr />

[1] N. Del Re, "Martiri di Inghilterra", in *Bibliotheca Sanctorum* 7:801–13.

the subdiaconate order on August 27, 1581, and, on September 3, 1581, ordination to the diaconate. Soon afterward he left the city of Rome, since it did not agree with his health, which had been weakened by illness. On November 2, 1581, he arrived in Reims, where, in 1578, the English college had been temporarily relocated. On December 21, 1581, George Haydock was ordained a priest. He celebrated his First Mass on January 4, 1582. After twelve days, the newly ordained priest left the mainland and traveled secretly to England with the clear understanding that, if his priestly vocation was discovered, he would be most severely punished as a traitor. In London he found a hiding place and from that base began his pastoral work. But as soon as February 6, 1582, he was arrested, because a certain Hawkinson had betrayed him. A meeting with a churchman who had Calvinist opinions ensued, who made it clear to the young priest that he would regain his freedom only if he rejected the papal primacy. That, however, George Haydock vehemently refused to do. Finally, he was put in the Tower of London, where he languished for two years. Several times Protestant ministers attempted to induce the Catholic priest George Haydock to denounce the Pope. He remained firm, however, in his loyalty to Rome. He even provoked his opponents with the sentence that he wrote on the door of his prison cell: "Gregory XIII is head of the English and of the universal Church, to whom both Queen Elizabeth and all the rest of the world must be subject, if they wish to be saved."

On the feast of Saint Peter's Chair at Rome, January 18, 1584, legal proceedings against George Haydock began. He declared that he was ready, with heartfelt gladness, to suffer anything for his Catholic faith, and he said once again quite emphatically that he was obliged to reject the supposed "supreme spiritual authority of the queen", because in the Church this belongs exclusively to the pope in Rome. In subsequent trials, George Haydock was accused of plotting a conspiracy against the queen to assassinate her. He energetically denied this accusation. Nevertheless, he, together with John Munden, John Nutter, and Thomas Hemerford, was sentenced to death on February 7, 1584, and was executed on February 10, 1584, at Tyburn. As a martyr who shed his blood in witness to fidelity to the Pope in Rome, he truly merits the title "blessed", together with eighty-four companions, whose names and dates follow:

From Yorkshire:
1. Marmaduke Bowes, husband and father, d. 1585 in York.
2. Francis Ingleby, diocesan priest, thirty-six years old, d. 1586 in York.
3. John Fingley, diocesan priest, thirty-three years old, d. 1586 in York.
4. Robert Bickerdike, apprentice, d. 1586 in York.
5. Alexander Crow, diocesan priest, thirty-six years old, d. 1586 in York.
6. Edmund Sykes, diocesan priest, thirty-seven years old, d. 1587 in York.
7. Richard Simpson, diocesan priest, thirty-four years old, d. 1588 in Derby.
8. William Spenser, diocesan priest, thirty-four years old, d. 1589 in York.
9. Robert Hardesty, domestic servant, d. 1589 in York.
10. Nicholas Horner, tailor, d. 1590 in Smithfield.
11. Richard Hill, diocesan priest, twenty-five years old, d. 1590 in Durham.
12. John Hogg, diocesan priest, twenty-five years old, d. 1590 in Durham.
13. Richard Holliday, diocesan priest, twenty-five years old, d. 1590 in Durham.
14. Robert Thorpe, diocesan priest, thirty-one years old, d. 1591 in York.
15. Thomas Watkinson, widower, d. 1591 in York.
16. Joseph Lambton, diocesan priest, twenty-four years old, d. 1592 in Newcastle.

17. William Knight, layman, twenty-three years old, d. 1596 in York.
18. William Gibson, layman, d. 1596 in York.
19. John Bretton, married man, sixty-nine years old, d. 1598 in York.
20. Peter Snow, diocesan priest, ordained 1591, d. 1598 in York.
21. Ralph Grimston, married man, d. 1598 in York.
22. Christopher Wharton, diocesan priest, sixty years old, d. 1600 in York.
23. Edward Thwing, diocesan priest, thirty-five years old, d. 1600 in Lancaster.
24. Thomas Palaser, diocesan priest, thirty years old, d. 1600 in Durham.
25. John Talbot, married man, d. 1600 in Durham.
26. Robert Middleton, S.J., Jesuit priest, thirty years old, d. 1601 in Lancaster.
27. Thurstan Hunt, diocesan priest, forty-six years old, d. 1601 in Lancaster.
28. Matthew Flathers, diocesan priest, forty-eight years old, d. 1608 in York.
29. Thomas Atkinson, diocesan priest, seventy-one years old, d. 1616 in York.
30. Nicholas Postgate, diocesan priest, eighty-two years old, d. 1679 in York.

From Lancashire:
31. William Thomson, diocesan priest, twenty-six years old, d. 1586 at Tyburn.
32. John Sandys, diocesan priest, thirty-four years old, d. 1586 in Gloucester.
33. George Beesley, diocesan priest, twenty-nine years old, d. 1591, in Fleet Street, London.
34. Edward Osbaldeston, diocesan priest, thirty-four years old, d. 1594 in York.
35. Robert Nutter, O.P., Dominican priest, forty-three years old, d. 1600 in Lancaster.

36. John Thules, diocesan priest, forty-eight years old, d. 1616 in Lancaster.
37. Roger Wrenno, weaver, forty years old, d. 1616 in Lancaster.
38. Edward Bamber, diocesan priest, forty-six years old, d. 1646 in Lancaster.
39. John Woodcock, O.F.M., friar and priest, forty-three years old, d. 1646 in Lancaster.
40. Thomas Whitaker, diocesan priest, thirty-five years old, d. 1646 in Lancaster.

From Durham:
41. Hugh Taylor, diocesan priest, twenty-six years old, d. 1585 in York.
42. Edward Burden, diocesan priest, forty-eight years old, d. 1588 in York.
43. John Norton, husband, d. 1600 in Durham.
44. William Southerne, diocesan priest, thirty-nine years old, d. 1618 in Newcastle.

From Gloucestershire:
45. Richard Sergeant, diocesan priest, twenty-eight years old, d. 1586 at Tyburn.
46. Henry Webley, layman, thirty years old, d. 1588 in Mile End Green, London.
47. William Lampley, glover, d. 1588 in Gloucester.

From London:
48. William Carter, printer, thirty-five years old, d. 1584 at Tyburn.
49. John Lowe, diocesan priest, thirty-three years old, d. 1586 at Tyburn.
50. Alexander Blake, stableman, d. 1590 in Grays Inn Lane, London.

From Warwickshire:

51. Robert Dibdale, diocesan priest, twenty-eight years old, d. 1586 at Tyburn.

52. Robert Grissold, layman, d. 1604 in Warwick.

From Buckinghamshire:

53. Thomas Belson, student, twenty-five years old, d. 1589 in Oxford.

54. Robert Drury, diocesan priest, thirty-nine years old, d. 1607 at Tyburn.

From Derbyshire:

55. Nicholas Garlick, diocesan priest, thirty-three years old, d. 1588 in Derby.

56. Robert Ludlam, diocesan priest, thirty-seven years old, d. 1588 in Derby.

From Dorset:

57. John Adams, diocesan priest, forty-three years old, d. 1586 at Tyburn.

58. William Pike, cabinetmaker, d. 1591 in Dorchester.

From Herefordshire:

59. Nicholas Wheeler, diocesan priest, thirty-six years old, d. 1586 at Tyburn.

60. Roger Cadwallader, diocesan priest, forty-four years old, d. 1610 in Leominster.

From Kent:

61. Edmund Duke, diocesan priest, twenty-seven years old, d. 1590 in Durham.

62. Roger Filcock, S.J., Jesuit priest, twenty-nine years old, d. 1601 at Tyburn.

From Lincolnshire:

63. Richard Yaxley, diocesan priest, twenty-nine years old, d. 1589 in Oxford.
64. Thomas Pormort, diocesan priest, thirty-two years old, d. 1592 in Saint Paul's London.

From Oxfordshire:

65. Stephen Rowsham, diocesan priest, thirty-two years old, d. 1587 in Gloucester.
66. George Nichols, diocesan priest, thirty-nine years old, d. 1589 in Oxford.

From Staffordshire:

67. Robert Sutton, diocesan priest, ordained 1578, d. 1588 in Stafford.
68. John Sugar, diocesan priest, forty-six years old, d. 1604 in Warwick.

From Sussex:

69. Thomas Pilcher, diocesan priest, thirty years old, d. 1587 in Dorchester.
70. Thomas Bullaker, O.F.M., friar and priest, thirty-nine years old, d. 1642 at Tyburn.

From Cornwall:

71. John Hambley, diocesan priest, twenty-seven years old, d. 1587 in Salisbury.

From Cumbria:

72. Christopher Robinson, diocesan priest, thirty years old, d. 1597 in Carlisle.

From Middlesex:

73. Anthony Page, diocesan priest, ordained 1591, d. 1593 in York.

From Norfolk:

74. Thomas Hunt, diocesan priest, twenty-six years old, d. 1600 in Lincoln.

From Northamptonshire:

75. Henry Heath, O.F.M., friar and priest, forty-four years old, d. 1643 at Tyburn.

From Northumberland:

76. George Errington, layman, forty-two years old, d. 1596 in York.

From Suffolk:

77. Montford Scott, diocesan priest, forty-one years old, d. 1591 in Fleet Street, London.

From Westmorland:

78. Thomas Sprott, diocesan priest, twenty-nine years old, d. 1600 in Lincoln.

From Worcestershire:

79. Arthur Bell, O.F.M., friar and priest, forty-two years old, d. 1643 at Tyburn.

From Scotland:

80. George Douglas, diocesan priest, d. 1587 in York.

From Wales:

81. Richard Flower (Lloyd), layman, twenty-two years old, d. 1588 at Tyburn.
82. Humphrey Pritchard, domestic servant, d. 1589 in Oxford.
83. William Davies, diocesan priest, thirty-five years old, d. 1593 in Beaumaris, Anglesey.
84. Charles Meehan, O.F.M., friar and priest, thirty-nine years old, d. 1679 in Ruthin Denbighshire.

In reading this apparently meaningless list, one should not forget that every single name is that of a blessed soul in heaven who—in many instances at a very young age—gave up his life to remain loyal to the Pope in Rome. Especially in our day, which is often "distinguished" by its anti-Roman sentiment—even within the ranks of the priests—these beatified martyrs deserve our veneration and imitation; each one of these Catholic heroes died *pro ecclesia et pontifice.*

In his homily at the beatification ceremony in Saint Peter's Basilica in Rome on November 22, 1987, the Pope struck a conciliatory, ecumenical note and said, among other things: "We must all rejoice that the hostilities between Christians, which so shaped the age of these martyrs, are over, replaced by fraternal love and mutual esteem." The Pope called for prayers that "the blood of those martyrs would be a source of healing for the divisions between Christians". He thanked God for the progress that had been made in recent years along the path leading to greater unity between Anglicans and Catholics.

SAINTS

Canonized by Pope John Paul II in the years 1984 to 1987

*View of the high altar of Saint Peter's Basilica in Rome
on the occasion of the beatification of George Haydock and
his eighty-four companions on November 22, 1987.*

Saint
Paola [Paula] Frassinetti

Foundress

b. March 3, 1809, Genoa
d. June 11, 1882, Rome

Canonized March 11, 1984

Saint Paula Frassinetti[1] arrived at beatification and canonization earlier than her saintly priest-brother. Whereas for him—Giuseppe Frassinetti, born on December 15, 1804; ordained a priest in 1827; died on January 2, 1868—the process of beatification was not introduced until 1939 and still [as this is being written] has not been concluded, his sister Paula, even though she died fourteen years after her brother, was beatified by Pope Pius XI on June 8, 1930, and canonized by Pope John Paul II on March 11, 1984.

Paula Frassinetti was born in Genoa on March 3, 1809; she was the third child of Giovanni Battista Frassinetti and his wife, Angela, née Viale. Her parents followed a good, industrious, and conscientious way of life; they gave to this child also an excellent upbringing and dedicated her to the Blessed Virgin Mary in the Marian shrine in Genoa.

During the years of her adolescence, Paula grew up in the shadow of her oldest brother's parish church; Giuseppe, who, like three other brothers, had become a priest, had been assigned at

---

[1] A. Capecelatro, *Vita della Serva di Dio Paola Frassinetti, Fondatrice delle Suore di Santa Dorotea* (Rome, 1900).

age twenty-eight to serve as pastor of the parish in Quinto al Mare, in the vicinity of his hometown of Genoa. This zealous, saintly priest earned for himself the honorary title of the Italian "Curé of Ars" and was an important spiritual writer (from his pen came eighty-six theological and ascetical books, some of which have been translated into foreign languages). From him Paula was able to learn a great deal, and he also provided much encouragement, not only for her personal spiritual life and aspirations, but also concerning her cooperation in pastoral work and the founding of her religious order. Her brother Giuseppe founded several pious associations and the religious order called the Sons of the Immaculate (*Figli di Santa Maria Immaculata*), which, in the course of thirty years, was able to place more than three hundred priests at the disposal of the archdiocese of Genoa. Similarly, Paula became more and more involved in the education of girls, and for this purpose she formed the religious congregation of the Sisters of Saint Dorothy in 1834. This ecclesial community grew and developed despite great difficulties. Quite early on, in 1841, the foundress moved the main house of her congregation to Rome, to the convent of Sant'Onofrio, on the Gianicolo. Paula showed a marvelous talent for organization and wonderful balance between firmness and kindness, between fortitude in all difficulties and a complete dedication to God and his holy will. During her lifetime, houses of the Sisters of Saint Dorothy were erected throughout Italy, and then in Portugal and Brazil as well. Today this congregation of teaching sisters numbers more than two thousand members in about ninety houses.

The spiritual character of the foundress Paula Frassinetti is most evident from her favorite saying: *"Volontà di Dio—paradiso mio!"* (The will of God is my paradise.) With complete self-control she managed to combine the exuberance of her fiery nature with the requirements of composure and gentleness; with the utmost simplicity she thereby aligned all of her human plans and actions, to the last detail, with the holy will of God, and she regarded herself as a very humble instrument in God's hand. "Everything as God wills." With these words upon her lips, Paula Frassinetti died on June 11, 1882, in the convent of Sant'Onofrio on the Gianicolo in Rome. In the chapel of this house her holy relics are revered. There, too, are preserved the memoirs (*Memorie*) and the letters of this saint. Pope John Paul II described her as follows at the canonization ceremony:

Paola Frassinetti is in fact a splendid fruit of the Redemption, always active within the Church. It has been said that, in order to determine if a work is Christian, it is necessary to see if there is the seal of the redeeming Cross. Now the Cross of Christ extensively cast its shadow, or better, its light, on the Saint's entire life and on all her works. In fact, she was convinced that whoever wants to undertake a path to perfection cannot renounce the cross, mortification, humiliation and suffering, which assimilate the Christian to the divine model, who is the *Crucified*. In her fervent immolation for the salvation of all souls, she held that, compared with the sufferings of Christ, what one might suffer is nothing. Not only did the cross not frighten her, but it was for her the powerful spring which moved her, the secret source from which sprang her tireless activity and her indomitable courage. She blessed the year which opened with some cross, deeming any relief of it as punishment: "Ah, any punishment at all—she said—but do not take my cross away."

Inner torments and the torments of persecution were not lacking for the Saint: calumnies, insults, affronts, mockery and outrages. But she knew how to bear all this with Christian fortitude, convinced that just as the earth needs fertilizing [fructifying] rain, so her new-born institute had to be sprinkled with her tears.

The inner strength which led her to live the "folly" of the cross so completely can be found in her tender devotion to the Heart of Jesus Christ. With her authentically apostolic sensitivity, the Saint perceived that no one can carry out a true apostolate if he does not have the stigmata of Christ engraved in his heart, if that ineffable intertwining of love and pain which is epitomized in the Most Sacred Heart of Jesus is not at work in him. Thus she wanted devotion to the Heart of Jesus to be professed in her institute as a rule: as a rule, one fasted on the eve of the feast of the Sacred Heart; every first Friday the sisters and students took turns in adoration before the divine Sacrament.

In 1872 she consecrated the entire institute to the Heart of Jesus.

The inner charge of St Paola Frassinetti could not but overflow into an intense apostolic activity, with a special interest for the Christian education of children and abandoned young people. She founded the Institute of the Sisters of St Dorothy precisely for this purpose. . . . [T]he message which flows from the simple but deeply devout life of St Paola, all purity and poverty, but also all charged with ardent zeal for the young people pushed to the sidelines of society, is a reminder of the true values of woman, of the expression of the most delicate feminine gifts, of the affirmation of the identity and dignity of woman, whom the Church has always protected and supported for the moral growth of society and for the coming of the Kingdom of Christ.

This message . . . constitutes an invitation to put the Redemption into practice, helping woman become aware of herself and of the place she occupies in the Christian community and in civil society, to prepare her according to her condition to assume her responsibilities and fulfil her role. I hope that this message will encourage the well-deserving Sisters of St Dorothy to continue to bring the spirit and the zeal of their holy Foundress to all the continents where they have their houses.[2]

[2] *L'Osservatore Romano*, March 26, 1984, p. 3.

Saints
Andrew Kim, Paul Chong, Laurent Imbert, François Siméon Berneux, and Ninety-nine Companions

Korean Martyrs[1]

d. between 1839 and 1867
Canonized May 6, 1984

The Catholic Church in Korea has existed, in a hierarchically organized form, only since September 9, 1831, when Pope Gregory XVI erected an apostolic vicariate for Korea, separated from the diocese of Peking [Beijing]. As early as 1791, however, Korea had brought forth Catholic martyrs, including the noblemen Paul Yun and his cousin James Kwon Sang-Yon, both of whom witnessed to their faith in Christ by shedding their blood on December 8, 1792. Other martyrs followed in the years 1793 to 1795, 1801 to 1802, 1815, and 1827. The greatest number of victims of the bloody persecution of Christians, however, died in the years from 1839 to 1846 and 1866 to 1867. During these years, the first Korean priest, Father Andrew Kim, the catechist Paul Chong, and the two French missionary bishops Laurent Imbert and François Siméon Berneux were martyred. They were killed together with ninety-nine other priests and lay people who gave witness by shedding their blood. In this group, then, there are altogether 103 Korean martyrs. They were canonized on May 6, 1984, by Pope John Paul II in the cathedral of Seoul, after seventy-nine of them had been beatified on July 5, 1925, by Pope Pius XI, and twenty-four of them on October 6, 1968, by Pope Paul VI.

The names of these 103 canonized Korean martyrs, listed chronologically according to the date of their martyrdom, are as follows:

[1] N. Del Re, "Martiri della Corea", in *Bibliotheca Sanctorum* 1:364–70.

1. Peter Yi, d. November 25, 1838.
2. Protasius Chong, d. May 20, 1839.
3. Agatha Yi, sister of Peter Yi, d. May 24, 1839.
4. Ann Pak, wife and mother, d. May 24, 1839.
5. Madeleine Kim, wife and mother, d. May 24, 1839.
6. Barbara Han, wife and mother, d. May 24, 1839.
7. Agatha Kim, wife and mother, d. May 24, 1839.
8. Peter Kwon, d. May 26, 1839.
9. Damian Nam, catechist, d. May 26, 1839.
10. Augustine Yi, catechist, d. May 26, 1839.
11. Lucy Pak, lady-in-waiting at the royal court, d. May 26, 1839.
12. Joseph Chang, d. May 26, 1839.
13. Barbara Yi, orphan girl, d. May 27, 1839.
14. Barbara Kim, maidservant, d. May 27, 1839.
15. John Yi, brother of Augustine Yi, d. July 20, 1839.
16. Rose Kim, widow, d. July 20, 1839.
17. Madeleine Yi, d. July 20, 1839.
18. Teresa Yi, widow, d. July 20, 1839.
19. Martha Kim, widow, d. July 20, 1839.
20. Lucy Kim, virgin, d. July 20, 1839.
21. Anna Kim, widow, d. July 20, 1839.
22. Mary Won, virgin, d. July 20, 1839.
23. Lucy Kim, virgin, d. September 2, 1839.
24. John Pak, d. September 3, 1839.
25. Mary Pak, d. September 3, 1839.
26. Barbara Kwon, wife of Augustine Yi, d. September 3, 1839.
27. Barbara Yi, sister of Madeleine Yi, d. September 3, 1839.
28. Mary Yi, wife of the catechist Damian Nam, d. September 3, 1839.
29. Agnes Kim, virgin, d. September 3, 1839.
30. Francis Ch'oe, d. September 3, 1839.
31. Laurent Imbert, titular bishop of Capsa, apostolic vicar of Korea, d. September 21, 1839.
32. Pierre Philibert Maubant, missionary priest, d. September 21, 1839.

Korean martyrs who were beheaded for the sake of their faith:
Upper left: Pierre Philibert Maubant, beheaded September 21, 1839.
Upper right: Just Ranferde Brettnières, beheaded March 8, 1866.
Lower left: Marie Nicolas Daveluy, beheaded March 30, 1866.
Lower right: Pierre Aumaître, beheaded March 30, 1866.

33. Jacques Honoré Chastan, missionary priest, d. September 21, 1839.
34. Paul Chong, catechist, who fwas the first layman to lead the Christians in Korea for twenty years, during the period in which they were without priests, d. September 22, 1839.
35. Augustine Yu, catechist, d. September 22, 1839.
36. Charles Cho, d. September 26, 1839.
37. Sebastian Nam, d. September 26, 1839.
38. Ignatius Kim, d. September 26, 1839.
39. Madeleine Ho, mother of Madeleine and Barbara Yi, d. September 26, 1839.
40. Madeleine Pak, d. September 26, 1839.
41. Agatha Chon, d. September 26, 1839.
42. Perpetua Hong, d. September 26, 1839.
43. Columbia Kim, sister of Agnes Kim, d. September 26, 1839.
44. Julitta Kim, virgin, d. September 26, 1839.
45. Catharine Yi, d. September 30, 1839.
46. Madeleine Cho, daughter of Catharine Yi, d. September 30, 1839.
47. Peter Yu, thirteen-year-old son of Augustine Yu, d. October 31, 1839.
48. Cecilia Yu, mother of the catechist Paul Chong, d. November 23, 1839.
49. Peter Ch'oe, d. December 20, 1839.
50. Benedicta Hyon, widow, d. December 20, 1839.
51. Madeleine Yi, virgin, d. December 20, 1839.
52. Madeleine Han, widow, d. December 20, 1839.
53. Elizabeth Chong, virgin, sister of Paul Chong and daughter of Cecilia Yu, d. December 20, 1839.
54. Barbara Cho, wife of Sebastian Nam, d. December 20, 1839.
55. Barbara Ko, wife of the catechist Augustine Pak, d. December 20, 1839.
56. Agatha Yi, d. January 9, 1840.
57. Teresa Kim, widow, d. January 9, 1840.
58. Andrew Chong, d. January 23, 1840.

59. Stephen Min, catechist, d. January 30, 1840.
60. Augustine Pak, catechist, d. January 31, 1840.
61. Peter Hong, catechist, d. January 31, 1840.
62. Mary Yi, virgin, d. January 31, 1840.
63. Madeleine Son, wife of Peter Ch'oe, d. January 31, 1840.
64. Agatha Kwon, daughter of Madeleine Han, d. January 31, 1840.
65. Agatha Yi, d. January 31, 1840.
66. Paul Ho, the first Christian soldier in Korea, d. January 31, 1840.
67. Barbara Ch'oe, daughter of Peter Ch'oe and wife of Charles Cho, d. February 1, 1840.
68. Paul Hong, brother of Peter Hong, d. February 1, 1840.
69. John Yi, catechist, d. February 1, 1840.
70. Anthony Kim, d. April 29, 1840.
71. Andrew Kim, the first Korean priest, d. September 16, 1846.
72. Charles Hyon, catechist, brother of Benedicta Hyon, d. September 19, 1846.
73. Susanna U, d. September 20, 1846.
74. Teresa Kim, d. September 20, 1846.
75. Agatha Yi, d. September 20, 1846.
76. Catharine Chong, d. September 20, 1846.
77. Lawrence Han, d. September 20, 1846.
78. Peter Nam, d. September 20, 1846.
79. Joseph Kim, d. September 20, 1846.
80. Peter Yu, catechist, d. February 17, 1866.
81. Siméon François Berneux, titular bishop of Capsa, apostolic vicar of Korea, d. March 8, 1866.
82. Just Ranferde Brettnières, missionary priest, d. March 8, 1866.
83. Pierre Henri Dorié, missionary priest, d. March 8, 1866.
84. Louis Bernard Beaulieu, missionary priest, d. March 8, 1866.
85. John Baptist Nam, d. March 8, 1866.
86. Peter Ch'oe, d. March 10, 1866.
87. John Baptist Chon, d. March 10, 1866.
88. Mark Chon, catechist, d. March 11, 1866.

Korean martyrs who were beheaded for the sake of their faith:
Upper left: Pierre Henri Dorié, beheaded March 8, 1866.
Upper right: Jacques Honoré Chastan, beheaded September 21, 1839.
Lower left: Louis Bernard Beaulieu, beheaded March 8, 1866.
Lower right: Siméon François Berneux, beheaded March 8, 1866.

89. Alex U, d. March 11, 1866.
90. Marie Nicolas Daveluy, titular bishop of Akka, apostolic vicar of Korea, d. March 30, 1866.
91. Pierre Aumaître, missionary priest, d. March 30, 1866.
92. Luke Huin, missionary priest, d. March 30, 1866.
93. Luke Hwang, catechist, d. March 30, 1866.
94. Joseph Chang, catechist, d. March 30, 1866.
95. Thomas Cho, d. December 13, 1866.
96. Peter Cho, d. December 13, 1866.
97. Joseph Cho, d. December 13, 1866.
98. Peter Yi, d. December 13, 1866.
99. Bartholomew Chong, d. December 13, 1866.
100. Peter Son, catechist, d. December 13, 1866.
101. Joseph Han, d. December 13, 1866.
102. Peter Chong, d. December 13, 1866.
103. John Yi, d. January 30, 1867.

To this list of the names of the 103 Korean martyrs, whose feast day has been celebrated each year on September 20 ever since their canonization, we add an abridged version of the homily that Pope John Paul II gave at the canonization ceremony on May 6, 1984, in the cathedral of Seoul:

The truth about Jesus Christ also reached Korean soil. It came by means of books brought from China. And in a most marvellous way, divine grace soon moved your scholarly ancestors first to an intellectual quest for the truth of God's word and then to a living faith in the Risen Saviour.

Yearning for an ever greater share in the Christian faith, your ancestors sent one of their own in 1784 to Peking, where he was baptized. From this good seed was born *the first Christian community in Korea*, a community unique in the history of the Church by reason of the fact that it was founded entirely by *lay people.* This fledgling Church, so young and yet so strong in faith, withstood wave after wave of fierce persecution. Thus, in less than a century, it could already boast of some ten thousand martyrs. The years 1791, 1801, 1827, 1839, 1846, and 1866 are forever signed with the holy blood of your martyrs and engraved in your hearts.

Even though the Christians in the first half century had only two priests from China to assist them, and these only for a time, they deepened their unity in Christ through prayer and fraternal love; they disregarded social classes and encouraged religious vocations. And they sought ever closer union with their bishop in Peking and the Pope in faraway Rome.

After years of pleading for more priests to be sent, your Christian ancestors welcomed the first *French missionaries* in 1836. Some of these, too, are numbered among the martyrs who gave their lives for the sake of the Gospel, and who are being canonized today in this historic celebration.

The splendid flowering of the Church in Korea today is indeed the fruit of the heroic witness of the martyrs. Even today, their undying spirit sustains the Christians in the Church of silence in the North of this tragically divided land.

Today then it is given to me, as the Bishop of Rome and Successor of Saint Peter in that Apostolic See, *to participate in the Jubilee of the Church on Korean soil. . . .* For behold: *through this Liturgy of Canonization* the Blessed *Korean Martyrs* are inscribed in the list of the Saints of the Catholic Church. These are true sons and daughters of your nation, and they are joined by a number of missionaries from other lands. They are your *ancestors*, according to the flesh, language, and culture. At the same time they are *your fathers and mothers in the faith*, a faith to which they bore witness by the shedding of their blood.

From the thirteen-year-old Peter Yu to the seventy-two-year old Mark Chong, men and women, clergy and laity, rich and poor, ordinary people and nobles, many of them descendants of earlier unsung martyrs—they all gladly died for the sake of Christ.

Listen to the last words of Teresa Kwon, one of the early

martyrs: "Since the Lord of Heaven is the Father of all mankind and the Lord of all creation, how can you ask me to betray him? Even in this world anyone who betrays his own father or mother will not be forgiven. All the more may I never betray him who is the Father of us all."

A generation later, Peter Yu's father Augustine firmly declares: "Once having known God, I cannot possibly betray him." Peter Cho goes even further and says: "Even supposing that one's own father committed a crime, still one cannot disown him as no longer being one's father. How then can I say that I do not know the heavenly Lord Father who is so good?"

And what did the seventeen-year-old Agatha Yi say when she and her younger brother were falsely told that their parents had betrayed the faith? "Whether my parents betrayed or not is their affair. As for us, we cannot betray the Lord of heaven whom we have always served." Hearing this, six other adult Christians freely delivered themselves to the magistrate to be martyred. Agatha, her parents and those other six are all being canonized today. In addition, there are countless other unknown, humble martyrs who no less faithfully and bravely served the Lord.

The Korean Martyrs have borne witness to the crucified and risen Christ. *Through the sacrifice of their own lives they have become like Christ* in a very special way.[2]

In concluding his sermon, which was given in English, the Pope also said in Korean:

And can we fail to recall with intense gratitude and admiration the French missionaries of the Foreign Missions of Paris, who came from far away to bring to this new-born Church their evangelical zeal, in order to deepen their faith and the grace of their episcopal and priestly ministry, which alone gives ecclesial structure to the community by uniting the faithful to Christ the

---

[2] *L'Osservatore Romano,* May 14, 1984, p. 5.

Head and by situating them within the Universal Church. I would like at least to mention Monsignor Imbert who was the first Bishop to preach the word of God upon this land, Monsignor Berneux who devoted himself to the task of making available to the faithful books of Christian doctrine and spirituality; and we commemorate also the zeal and the martyrdom of a dozen French missionary priests: with these, they would spend themselves day and night for the cause of the Gospel, strengthening the faith in a time of persecution and even seeking to arouse priestly vocations in the country, and they would accept the sacrifice of their lives for Christ.[3]

[3] Ibid., p. 6.

Saint
Miguel Francisco Febres
Cordero

Christian Brother

b. *November 11, 1854,*
   Cuenca, Ecuador
d. *February 9, 1910,*
   Premiá, Spain

Canonized October 21, 1984

By its fruits you can tell the value and quality of a tree. That is also true of a religious community. For the Christian Brothers of Saint Jean Baptiste de la Salle, the canonization of Brother Miguel Francisco Febres Cordero was proof that in their ranks not only are capable teachers and educators employed, but saints are also being formed.

Francisco Febres Cordero,[1] later, Brother Miguel of the Christian Brothers, was born on November 7, 1854, in Cuenca, in the Latin American country of Ecuador, the son of Francisco Febres Cordero and Ana Muñoz Cárdenas. The boy was just nine years old when the Christian Brothers, at the invitation of that country's heroic Catholic president, García Moreno, founded a school in Cuenca. Francisco was among their first pupils. He stood out from among the other students by his intelligence and attentiveness, but even more so by his great piety and exquisite good manners. He thereby earned the esteem of his teachers, and he was well-liked by his classmates.

---

[1] A. M. Lozano, "Michele Francesco Febres Cordero", in *Bibliotheca Sanctorum* 9:450–52.

Already at the age of fourteen, after considering the question thoroughly and consulting with experienced persons, Francisco made the decision to enter the religious community of his teachers and to become a Christian Brother, too. His parents would rather have seen him go to the diocesan seminary as a candidate for the priesthood; but he abided by his decision and entered the Community of the Brothers of the Christian Schools on March 24, 1868, taking the religious name Miguel (Michael).

After his religious formation in the novitiate, Brother Miguel began his apostolic and pedagogical work, at first in his native city of Cuenca. In 1869, however, he was transferred to Quito, where for thirty-five years he edified the people of this city by his words and his exemplary way of life. He was admired for his great knowledge but, above all, on account of his virtuous conduct. In the classroom he proved to be a model teacher who, in addition to his excellent teaching, composed several textbooks and inspirational religious books, among them a catechism that was very well written, with respect to both doctrine and method. Besides this he acquired an excellent knowledge, not only of the Spanish language and its literature, but also of English and French. He even became an honorary member of the Spanish and French Academies of Language and a corresponding member of the Academy of Sciences in Venezuela. During his career he advanced to become, not only a professor and a director in the Christian Brothers schools in Quito, but also an inspector. First and foremost, however, he set an example of striving for perfection and holiness in following Christ, the Crucified. Thanks to his example, many of his pupils became priests, and even bishops; among them was his student, the first cardinal of Ecuador, the archbishop of Quito, Carlos Maria de la Torre.

In 1907 Brother Miguel was reassigned by his religious superiors to Lembecq-lez-Hal in Belgium, where at that time the generalate of the Christian Brothers was located. Here Brother Miguel was supposed to work in peace and recollection on additional textbooks. For health-related reasons, however, this Belgian stay lasted only a very short time. Brother Miguel was sent to Premiá de Mar, in Spain, to recuperate. There he taught class again. Much too soon, however, on February 9, 1910, a serious illness put an end to his life and work.

After his death, this Christian Brother's reputation for sanctity spread very quickly, and confidence in his power to intercede for various intentions grew quite strong. And so, on November 13, 1935, the process of beatification for Brother Miguel was introduced, which was successfully concluded with his beatification on October 30, 1977.

Only seven years later, on October 21, 1984, Pope John Paul II was able to canonize this exemplary educator and religious in Saint Peter's in Rome. On this occasion the Pope said the following:

> *"Before I formed you in the womb I knew you."*
> These words of the Divine Creator to the Prophet Jeremiah, on which today's liturgy invites us to meditate, are totally true also for each one of us, who on this Mission Sunday are assembled here for the solemn canonization ceremony of a son of Ecuador, Brother Miguel Febres Cordero.
>
> God knows each one of us as no one else could. He knows us better even than those who begot us.
>
> He knew us even before we existed, even before we were conceived. God knows us even better than we know ourselves.
>
> And knowing us so intimately and so deeply, God anticipates us with his graces, to enable us to make use of the gifts which his goodness has given us and continues to give us.
>
> God's gifts are infinitely diverse. It is up to us to recognize the gifts which God gives us and to put them to work in order to respond to the vocation to holiness which is addressed to each and every one.
>
> It is not rare that God's gift assumes the form of a call to serve him in one or another aspect of consecrated life. This call was addressed to some of you, dear brothers and sisters, and God has given you also the grace to listen to it and to respond

to it. The same call is addressed yet today to so many others who perhaps hesitate or delay in responding to it. The Prophet himself, as is seen in the passage just read, tried to evade it, giving his youth and his inability as a reason: "I know not how to speak; I am too young." To have a right feeling of one's own poverty and inability is certainly very praiseworthy, so long as it does not lead to disregarding God's gift and the omnipotence of grace.

If it is God who calls, it will be he who will never allow his grace to be lacking for those who listen to his voice with a docile heart.

From his earliest years, our new saint was preceded by a special grace which almost irresistibly attracted him to share the life of his religious teachers, the Brothers of the Christian Schools, who had arrived in Ecuador a few years earlier.

More than one member of his family thought it their duty to oppose this plan. Young Francesco had to suffer more than one refusal. Then for several years he was forced to endure an attitude of extreme coldness on the part of his father, who was nevertheless a sincere Christian.

But young Miguel never for even a moment doubted the divine call. He wrote, "I assure you of God's presence and, without any human respect, I assure you that I believe I am called to the Institute of the Brothers of the Christian Schools, and that in no other place will I feel I am in my true place as there. Please communicate these feelings to my father. If he truly desires my happiness, that is, my eternal happiness, he will allow me to follow the path which the good God has marked out for me."

Faithful to God's call from the very beginning, St Miguel Febres Cordero continued to be so without the slightest hesitation during the forty years of his religious and apostolic life; and God, as he had promised the Prophet, "placed his words in his mouth", opening to him the way to the hearts of those who approached him.

His confrères and former students—among whom were various priests and some bishops—competed to attest to how this humble and gentle man proved to be capable of moving them and drawing them to good.

He talked about the principal mysteries of our religion with the stress of a profoundly convinced Christian.

Those who were older, coming to the end of their lives, recalled with emotion the teaching which Brother Miguel had given them decades earlier.

He never hesitated to present an exacting and demanding Christianity to the young men who went to him.

As St Paul had done earlier with his dear Corinthians, he "preached Jesus crucified".

The crucifix presided over his entire life and all his occupations: in the classroom, at his writer's desk, as well as in the chapel and the community rooms, his gaze was often fixed on the image of the Divine Crucified.

During their spiritual retreat he had the boys who were preparing for confession contemplate Christ on the Cross, showing them his wounds and emphasizing that they had been suffered in expiation for sins.

And these young men, whose minds were deeply sensitive, never resisted the salve of his words. Various witnesses confirm that many boys were moved to tears and left the school without saying a word, visibly saddened by the memory of the Saviour's sufferings.

The new Saint Miguel Febres Cordero shared heroically in the sufferings of Christ crucified. Among the various crosses which he had to bear during his life, not the least was a malformation of his feet, which caused him considerable pain when walking. But from weakness he drew strength; from pain, a reason for joy, making his own life "the message of the cross" (1 Cor 1:18), a scandal and madness for those who refused to accept Christ crucified as Saviour and Lord.

The joyful acceptance of his cross was for many a reason for edification and of Christian example. First in his native Ecuador and later in Europe—especially in Premia de Mar, where he spent the last months of his life—his joy in his suffering aroused profound respect and admiration in his community among the students and among those who associated with him. Clear proof that he had deeply assimilated the Pauline teaching: "God's weakness is more powerful than men" (1 Cor 1:25).

At the same time, he welcomed everyone with great simplicity and cordiality. Following the example of Christ, Brother Miguel spent himself visiting the poor and the needy, counselling young people, teaching children, giving himself to everyone. From Christ's Cross—the greatest expression of love for man—he drew strength and inspiration to give of himself unreservedly to others, often at the cost of his very self.

Precisely on 19 February 1888 . . . the new saint was present in this very Basilica of Saint Peter's participating in the beatification ceremony of the Venerable John Baptist de La Salle, founder of the Christian Schools.

This religious institute, of which he was a member for almost twenty years, made the words of the Gospel which we have just heard a motto for its apostolic and educational activity: "Whoever welcomes a child such as this for my sake welcomes me" (Mk 9:37).

For Brother Miguel, these words were a rule of life, a constant incentive in his vocation as educator. All of his efforts centred on the integral education of the new generations, moved by the conviction that the time dedicated to the religious and cultural formation of youth is of great transcendency for the life of the Church and of society.

What love and dedication this "apostle of the school" gave to the thousands of children and young men who passed through his classrooms during the long years of his life as educator!

Both at the "El Cebollar" school in Quito and in the small school where he taught at the beginning of his apostolate, he took upon himself the pleasant task of preparing the children—the "new living tabernacles" as he called them—for their First Communion.

Faithful follower of Jesus, he had made part of his life the Master's teaching: "If anyone wishes to rank first, he must remain the last one of all and the servant of all" (Mk 9:35). For this reason, in the spirit of service and love for his neighbour, he dedicated many years of work and effort to the publication of works of a didactic nature, for which work—and in the sunset of his life—he was called to Europe, having to leave his beloved homeland.

As a man of culture his reputation was on the rise, resulting in his being elected a member of the Ecuadorian Academy of Language. But neither this honour nor his recognized prestige as a grammarian could blemish the humble and unaffected way in which he treated everyone. Because he was convinced that "God chose those whom the world considers absurd to shame the wise" (1 Cor 1:27).

Nevertheless, his work as a scholar was always at the service of his immediate teaching activity. And with a truly evangelical spirit he always sought to devote himself preferably to the teaching of children who were most economically, culturally and spiritually poor, seeing in them the person and the countenance of Christ.

We can well say, therefore, that the exemplary itinerary of his life as a teacher is a valid model for Christian educators of today, as well as a stimulus for evaluating the great importance of the apostolate and ideals of Catholic instruction which has as its aim the offering of a solid culture steeped in the light of the Gospel to the new generations.

Brother Miguel—chosen soul who spared no effort in his devotion to God and to neighbour—left an imperishable remembrance among those who knew him. Twenty-seven years after passing from this world to the Father, his mortal remains were received with great emotion and joy in his native Ecuador, where the admiration and affection for this son of the Church, glory of his homeland also, remains ever alive.

Today, Mission Sunday, his glorification is a reason for new joy for the universal Church. She, like the Church in Ecuador, looks to St Miguel Febres Cordero, apostle of the school, who was also an exemplary missionary, an evangelizer of Latin America.[2]

[2] *L'Osservatore Romano*, November 12, 1984, pp. 6–7.

Saint
Francesco Antonio
Fasani

Conventual Franciscan Priest

b August 6, 1681,
  Lucera, Italy
d. November 29, 1742,
  Lucera

Canonized April 13, 1986

Beatified by Pope Pius XII on April 15, 1951, the Conventual
Franciscan friar Father Francesco Antonio Fasani[1] was canonized
by Pope John Paul II on April 13, 1986. This saintly priest and
religious was born on August 6, 1681, in Lucera, a city in the
southern Italian region of Puglie, the son of a poor peasant, Giuseppe Della Monaca. In the sacrament of baptism he received the
name Donato Antonio Giovanni. While still a very small child, he
lost his father. His mother's second husband, like the first, made a
sincere effort to give the boy a good upbringing. He also saw to it
that he received instruction in grammar and Latin from the Conventual Franciscans in Lucera.

When he was not quite fifteen years old, Giovanniello, as he
was affectionately called within the family, entered the order of his
teachers and, with the habit, received the names of the order's
two great saints, Francis and Anthony. The Conventuals, in many
places called the Friars Minor or the Black Franciscans, were then,

---

[1] G. Stano, *Il Beato Francesco Antonio Fasani* (Rome, 1951); F. Baumann, *Pius XII.
erhob sie auf die Altäre* (Würzburg, n.d.), pp. 280–85.

just as today, the custodians of the grave of the Seraphic Saint in Assisi and that of the great wonderworker in Padua.

After his novitiate in Monte Sant'Angelo in the Gargano mountains, Francesco Antonio Fasani took vows and made his religious profession on August 23, 1696, and then began his studies of philosophy and theology in various houses of his order: in Venafro, Montella, Naples, Aversa, and Foggia. Then in 1703 he went to Assisi. There, on September 11, 1705, he was ordained a priest. To round out his studies, Father Francesco Antonio Fasani subsequently stayed for a short time at San Bonaventura College in Rome and earned a master's degree in theology. Later this title became the customary form of address for the saintly friar: *Padre Maestro—Pater Magister,* because of his excellent training in philosophy and theology, but even more so because he stood out from his fellow friars as the master of all the virtues that ought to adorn a religious. One of his confrères, Father Antonio Lucci, later the bishop of Bovino, made the following statement about him as part of the beatification process for Father Francesco Antonio Fasani: "He always kept aloof from anything that seemed to him even the least bit unsuitable for a religious. Indeed, he even went without permitted forms of recreation so as to mortify himself. People considered him a saint, and this ever growing reputation had its origin in the virtues that he practiced to perfection."

After completing his studies in Rome, the young priest returned again to Assisi, where he remained until 1707, devoting himself to the preaching ministry there and in the villages of Umbria.

From 1707 until his death on November 29, 1742, Father Fasani labored in his hometown of Lucera: at the podium of the college as a lecturer; in the pulpit as a model preacher; in the confessional as a much sought-after confessor; among his confrères as the guardian of the convent; as novice master, and as provincial of the Sant'Angelo province of the order.

Father Fasani left to posterity several homiletic works, for instance, a *Quaresimale* (sermons for Lent), a *Mariale* (sermons about Mary), and a commentary on the Lord's Prayer and the *Magnificat*.

His particular concern in preaching was to proclaim the good news in a way that all could understand and to instill love for God and for the Blessed Virgin. He venerated Mary especially in her Immaculate Conception. In her honor he wrote the lyrics and composed the music for a popular song that is still sung today in southern Italy. He called Mary "the key to paradise", because one can obtain everything through her. Every evening he could be seen kneeling and praying for at least a half-hour before the statue of the Immaculata that he had procured for the church of San Francesco in Lucera. Again and again he would recall Mary's virtues and say, "Let us love God as Mary loved him; let us have a faith such as Mary had; let us trust in God as Mary did." Through his great confidence in Mary, Father Fasani obtained quite extraordinary favors for himself and for others.

Toward the end of 1742, during his sixty-first year, Father Fasani indicated that he was near death. Soon afterward, the aches and pains from which he had been suffering for years worsened, and five days later he died. Among his last words on the day that he died, November 29, 1742, was that he was "happy that he was now permitted to go to a place where no one could offend God any more".

At the canonization of Father Francesco Antonio Fasani, on April 13, 1986, Pope John Paul II said:

In the last analysis, the sanctity of man is decided by love.

It is of this love that the Conventual Franciscan Francesco Antonio Fasani has given exemplary proof. Today the Church officially numbers him among the Saints.

He made the love taught us by Christ the fundamental characteristic of his existence; the basic criterion of his thought and activity; the supreme summit of his aspirations. For him, too, the "question regarding love" was the guiding criterion of his whole life, a life which therefore was nothing but the result of an ardent and tenacious will to respond affirmatively—like Peter—to that question. . . .

Francesco Antonio's love was one of total adherence to the Lord's example. The new Saint showed with his life—like the Apostles—that it is always necessary to "obey God rather than men" (Acts 5:29), even at the price of suffering and humiliations, which he did not lack, along with the esteem and the agreement that his generosity won for him in the circle of his contemporaries. . . .

St Fasani presents himself to us in a special way as the perfect model of the *priest and pastor of souls*. For more than thirty-five years . . . he dedicated himself to the most varied forms of priestly ministry and apostolate, working in his town of Lucera, but with numerous visits to the surrounding areas as well.

A true friend to his people, he was brother and father to everyone, an eminent teacher of life, sought out by all as an enlightened and prudent counsellor, a wise and sure guide in the ways of the Spirit, a courageous defender and supporter of the humble and the poor. Witness to this is the reverent and affectionate title with which his contemporaries greeted him, and which is still familiar to the good people of Lucera: for them he is always, then as now, the "Padre Maestro".

As a religious he was *a true "minister"* in the Franciscan sense, that is, the servant of all the friars: charitable and understanding, but devoutly demanding when it came to the observance of the Rule, and particularly the practice of poverty; he himself provided an impeccable example of regular observance and austerity of life.

In an era characterized by great insensitivity on the part of the powerful as regards social problems, our Saint spent himself with inexhaustible charity *for the spiritual and material elevation of his people.* His preferences were towards the most neglected and exploited classes, above all towards the humble field workers, the sick and suffering, prisoners. He devised ingenious initiatives, soliciting the cooperation of the wealthiest classes, thus creating [a network of] concrete . . . forms of assistance. . . .

Father Fasani was *an authentic minister of the Sacrament of Reconciliation*, a tireless apostle of the confessional, where he sat for long hours each day, welcoming with infinite patience and great kindness those who—of every class and condition—came to seek God's pardon with a sincere heart. . . .

The gratitude that Father Fasani's penitents felt then in the secret of the confessional is now perpetuated in the joy that they share with him in heaven.[2]

[2] *L'Osservatore Romano*, April 21, 1986, p. 3.

Saint
Giuseppe Maria
Tomasi

Religious Priest,
Professor, Cardinal

b *September 12, 1649,*
    Licata, Sicily
d. *January 1, 1713,*
    Rome

Canonized October 12, 1986

This saint from the second half of the seventeenth and the beginning of the eighteenth centuries was beatified ninety years after his death, on September 29, 1803, but only now canonized by Pope John Paul II, on October 12, 1986. This was certainly not only because the miracles worked by his intercession with God, which are necessary for canonization, are now documented, but surely also because this religious priest, whom Pope Clement XI elevated to the rank of cardinal a half year before his death on January 1, 1713, can serve as an exemplary patron saint for the liturgists of our day.

Giuseppe Maria Tomasi, whose collected works in eleven volumes contain valuable treatises on the liturgy, was born on September 12, 1649, in Licata, province of Agrigento, Sicily, the fifth child of the Duke of Palma di Montechiaro and Prince of Lampedusa, Don Giulio Tomasi, and his wife, the Baroness Rosalia Traina della Torretta. Because he, the firstborn son, was expected, as the successor to the throne, to carry on the noble line of the Tomasis, he had in every respect the best possible upbringing and education. Before his birth, the aristocratic Sicilian couple already had children, three girls, named Francesca, Isabella, and Antonia. All three became nuns in the Benedictine abbey *Nostra Signora del Santo Rosario*, in Palma, during the rule of Abbess Antonia Traina, who was the maternal aunt of the three Tomasi daughters.

Duke and Duchess Tomasi had two other sons after Giuseppe Maria: one who died soon after birth and whose name is unknown, and one by the name of Ferdinand, who became the successor in the ducal line after Giuseppe Maria renounced his inheritance. Ferdinand died in 1672, four months after the death of his wife, Melchiora, Princess of Aragon.

From his early childhood, Giuseppe Maria, following the example of his uncle, Father Carlo Tomasi, was inclined to a priestly and religious vocation. At the age of fifteen, he entered the Clerics Regular (who were called the Theatine Fathers, after their saintly founder, Cajetan of Thiene), once his father, who had opposed his son's intention for a long time, finally gave his permission. After the four months of his postulancy, he began the novitiate on March 24, 1665, under the saintly novice master Father Francesco Maria Maggio, who was very learned, both in theology and, especially, in the history of the liturgy, and who had written two liturgical works (*De sacris ceremoniis* and *De Divino Officio et Choro*).

Before taking vows, the Theatine novice renounced the rights and titles vested in him as the firstborn son, in favor of his brother Ferdinand. Then he began his studies of philosophy and theology, during which he had to change his residence as a student again and again because of frail health: Messina, Rome, Ferrara, Modena, and then Rome again. There he was ordained subdeacon and deacon in 1671. Due to the death of his brother Ferdinand, he returned in 1672 to Palma di Montechiaro. Finally, after completing his studies in Palermo, he was ordained a priest in Rome in 1673. In the church of San Silvestro de Monte Cavallo in Rome, at the generalate house of his order, the new priest celebrated his First Holy Mass on Christmas Day 1673. From then on he spent most of his priestly life in Rome, with great piety and devotion to his sacred calling, and also in the service of scholarship and at the disposal of the authorities of the Apostolic See, especially in the service of the Pontifical Congregation of Rites.

At first his religious superiors had assigned the young priest with the excellent theological training to duties in his own order. He became the assistant novice master and spiritual director of the lay brothers at the generalate of the order, then also the assistant prefect of studies for the Theatine seminarians. Soon, though, he had to give up his work in those positions, because he was stricken with insuperable anxieties, especially scruples with regard to administering the sacrament of penance.

Then a new field of activity opened up for the young religious priest, which was quite suited to his intellectual abilities and inclinations. He became a great, highly esteemed scholar who researched the early Christian and patristic sources of the liturgy, and as such he edited works on that subject. In addition, he was consulted more and more as an expert by the authorities in the Holy See and was asked to collaborate especially with the Congregation of Rites. Based on his knowledge of the Hebrew, Arabic, Syro-Chaldaean, and Ethiopian languages, Father Tomasi researched biblical, patristic, and, above all, liturgical source materials. Besides many treatises on his investigations, he prepared editions of important texts. Of the collected works of Father Tomasi, which were published in eleven volumes by the Theatine priest A. F. Vezzosi during the years 1747 to 1769, in Rome, the following in particular should be mentioned: *Codices Sacramentorum, Responsalia et Antiphonaria, Antiqui Libri Missarum,* and *Institutiones Theologicae Antiquorum Patrum.* "The editions of Father Tomasi, furnished with extensive introductions and numerous annotations, have been replaced to some extent today by better ones, yet they were a great accomplishment at that time, and they had a seminal importance for liturgical research."[1] The spirit discernible in the works of Fa-

---

[1] H. Becker, "Tomasi, Giuseppe Maria", in *Lexikon der Theologie und Kirche,* 2d ed. (1957), 10:248; G. B. Mattoni, C.R., *Sul sentiero della sapienza: Vita di San Giuseppe Maria Tomasi, Teatrino, Cardinale di S. Romana Chiesa* (Palermo, 1986).

ther Tomasi had a strong influence on the liturgical reform of the Second Vatican Council. Father Tomasi, in any case, is rightly considered to be the precursor of modern liturgical scholarship and the "prince of the Roman liturgists".

The impressive thing about this priest-scholar, besides the immense diligence with which he combed the archives and libraries of Rome, was his admirable piety and humility, whereby he remained, despite his increasing renown among scholars and Roman officials, a simple, ascetical religious who lived a life of complete poverty, even after he had been named a cardinal (against his will) on May 19, 1712, with the titular church of San Martino ai Monti in Rome. While a cardinal he used to give the customary catechetical instructions himself in his titular church, and he would donate the greater part of his income to the poor.

We should mention here the touching fact that, as a priest, Father Tomasi did not hesitate to take lessons with the rabbi of the Eternal City at that time, Mosè da Cave, to deepen his knowledge of Hebrew so as to be able to produce a critical edition of the Psalter. And what happened? The highly regarded, learned Roman rabbi was so impressed by the humility and piety of the Catholic religious priest Tomasi, and also by his erudition, that he became a Catholic and at his baptism took the name of the priest who baptized him, Giuseppe Tomasi.

Father Giuseppe Maria Tomasi fell ill during the octave of Christmas in 1712 and died in the odor of sanctity in Rome on January 1, 1713. Because of his heroic virtues and on account of repeated miracles worked by God through his intercession, Cardinal Tomasi was beatified by Pope Pius VII in 1803. After the successful completion of the canonical process concerning a miraculous healing in very recent times, Pope John Paul II canonized him on October 12, 1986. The relics of this saint are revered in the Roman Theatine Church of Sant'Andrea della Valle in Rome; his feast day is celebrated there on January 3.

At the canonization, Pope John Paul II praised Saint Giuseppe Maria Tomasi, calling special attention to the following facts:

The reasons of pastoral timeliness for this canonization are numerous. The main one could be the importance of St Giuseppe Maria Tomasi in the field of liturgical worship, which he greatly promoted in his life and with his learned writings. The witness of this new saint is *particularly opportune in these days*, twenty years after the Second Vatican Council, which gave so much emphasis to renewal of the liturgical life. The saint whom we proclaim today helps us *to understand and bring about this renewal in its proper sense*. . . .

In the wake of and following the example of the Doctors of the Church and of the great theologians, he eminently fitted the figure of the priest who unites *love for learning and love of piety*; he recalls to us the model offered by the prophet Malachy when he said: "For the lips of a priest should guard knowledge, and men should seek instruction from his mouth, for he is the messenger of the Lord of hosts" (Mal 2:7).

Certainly the "knowledge" that the prophet is referring to is the knowledge in which Cardinal Giuseppe Maria shone so brightly—the knowledge, or better yet, the "experience" of *divine things*. But St Giuseppe Maria leads us to this mystical knowledge precisely through his witness as a *liturgical "scientist"* in the modern sense of the word.

Furthermore Tomasi shows all of us, and especially the shepherds of souls, how important it is for the priest to have *a healthy cultural sensitivity*, founded on an authentic *love of truth*, which is then translated into a generous commitment to *communicate it to one's brothers*. This commitment gave his ministry a special dignity and a particular effectiveness.

From his childhood St Giuseppe Maria experienced an intimate inclination and a strong preference for "*ecclesiastical things*"—for the *things of God*, as he used to say. Therefore he, the soul who was always listening, decided while very young, without any difficulty, to follow the divine inspiration which was calling him to a type of life in which the service and worship of God are guaranteed by a special and renewed consecration: *religious profession*. Therefore he entered the Order of the Theatines.

A member of a noble Sicilian family, had he remained in the world, he would have had immense riches and enormous social prestige, which were his as the heir to the Principality of Lampedusa and to the Duchy of Palma di Montechiara. However, attracted by other riches and the prospect of a glory immensely greater than that earthly one, *he renounced these rights in order to follow Christ, poor, chaste and obedient* in the discipline and austerity of religious life.

In imitation of our Lord, "who though he was rich, made himself poor" (II Cor 8:9), in order to enrich his brothers through his witness of total availability and disinterested love.

Cardinal Tomasi is the *model of a pastor*, because he first of all *followed the divine Pastor*; he went to his school, and sought to penetrate the mystery—*Mysterium pietatis*; most of all he sought to *live* this mystery in his life as a believer and as a priest, and in his work of study and research.

A true minister of the altar, Tomasi understood that it was necessary to seek Christ, most of all, as the psalmist says, "in his sanctuary" (Ps 62 [63]:3), *"dwelling in the house of the Lord"* (cf. Ps 22 [23]:6); he gave due honour to the sacred liturgy, not limiting

Glass sarcophagus with the mortal remains of Saint Giuseppe Maria Tomasi. Rome, Church of Sant'Andrea della Valle.

it to a ritualistic external action, but making the divine worship a *supreme fount of light and operative energy* for the Christian's entire day, making the day nothing else than the prolongation of the liturgical act, especially the Eucharistic sacrifice.

This was the special way in which he followed the divine shepherd and teaches us to follow him. Attending the school of the divine Master, he in his turn became our teacher. . . .

The promotion of liturgical life—to which he applied himself in a special manner—ranged from the publication of research and scholarship to the work which he performed for the liturgical education of the people and of the simple faithful.

His *spirit of service* and his *ardent love for souls*, cultivated by study and the conscientious observance of the Rule of his Order, rendered him available for charitable works with the poor and the sick as well as fulfilling his tasks in the Roman Curia, to the point of ultimately receiving from Pope Clement XI the honour of being made a Cardinal, although in his humility he had tried in vain to refuse it. After he completed the liturgical duties inherent in his role as cardinal, he began, like a simple parish priest, to explain the basics of faith and catechesis to the children and the other faithful, offering prizes to those who progressed in Christian doctrine.

Like the divine Pastor, Cardinal Tomasi knew how to *gather the flock* which is sometimes dispersed (cf. Ezek 34:12), and *to make them lie down in "verdant pastures near restful waters"* (cf. Ps 22 [23]:2). He knew how to lead it to *"the choicest pastures"* (Ezek 34:14)—those of the Word of God shown and "made flesh" in the eucharistic mystery of the holy liturgy.[3]

---

[3] *L'Osservatore Romano*, October 20, 1986, pp. 8–9.

Saints
Domingo Ibáñez de Erquícia,
Lorenzo [Lawrence] Ruiz of Manila,
Jacobo Kyushei Tomonaga,
and Thirteen Companions

Martyrs

d. between 1633 and 1637

Canonized October 18, 1987

These heroes of the faith, who were martyred in Nagasaki, Japan, during the persecution of Christians in the years 1633 to 1637, were beatified on February 18, 1981, by Pope John Paul II in Manila and canonized on October 18, 1987. These sixteen Japanese martyrs are listed by name in volume 1 of *New Saints and Blesseds of the Catholic Church* (pp. 64–70), together with a brief description of the life and death of each; the homily the Pope gave at the beatification ceremony in Manila is likewise reprinted there.

At the canonization on World Missions Sunday, October 18, 1987, in Saint Peter's in Rome, the Pope again gave an appreciation of the outstanding example and the missionary commitment of the new saints, among whom there were nine people of Japanese descent, four Spaniards, one Italian, one Frenchman and one Filipino, namely, Lorenzo Ruiz of Manila, the father of three children. John Paul II said that these new saints are an inspiration and example for Europe and Asia, as well as for the universal Church, of evangelization, in which lay people, too, must play a decisive role.[1]

---

[1] *L'Osservatore Romano*, October 26, 1987, pp. 9–10.

Saint
Giuseppe Moscati

Physician,
University Professor

b. July 25, 1880, Benevento, Italy
d. April 12, 1927, Naples

Canonized October 25, 1987

During the synod of bishops in October 1987, which discussed the theme of "The Layman in the Church", Pope John Paul II canonized the Italian physician and university professor Giuseppe Moscati, whom Pope Paul VI had beatified on November 16, 1975, thus demonstrating once again that sanctity is not only for bishops, priests, and religious, and that the Church, thanks to her sacraments and teachings, can also lead people in the lay state to holiness.

Giuseppe Moscati[1] was born on July 25, 1880, in Benevento, southern Italy, the son of the high-ranking nobleman and magistrate Francesco Moscati and Countess Rosa de Lucca.

At the beginning of 1881, his father was reassigned to the tribunal in Ancona. Thus the boy spent his childhood there until the year 1888. Then his father had to take up the duties of a council member in the court of appeals in Naples. There Giuseppe Moscate completed his secondary education with a diploma. He then enrolled in the medical school of the University of Naples,

[1] G. Papasogli, *Das Leben eines heiligen Arztes* (Stein am Rhein, 1982); F. Bea, *Storia di un medico* (Turin, 1961).

which at that time had famous physicians of world renown on its faculty; almost without exception, however, they paid homage to the worldview of positivism and materialism as expressed in the writings of Vogt, Moleschott, Büchner, and Feuerbach. As a medical student, Moscati nevertheless managed to keep his Catholic faith, and even to deepen it and to put it into practice more conscientiously.

On August 4, 1903, the student received the degree of doctor of medicine with highest honors. Soon afterward, he became an assistant with the United Hospitals of Naples and eventually an associate member of its administration. From 1904 on, Dr. Moscati worked at the famous hospital Santa Maria del Popolo in Naples, which was known throughout the world by the name of *Incurabili*. On two occasions during this period of his medical practice, Dr. Moscati voluntarily took part in relief efforts that revealed his characteristic selflessness and dedication: On April 4, 1906, Mount Vesuvius erupted, threatening the villages situated on its slopes with immediate destruction. Terrible confusion resulted among the fleeing inhabitants. Then it was Dr. Moscati who personally went into the danger zone, so that the evacuation of the houses could be conducted in an orderly manner and the people brought to safety. He demonstrated the same spirit and courage in helping others during the cholera outbreak in Naples in 1911.

In early 1911, Dr. Giuseppe Moscati became the medical superintendent (head physician) of the *Incurabili*. As such he supervised in particular several departments in this famous hospital that were staffed by specialists—for instance, pathological anatomy and the tuberculosis ward—and he also looked after the sick and wounded soldiers who were admitted as a result of the First World War.

In the same year, Dr. Moscati qualified as an instructor in the department of physiological chemistry and began to give lectures on general clinical medicine. He continued his medical practice on the side and in his free time devoted himself also to academic research. Over the course of many years, he published more than thirty scholarly works and participated in international medical congresses, for instance, in Budapest (1911) and in Edinburgh (1923).

Professor Dr. Moscati, who at the age of thirty-three was already a celebrity in the medical field and had become the forerunner of modern biochemistry, proved in that materialistic milieu to be a practicing Catholic with a deep faith who never concealed his convictions and his piety but manifested them openly. Before examining a patient or engaging in research, he would always place himself in the presence of God, the Creator of the universe. He received Holy Communion daily; he practiced the Christian virtues in a heroic manner; he treated poor patients without asking them for payment; he viewed his medical practice as a priestly ministry to his fellow men who were suffering; and he encouraged his patients, especially those who were about to undergo an operation, to receive the sacraments. For not quite twenty-five years he pursued his vocation as a physician and a professor of medicine in an exemplary way that testified to his faith.

He had been sick only a few days when death called on him during his forty-seventh year on April 12, 1927; that morning, as usual, he had received Holy Communion.

Beatification of Giuseppe Moscati, Rome, Saint Peter's Square, November 16, 1975.

The funeral ceremonies for the "saintly physician", as Dr. Moscati was already called then, turned into a triumphal procession through the streets of Naples in honor of this great personage. On November 16, 1930, three years after his death, the mortal remains of Dr. Moscati were disinterred and laid to rest in the Neapolitan church of Gesù Nuovo, where many people soon began to pray that he would be raised to the glory of the altars. On March 6, 1949, the process of beatification was introduced, which was successfully completed on November 16, 1975, with his beatification. Then, on October 25, 1987, Pope John Paul II was able to proceed with the canonization of this exemplary layman. On that occasion the Pope emphasized, "[Giuseppe Moscati] was thus a forerunner and protagonist of the humanization of medicine felt today to be a necessary condition for renewed attention and assistance with respect to those who are suffering." [2] As a university professor, the Pope said, Moscati focused his attention in particular on the education of young medical students. Furthermore, he did not hesitate to denounce abuses, and he worked to abolish practices and systems that were injurious to true professionalism and science, to the patients, or to the students. In his writings we find the words, "Not science but charity has transformed the world." Physicians and all those employed in the field of medicine should see in Saint Giuseppe Moscati an example worthy of imitation.

[2] *L'Osservatore Romano*, November 9, 1987, p. 10.

*In the background, to the left, Saint Peter's Basilica in Rome.
To the right, the Jesuit Generalate, at Borgo San Spirito, 4,
where the General Postulator's office is also located.*

AFTERWORD

by Professor Paolo Molinari, S.J.

General Postulator of the Society of Jesus

In the time between 1984 and 1987, Pope John Paul II carried out forty-nine beatifications in twenty-eight solemn liturgies and seven canonizations in as many liturgical celebrations. During these ceremonies—in a few cases they dealt with groups of martyrs—233 persons were declared blessed and 124 persons were proclaimed to be saints. This is a remarkable number, which—as has already been emphasized in various articles and publications—far surpasses the scope of his predecessors' activity in this field.

This fact and the accompanying statistics have prompted many very respectable people, who are to be taken seriously, to ask whether the increasing number of beatifications and canonizations might not bring with it the risk of causing an "inflation" of such ceremonies, with the dangerous consequence of devaluing the recognition and appreciation for what the Church intends to accomplish in proclaiming blesseds and saints.

It is precisely this consideration which we take as our starting point in presenting the book of Professor [Monsignor] Ferdinand Holböck, *New Saints and Blesseds of the Catholic Church: Blesseds and Saints Canonized by Pope John Paul II during the Years 1984 to 1987,* [original German edition published by] Christiana-Verlag, Stein am Rhein, 1992.

This book is the continuation of a volume that was previously published on the same subject for the years just before the period covered in this one. It is the result of a keen and meticulous investigation on the basis of what has been written and published about the saints and blesseds who were raised to the glory of the altars in the years 1984 through 1987 during the pontificate of Pope John Paul II.

We want to emphasize, above all, that the doubt which is expressed with regard to the rapid numerical increase of new saints and blesseds must not be seen as a destructive criticism, nor as the result of an embittered estrangement from the Church. It is, rather, as we have already indicated, the expression of a certain concern that the value of canonizing and beatifying could lose some of its meaning. It is feared that, because of the frequency of such ceremonies, the faithful will no longer pay attention to the message that the saints and blessed have to communicate to us by the fact that they embodied in an outstanding way the spirit of the Gospel. The consequences of that trend would be detrimental to the exemplary character of the saints.

Therefore we take the above-mentioned doubt and the concerns in this regard as the starting point for a short theological reflection about several decisive points in the discussion about canonizations. In our opinion, that is in fact the best presupposition, and an objective one, for what we believe we must say in reference to this volume by Professor Holböck.

It must be recalled here, first of all, that God not only brings forth saints in the Church, but also calls the attention of the faithful to them, when he awakens in the faithful a feeling of respectful admiration and appreciation, which is then converted into that phenomenon which surrounds many individuals in a particular way and which is known to us by the name of *fama sanctitatis*, "the odor of sanctity".

Whenever there is an authentic odor of sanctity—fruit of the spiritual intuition that is extremely vivid among the people of God—one must see in this *sensus fidelium* a sign of divine activity. If this sense proves to be true, is it permissible, from a theological and pastoral point of view, for the Church, the hierarchy, and the faithful to ignore this "sign from God" and *not* to make a thorough investigation of its character and message?

As if in answer to this question, we have a weighty statement from the Pope, who in the foreword to the apostolic constitution *Divinus Perfectionis Magister* explicitly says:

Accepting these signs and the appeal of the Lord with great reverence and docility, the Apostolic See from time immemorial—pursuant to the difficult office entrusted to it of teaching, sanctifying and governing the People of God—has placed before the faithful, for their imitation, veneration and invocation, men and women who are outstanding for their love of neighbor and other splendid evangelical virtues, and whom it declares, after carrying out the necessary investigations, to be saints in a solemn act of canonization (*Acta Apostolicae Sedis*, 75 [1983], p. 350).

This is precisely what the Second Vatican Council had said quite clearly:

To look on the life of those who have faithfully followed Christ is to be inspired with a new reason for seeking the city which is to come (cf. Heb 13:14 and 11:10), while at the same time we are taught to know a most safe path by which, despite the vicissitudes of the world, and in keeping with the state of life and condition proper to each of us, we will be able to arrive at perfect union with Christ, that is, holiness. God shows to men, in a vivid way, his presence and his face in the lives of those companions of ours in the human condition who are more perfectly transformed into the image of Christ (cf. 2 Cor 3:18). He speaks to us in them and offers us a sign of this kingdom, to which we are powerfully attracted, so great a cloud of witnesses is there given (cf. Heb 12:1) and such a witness to the truth of the Gospel (*Lumen gentium*, 50).

That is why the Church, in her two-thousand-year history, has again and again presented to the faithful and to all mankind the figures of countless persons who opened themselves to God's grace and, by allowing themselves to be seized by the Spirit of Christ and to be conformed to him, manifested the inexhaustible riches of his love in ways and forms that are ever new. This has found expression, according to the gifts and abilities conferred by God, in various walks of life: martyrs and confessors of the faith; people who felt drawn to live as hermits and contemplatives; scholars and teachers of the spiritual life; founders and foundresses of new forms of community life according to the evangelical counsels; heroic missionaries and outstanding apostles of social justice; first-rate educators; far-sighted persons who dedicated themselves courageously to the service of love of neighbor among the poor and the outcast in hospitals and leprosariums. Yet besides these great "pioneers", the Church—heeding the signs granted to her by her divine Founder—has presented and recommended as models other people, who practiced their Christian faith in an exemplary way in quite ordinary circumstances, in whom there was nothing unusual except the heroism of perfectly fulfilling their duties in the monotony of everyday routine: mothers and housekeepers, young people and children, workers and even beggars, insignificant employees or unassuming porters—simple, modest citizens, who did good in the social milieu that was typical of their time.

For not all Christians receive special gifts and charisms from God that single them out to complete some special task in the Church and in the world. Indeed, to the great majority of the faithful, God assigns the task of living their ordinary, everyday lives in an exemplary Christian manner.

In this connection we would like to emphasize that the doctrine whereby all Christians are called—each according to his vocation—to the perfection of holiness and to the fullness of charity is not a discovery of our [twentieth] century, even though it was first presented in a dogmatic constitution by the Second Vatican Council. This is, after all, a perennial teaching of the Church.

The Church, precisely in undertaking so many beatifications and canonizations, intends to help all the faithful now. Through these ceremonies the Church wishes to offer to Christians of every age and nationality, of every culture, every occupation and condition of life, living examples who can serve as models. The Church has done this through the centuries and not only in recent times. In fact, as early as March 12, 1622, Gregory XV canonized four great and splendid figures from ecclesiastical life: Ignatius of Loyola, Francis Xavier, Philip Neri, Teresa of Avila; yet he added a fifth saint: a simple, uneducated farmer, Saint Isidore.

To this first consideration, we would like to add a further observation, which is closely connected with the previous one. It is to point out something that is already commonplace among scholars: we mean the fact that, through an inadequately enlightened hagiography (depiction of the lives of the saints), the impression is not infrequently conveyed that the life of a saint must be distinguished by a series of extremely difficult deeds and be endowed with all sorts of charismatic and mystical gifts, which are not accessible to all people.

Precisely in the light of these theological observations and considerations, which have a considerable breadth of application, it is our honor and pleasure to present the book of Professor Ferdinand Holböck.

A careful reading of his book shows that there are many persons, especially among the saints and blesseds of our [twentieth] century, who have reached the summit of sanctity in quite different ways and by various paths: to have demonstrated this to the reader is one of the most remarkable merits of this work.

Besides this merit, it seems to us especially noteworthy that Professor Holböck does not only present the essential facts about the life and work of the individual blesseds or saints (or about groups of them), but also emphasizes their pastoral significance. The author then follows these interesting biographical sketches, which are written in a simple, elegant, and versatile style, with the most important excerpts from the homilies that the Holy Father gave at the respective ceremonies.

In this comprehensive volume, then, the author offers a wealth of material, which has been compiled by patient, painstaking work. Consequently, the book provides a splendid proof for the above-mentioned teaching of the Church. For it cannot escape the reader's notice that, among the saints and blesseds treated in this book, there is a broad representation of the various groups within the people of God: persons of various ages and of both sexes; persons from various nations and continents, enjoying quite different levels of culture; persons of every state and from all walks of life: bishops, priests, monks, friars and nuns, lay men and women.

It seems to us fitting to point out, in this connection, that the new saints and blesseds who are the subjects of the present volume died between the years 1584 and 1964, that is, during a period of time that extends into our own days; of the forty-nine beatifications, thirty-one concern persons who died in our [twentieth] century; in the case of the canonizations, two of the new saints belong likewise to our time.

In reading Professor Holböck's book, we were reminded more than once of the words that Pope Pius XI spoke about one of these humble saints. With these words we wish to conclude our epilogue to this excellent book. For they are genuinely encouraging and important for everyone whom the Lord is calling to follow him, and that is, after all, the goal that the author set for himself in writing his book. We are referring to the address Pope Pius XI gave when he declared the heroic character of the virtues of Brother Benilde:

The Venerable Brother Benilde of the Brothers of the Christian Schools was a humble Servant of God, whose life was quite modest and quiet, a thoroughly ordinary, everyday sort of life.

But how much there was that was not at all ordinary, not at all quotidian, in that ordinary, everyday existence! The recurring everyday routine, which always brings the same occupations, the same situations, the same difficulties, the same temptations, the same weaknesses, the same needs, has accurately been called the "terrible routine". How much strength it requires to defend oneself against this terrible, oppressive, monotonous, boring routine! How much extraordinary virtue is demanded to carry out all the ordinary things that fill our daily life with extraordinary fidelity, or, to express it better, not with the ordinary and everyday inexactitude, looseness, neglect, and carelessness that are so common, but rather with attention, devotion, and an inner spiritual fervor!

Never does the Church show a greater appreciation for holiness or prove herself more convincingly to be the wise teacher thereof, than when she points to these humble lights, who were very often unknown even to those who had the good fortune to see them shining before their own eyes.

Extraordinary things, great events, marvelous deeds, by their very occurrence, arouse and awaken the best instincts, generosity and magnanimity, the powers that very often slumber in the depths of souls. Great occasions are like an exquisite theme for an artist and a poet, which by its mere appearance leads inspiration to the loftiest heights. But things that are ordinary, lowly, everyday, devoid of significance or brilliance, certainly have no exciting or fascinating qualities in and of themselves. Yet that is what the life of most people is like, namely, that it usually consists of nothing but ordinary things and everyday occurrences.

That is why the Church appears to us so wise, when she invites us to admire and imitate the examples of quite ordinary and modest everyday virtues, which are all the more valuable, the more humble and ordinary they are (*L'Osservatore Romano*, January 7–8, 1928, *"Inviti all'eroismo"*, from *Discorsi di S.S. Pio XI. nell'occasione della lettura dei Brevi per le Canonizzazioni, le Beatificazioni, le proclamazioni dell'eroicità delle virtù dei Santi, Beati e Servi di Dio*, vol. 2, published by *La Civiltà Cattolica*, Rome 1942, pp. 155–56 ["Invited to heroism", from a volume entitled: Addresses of His Holiness Pius XI upon reading the briefs for the canonizations, beatifications and proclamations of the heroic virtues of the saints, blesseds and servants of God]).

With these reflections, we believe, we have set forth the extremely valuable merits of this book and can only hope that, given its magnificent qualities, it will accordingly find a wide circulation.

APPENDIX

Martyrs of France (1794)

98 Companions of Guillaume Répin

Priests
1. Laurent Bâtard
2. François-Louis Chartier
3. André Fardeau
4. Jacques Laigneau de Langellerie
5. Jean-Michel Langevin
6. Jacques Ledoyen
7. Jean-Baptiste Lego
8. René Lego
9. Joseph Moreau
10. François Peltier
11. Pierre Tessier

Religious
12. Odile Baumgarten
13. Rosalie du Verdier de la Sorinière
14. Marie-Anne Vaillot

Laymen
15. Pierre Delépine
16. Antoine Fournier
17. Pierre Frémond
18. Jean Ménard

Laywomen
19. Gabrielle Androuin
20. Perrine Androuin
21. Suzanne Androuin
22. Victoire Bauduceau Réveillère
23. Françoise Bellanger
24. Louise Bessay de la Voûte
25. Perrine Besson
26. Madeleine Blond

27. Françoise Bonneau
28. Renée Bourgeais Juret
29. Jeanne Bourigault
30. Perrine Bourigault
31. Madeleine Cady
32. Renée Cailleau Girault
33. Marie Cassin
34. Marie-Jeanne Chauvigné Rorteau
35. Simone Chauvigné Charbonneau
36. Catherine Cottenceau
37. Carole Davy
38. Louise-Aimée Dean de Luigné
39. Marie de la Dive du Verdier
40. Anne-Françoise de Villeneuve
41. Catherine du Verdier de la Sorinière
42. Marie-Louise du Verdier de la Sorinière
43. Marie Fasseuse
44. Renée-Marie Feillatreau
45. Marie Forestier
46. Jeanne Fouchard Chalonneau
47. Marie Gallard Queson
48. Marie Gasnier Mercier
49. Marie Gingueneau Couffard
50. Jeanne Gourdon Moreau
51. Marie Grillard
52. Renée Grillard
53. Perrine Grille

54. Jeanne Gruget Doly
55. Victoire Gusteau
56. Marie-Anne Hacher du Bois
57. Anne Hmard
58. Marie Lardeux
59. Perrine Laurent
60. Perrine Ledoyen
61. Jeanne-Marie Leduc Paquier
62. Marie Lenée Lepage Varancé
63. Marie Leroy Brevet
64. Marie Leroy
65. Carola Lucas
66. Renée Martin
67. Anne Maugrain
68. Françoise Michau
69. Françoise Micheneau Gillot
70. Jacqueline Monnier
71. Jeanne Onillon
72. Françoise Pagis Roulleau
73. Madeleine Perrotin Rousseau
74. Perrine Phélyppeaux Sailland
75. Marie Pichery Delahaye
76. Monique Pichery
77. Marie Piou Supiot
78. Louise Poirier Barré
79. Perrine-Renée Potier Turpault
80. Marie-Geneviève Poulain de la Forestrie
81. Marthe Poulain de la Forestrie
82. Félicité Pricet
83. Rose Quenion
84. Louise Rallier de la Tertinière Dean de Luigné
85. Renée Regault Papin
86. Marguerite Rivière Huau
87. Marguerite Robin
88. Marie Rochard
89. Marie Roger Chartier
90. Marie Rouault Bouju
91. Jeanne-Marie Sailland d'Epinatz
92. Madeleine Sailland d'Epinatz
93. Perrine-Jeanne Sailland d'Epinatz
94. Madeleine Sallé
95. Renée Seichet Dacy
96. Françoise Suhard Ménard
97. Jeanne Thomas Delaunay
98. Renée Valin

INDEX OF SAINTS AND BLESSEDS